AYN RAND CONTRA HUMAN NATURE

AYN RAND CONTRA HUMAN NATURE

▼

Greg S. Nyquist

Writers Club Press
San Jose New York Lincoln Shanghai

Ayn Rand Contra Human Nature

Writers Club Press
an imprint of iUniverse.com, Inc.

For information address:
iUniverse.com, Inc.
5220 S 16th, Ste. 200
Lincoln, NE 68512
www.iuniverse.com

ISBN: 0-595-19633-0

Printed in the United States of America

EPIGRAPH

▼

"Human beings inherit a propensity to acquire behavior and social structures, a propensity that is shared by enough people to be called human nature."

—Edward O. Wilson

CONTENTS

▼

INTRODUCTION

---▼---

"The centuries roll by, human nature remains the same!"
—Vilfredo Pareto

For many years, Ayn Rand's pretensions as a philosopher were scarcely taken seriously by the academic and cultural establishments of this country. Most establishment critics and scholars considered Rand's philosophy the work of a mere amateur whose ideas were hardly worth the trouble of refuting. Some of her critics even went so far as to accuse Rand of trying to rationalize rapacious and exploitative behavior. Gore Vidal accused Rand of having "a great attraction for simple people…who object to paying taxes, who dislike the 'welfare' state, who feel guilty at the thought of the suffering of others but who would like to harden their hearts." (1961, 26) During her lifetime, Rand, despite the financial success of her books and a large, adoring audience, was a persona non grata among the cognoscenti. The liberal and radical left intellectuals who dominated the Universities and the media wanted no part of Rand. Her ideas frightened and shocked them.

Since her death in 1982, Rand's stock has somewhat risen. Although most intellectuals still do not take her seriously as a philosopher, her importance as a cultural figure has been established beyond any doubt. The publisher Twayne has included Rand in its series of books on important American authors, and Barbara Branden's biography of Rand, which, though critical of Rand's character, praised her accomplishments as a thinker and writer, was well reviewed by the press and briefly appeared on several best seller lists. Rand's books continue to sell over a half-a-million copies each year, making her one of the most enduring American writers of her (or any other) generation. Her philosophical books alone have sold well enough to make her one of the most widely read philosophers of the twentieth century. And while her ideas may not yet enjoy an extensive influence over society at large, they have been very influential over that segment of the population which has read her novels and philosophical essays. Rand had a unique talent for inspiring cult-like devotion in her admirers. And although these admirers do not make up a particularly large percentage of the total American population (probably less than 0.5% of the adult public), they nevertheless can be found in nearly all walks of life, including even in academia.

Ayn Rand's influence is not, of course, confined merely to her diehard admirers. There are literally millions of people who, although they do not consider themselves "Objectivists," have nevertheless been profoundly influenced by her ideas. Many libertarians and conservatives have drawn heavily on Rand's ideas. The Libertarian Party which, before the emergence of Ross Perot's Reform Party and Nader's Green Party, was the nation's third largest political party, would be unthinkable without Rand's influence. Even an establishment conservative like Rush Limbaugh has occasionally shown signs of having been influenced by Rand's ideas, albeit indirectly, through second or third-hand sources. His attempt to defend the "greed" of the eighties borrows heavily from Rand. Before Rand, only a handful of iconoclasts and other eccentrics would have dared defend greed in public.

Her influence, then, has not been confined entirely to a small group of ardent admirers. Faint echoes of her ideas can be heard in all segments of American life. There is some evidence to suggest that this influence may be growing. Ironically, it is in academia, where hostility to her ideas has been the most intense, that Objectivist ideas have made the greatest progress in recent years. Admittedly, this progress has thus far been rather on the slow side, a mere trickle at best, but though dilatory, it has been steady. Individuals sympathetic to Rand and her Objectivist philosophy are gradually beginning to infiltrate the academic establishment, and a few colleges have even gone so far as to offer classes in Rand's philosophy. Objectivist ideas are also beginning to appear in college textbooks and in classroom discussion. Even the American Philosophical Association, which for years would have nothing to do with Rand, now includes, as an affiliate to its Eastern division, something called the "Ayn Rand Society." And since Objectivists have made no secret of their determination to infiltrate the academic establishment, it is not unreasonable to expect these developments to continue well into the future, until finally the Randites manage to carve up a respectable niche of their own within the academic pie.

Despite Rand's obvious importance both as a controversial polemicist and as an American cultural figure, her philosophy has largely escaped the scrutiny of a genuinely intelligent and penetrating criticism. Objectivists would probably ascribe this phenomenon to the soundness and irrefutability of Rand's ideas. You cannot, after all, effectively criticize true ideas, because the truth is above criticism. If Rand's philosophy were in fact largely true, you would expect her critics to have a rough time explaining what is wrong with it. However, I do not believe this explains why Objectivism thus far has been, a few exceptions notwithstanding, so ill criticized. The reason most of the criticisms leveled against Rand's philosophy are weak, unfair, irrelevant, and/or invalid has nothing to do with the intrinsic soundness of Objectivism. It results, not from the irrefutability of Rand's ideas, but from the philosophical imbecility of her critics.

As I will seek to demonstrate over the course of this book, Rand's philosophy of Objectivism is open to many serious objections. Rand was a surprisingly sloppy and even maladroit thinker who apparently believed that matters of fact can be determined by the manipulation of logical and rhetorical constructions. Indeed, some of the most important doctrines in her philosophy, such as her theories of human nature and value, are based on nothing more than a mere play on words. But this is not the least of it. What is most astonishing about Rand is not that she made errors (all philosophers make errors), but that she made stupid errors—the kind of errors philosophers make when they are too precipitous in their judgments and haven't stopped to really think things through. Even when Rand's philosophical conclusions are substantially correct, she is often right for the wrong reasons. Her rejection of philosophical idealism (i.e., the belief that reality is primarily mental) represents a case in point. As I will explain in detail throughout the course of this book, none of Rand's arguments against philosophical idealism are relevant. Yet I believe she is right to consider idealism an invalid theory. She is simply unable to explain *why* she is right.

Although I am sharply critical of many of Rand's philosophical views and formulations, this book is not meant to be a refutation of Objectivism. I do not believe that philosophical systems can in fact be refuted. Every philosophical system, no matter how false or mendacious, contains at least some truth. And this is certainly the case with Objectivism. I would even go so far as to say that there is quite a bit of truth in Objectivism. The problem is that this truth is, in a great many instances, so inextricably mixed with falsehoods and errors that it is sometimes not that easy to separate the former from the latter. Objectivism is in many respects a compendium of half-truths. The failure of her detractors to recognize this is one of the reasons why their attacks against her philosophical system have so often proved ineffective. Before you can determine what is wrong with Objectivism, you must first determine what is right. Many of Rand's most controversial doctrines, including her denunciations of altruism, superstition and the welfare state on the one side and her support of selfishness, atheism, and laissez-faire capitalism on the other, have an element of truth in them. Failure to acknowledge this element of truth can only lead to criticism that is confused and inept.

Despite my low opinion of Rand's philosophical expertise, I nevertheless regard Rand as an important and

perhaps even a great thinker. For even though her philosophy is riddled with non sequiturs, over-generalizations,
incompetent formulations, pseudo-empirical inferences,
and other palpable bunglings, this does not mean that she
cannot in fact be regarded as a great philosopher. Many a
philosopher considered great by the denizens of academia
is every bit, if not more, culpable of the sort of violations
of logic and evidence which characterize Rand and her
disciples. Think of all the fallacies and other blatant
absurdities to be found in the philosophical systems of
Plato, Plotinus, Leibniz, Berkeley, Kant, Fichte, Hegel,
Russell, Whitehead, Husserl, Heidegger, and Sartre!
Schopenhauer believed in phrenology; William James
believed in spiritual mediums and ghosts. Nearly every
great philosopher has embraced at least one appalling
absurdity, and several have embraced scores of them.
Regrettably, the greatness of a philosopher rarely has anything to do with whether his philosophy is faithful to the
elemental facts of reality. On the contrary, in many
instances, the more a philosopher departs from reality, the
greater will be his reputation as a thinker of genius. The
reason for this paradox is not hard to fathom. The greatness of a philosopher is usually determined by intellectuals—in other words, by that very class of individuals who
are most afraid of reality. This being the case, is it at all
surprising that Plato and Hegel, two of the most implacable enemies of common sense that the world has ever
seen, should be regarded as great philosophers? What
your typical intellectual seeks in a philosophy is not
insight *into* reality, but a way *out* of reality.

In a confused sort of way, Rand understood this. She
knew that many philosophers and intellectuals resented

reality and sought to rationalize it away. Yet this did not prevent her from indulging in her own mendacious rationalizations. And I must say—in all fairness to Rand—she could rationalize with the best of them. Her philosophy might not have been as beautiful and poetic as Plato's, or as complex and imaginative as Hegel's, but if you feel any sympathy with its basic premises, you will have a devil of a time resisting its allure. It is not surprising that Rand is one of the most widely read and discussed philosophers of the twentieth century. She was a brilliant polemicist and an ingenious sophist. Her method consisted of having a seemingly cogent answer to all the major philosophical problems. Whether the issue dealt with abortion, the problem of universals, the fact-value dichotomy, or the standard of rights, she always had something to say about it that sounded logical and apposite. Of course, what she said was never as logical and apposite as it may have sounded, but only someone with a great deal of philosophical acumen would be capable of realizing this. Since most people are philosophically illiterate (including many contemporary philosophers), they cannot detect the numerous empirical and logical shortcomings in Rand's arguments. Even those individuals who, because of their greater experience of men and the world, *know* that Rand is wrong, are often unable to explain *why* she is wrong. In polemics, articulation is everything. Merely being able to verbalize one's point of view in semi-cogent fashion is often all that is necessary in order to seem as if one knows what one is talking about. Rand was clearly an absolute master of this method, and for this reason it was very difficult for anyone to get the better of her in debate. Like Socrates in Plato's dialogues, she would spin a verbal web in which her antagonists, unable to articulate a semi-cogent response of their own, would find themselves inextricably entangled.

But the truth of a philosophy is not gauged by how well it can be used in a debate. The ability to articulate a point of view and defend it against those who raise objections to it says little, if anything, as to its truth. Truth, especially in its deeper manifestations, can often be so inordinately complex that it defies articulation. This is the trouble with all these philosophies which, like Objectivism, seek to reduce the entire universe to a handful of rhetorical constructions. They assume that all truth, regardless of how complicated it may be, can ultimately be expressed by a few pithy phrases. I regard this assumption as fundamentally mistaken. It derives from a false view of knowledge—one which equates knowledge with articulation. But it should be obvious from everyday life that articulation is not necessary for knowledge. Knowledge comes, not from words, but from experience. The knowledge of any complex skill, whether it is cooking, judging the motives of other people, or writing a novel, can only be learned from immersing oneself in the activity from which the knowledge springs. To learn how to cook, you go into the kitchen; to learn how to judge the motives of other people, you begin by sharply observing those around you; to learn how to write a novel, you read other novels and attempt to write some of your own. Of course, learning in this way is difficult and time-consuming. Hence the appeal of philosophers who, like Rand, declare that knowledge comes from words. It is very flattering to think that, once one masters the vocabulary of a given subject, one has mastered the subject itself. Yet it should be obvious to anyone who has given the matter serious thought that, just because you are familiar with, say, the general concepts of cooking, this does not mean that you know how to cook. Knowledge of cooking must derive, not from the terms in which cooking is described, but from cooking itself.

Rand's entire theory of knowledge is tantamount to a denial of the old adage that wisdom comes from experience. While it is true that Rand's philosophy of Objectivism officially adopts the view that all knowledge ultimately comes from experience of the external world, this concession to empiricism turns out, on closer examination, to be shallow and unrigorous. All philosophers like to believe that their doctrines are in accord with empirical reality. The question, however, is whether this belief is justified. In Rand's case, I do not believe it is. As I will attempt to demonstrate during the course of this book, I believe that Rand is either wrong or confused about many of the central issues in philosophy. She is wrong about the nature of man, about the role of philosophical ideas in history, about the validity of induction, about the absolute objectivity of values, about the feasibility of laissez-faire capitalism, and about the nature of romanticism; and she is confused about philosophical idealism, the nature of consciousness, the relation between ideas and the things they represent in reality, the psychology of altruism, and the issue of a benevolent versus a malevolent sense of life. In this book, I will attempt to explain, in language as lucid as possible, why Rand is wrong on the former issues and confused about the latter.

*   *   *

Before commencing with a critique of Rand's views, I think it is only fair that I briefly indicate my own philosophical positions. There are few things more annoying in philosophical criticism than to have to guess the viewpoint of some particular critic who, in order to make himself appear impartial and objective, pretends that he has no point of view of his own. Any critic who will not come right out and say "This is what I believe, this is where I'm coming from" is probably trying to hide something. The honest critic should not be afraid to show his colors. If he has prejudices which might cause him to be unfair in his critique, he should own up to them in a forthright and unshrinking manner.

Every philosophy starts with a vision of the limits and possibilities of human nature. At one extreme is the *naturalistic* view, which holds that human beings will continue to behave as they have in the past, and that consequently the possibilities of human nature, at least in terms of moral or spiritual progress, are extremely limited. At the other extreme is the *utopian* view of human nature which holds that the possibilities for man's moral and spiritual progress are much greater than the historical record would lead us to believe, and that human nature can be regenerated either by changing social conditions or converting men to a more enlightened point of view. In addition to these two extremes, there exists a whole host of intermediate positions; and it is somewhere between the two extremes that you will find most social theorists.

On this issue, I consider myself to be pretty much of an extreme naturalist. If you cannot find any historical evidence for a certain theory of human nature, I will tend to believe that your theory is not in accord with the facts of reality. Hence, if someone tried to convince me that human beings, under a socialist form of government, could develop into creatures far less rapacious and self-centered than they have shown themselves to be historically, I will almost certainly dismiss such a claim as patent nonsense. *Where's the historical evidence for such a claim?* I would immediately wish to know. Answer: *There is none!* Then why should I believe such a claim? According to my philosophy, I shouldn't. Without empirical (i.e., historical) evidence, no belief about matters of fact is warranted.

Incidentally, it is on this issue of human nature where I find myself most at odds with Rand and her followers. Rand tended to adopt a rather utopian view of man. According to her theory of human nature, man is the product, not of his nature, but of his ideas. Again, I must ask, *Where is the empirical evidence for such a view?* It will be my contention that Rand offers *no relevant empirical evidence* for her view of man.

The question of evidence brings up another crucial subject in philosophy—namely, the subject of *epistemology*, which studies the nature of human knowledge. Most philosophers (including Ayn Rand) hold that man's theoretical knowledge about the universe derives from a process of induction whereby the general nature of some object or process is discovered through repeated observation. After I have seen an object or a particular process a certain (unspecified) number of times, I am justified in making various conclusions about it. Thus, if every swan I perceive turns out to be white, I am justified, according to this theory of knowledge, in assuming that *all* swans are white.

According to my philosophy, there is no such thing as induction: it is a mere fiction without any basis in either fact or logic. I agree with Karl Popper on this issue: theoretical knowledge about the empirical world is attained, not by induction, as so many credulous philosophers would have us believe, but through a process of trial and error. All theoretical knowledge is essentially hypothetical. There is no such thing, according to my philosophy, as a theory which can be regarded as certain. All theories are mere conjectures. Progress in knowledge is attained by rigorously trying to refute these conjectures. The longer a given conjecture can remain unrefuted, the more our faith in it will be justified. Those conjectures which survive our best efforts to refute them will be the ones that we will tend to follow in practice.

Even though this theory of knowledge, first formulated by Popper, constitutes one of the most influential epistemological theories of the twentieth century, it is still considered very controversial, and few contemporary philosophers would be willing to accept it *in toto*. For centuries, philosophers have been habituated to regarding knowledge as an inductive process involving the observation and classification of empirical data. For this reason, it would never occur to them to question whether this way of looking at the problem of knowledge was the only viable one. The inductive (i.e., traditional) view of knowledge, although mercilessly criticized by skeptics, is still so deeply rooted within the philosophical mind and so taken for granted that any philosopher who dares to replace it by an entirely different theory is bound to be regarded with incredulity and dismay.

Another epistemological issue that has aroused a great deal of contention is that relating to the duality of subject and object, the mental and the real. "There is little philosophy," wrote the twentieth century's greatest philosopher, George Santayana, "not contained in the distinction between things as they exist in nature, and things as they exist to opinion; yet both the substance and its appearance often bear the same name, to the confusion of discourse." (1926, 37) I am inclined to believe that, after the issue of human nature, this issue of the duality of the physical and the mental is the most important in all philosophy. Failure to distinguish between our ideas of things and the things themselves has led to an immense amount of philosophical confusion. If I see a cat walking across the wall, my perception of the cat and the cat itself will not be one and the same. This may seem like a trite observation, but the failure to distinguish what I perceive or think of the cat from the cat itself causes philosophers to regard perceptions and ideas as things and things as mere figments of the imagination. This confusion has led to a great many philosophical errors, including the most egregious of them all—namely, the belief that man's mind creates, or in some way *is*, reality.

Once the philosopher has clearly distinguished the idea from the thing it represents, he can proceed to clarify the relation existing between the data of the mind and the things this data represents in the material world. If this dualism between ideas and things, thoughts and objects really does exist, then it follows that all human knowledge must be merely symbolic in character. An idea, in and of itself, is not a substantive entity. Its existence is purely spiritual (i.e., purely intellectual); but that which it symbolizes (if, that is, the idea is true) has a purely material existence (or is related to or characteristic of some material existent). This consideration, when subjected to logical and empirical analysis, will inevitably lead to some rather startling conclusions. In the first place, if everything we veraciously perceive is material (i.e., substantive), and if the perceptions themselves, along with the thoughts pertaining to them, are spiritual, then spirit becomes merely, as Santayana puts it, "the light of awareness"—which means that spirit, properly conceived, is a quality or a process, not a thing. And since only things (i.e., material substances) can act, it follows that spirit cannot be viewed as an actor—or (what amounts to the same thing) as a power. *Spirit is impotent, but matter is blind.* It is only when spirit is wedded to matter, as it is in sentient creatures, that matter can see and spirit can act. Yet make no mistake about it: when an animal sees, it is the spirit in him, and not the matter, that does the seeing; and when he acts, it is the matter within him, rather then the spirit, that initiates the action.

Whether you agree with this point or not, it will nevertheless play an important role in my criticism of Rand's philosophy. Rand believed that man's spirit—his mind, his intellect, his reason—constitutes a power. Man's mind, she declared, is sovereign. It exercises total power within the human organism. The unstated implication of this view is that mind is more powerful than matter. According to my philosophy, this view of the relation between mind and matter is flat out wrong. Mind, intellect, spirit are all functions of matter, not vice versa. Although man's mind or spirit may appear, to a naive observer, to control the course of his life, this appearance is a mere illusion occasioned by not distinguishing properly between the experience of a thing and the thing itself. If we are entirely honest with ourselves, I believe we will have to admit that we are controlled by something deeper within us—I call it "the will"—rather than by our minds. The mind merely experiences this control; it does not actually participate in the control itself.

Rand's conviction that man's mind constitutes a power serves as the underlying rationale of some of her most egregious philosophical errors, the most notable being her theory of history. Philosophical ideas, Rand claimed, determine the course of history. But this hypostatizes ideas into powers. Ideas, we must remember, are purely spiritual phenomena, and as such cannot be considered as powers, because spirit, in and of itself, is impotent. The ideas a man holds may appear to determine the course of his life; but it is not spirit or reason or any other abstract function or quality of the mind that chooses these ideas; no, it is man's *will* that chooses them. Spirit merely identifies and records the choices of the will; it does not, nor can it, make them.

From issues of the relation between spirit and matter we turn to issues of morality. My ethical philosophy is grounded in a firm and unrepentant naturalism. I believe in the validity of the is-ought gap, which asserts that no moral value can be proven on the basis of fact alone. If Peter and Paul entertain a difference of opinion about the weight of a certain rock, they can settle their differences merely by weighing the rock. If, however, they entertain a fundamental disagreement about moral values, then there is no way either of them will ever be able to reconcile their differences by reason alone. Since a fundamental disagreement over moral values stems from an individual's basic character, it cannot be resolved by logical argumentation. Character is something rooted within man's very nature. It is what it is: like the weather or the stars, it is impervious to rational argument.

Ayn Rand, needless to say, held a different view. She believed that an absolute code of values applicable to all men could be established by reason alone. Ethics, in her view, is an objective science in the same way that physics and chemistry are objective sciences. When founded on fact and logic, ethics would yield conclusions which all rational man, regardless of differences in fundamental character, must accept. Moral absolutes, Rand declared, not only exist, but can be objectively validated.

I do not necessarily disagree with Rand, by the way, on the question of whether moral values can be objectively validated. Where I disagree with her is on the question of whether *moral absolutes* can be objectively validated. I do not believe they can. A moral absolute is an ethical value or judgment that applies to all human beings, despite congenital differences of character. Even the value expressed by the judgment "life is good" cannot be proven to be rationally absolute, for there are clearly some people (suicides for example) who believe that life is *not* good, and it is conceivable that, at least from their point of view, they are "right." Values, according to the naturalist, are determined by the fundamental character of each individual; and since no two individuals have exactly the same character, it follows that no two individuals are likely to have exactly the same values—at least not in the sense meant here. Of course, the values an individual professes are not always the values most in harmony with his inner nature.

But this only proves that most people don't know themselves as well as they should. It proves nothing against the naturalist point of view in general.

Rand would have considered this ethical naturalism to be merely another form of moral subjectivism. The subjectivist holds that not only are there no moral absolutes, but that there is no objective standard of morality either. One can hold whatever values one wishes. One person can say that murder is good and another that it is evil and, according to the subjectivist, they would both be right. Nor would they have to give any reasons for holding their respective opinions. Subjectivism grants the individual *carte blanche* when it comes to values. Whatever he *feels* is right, *is* right.

It is a mistake to confuse, as Rand does, naturalism and subjectivism. While it is true that the naturalist rejects moral absolutes, he does not, for this reason, reject objectivity. If anything, he is even more objective than those who, like Rand, believe in moral absolutes, because he at least recognizes the all too obvious fact that different individuals will tend to value different things. If the truth be told, it is the moral absolutist, not the moral naturalist, who is the subjectivist, for it is the absolutist who dogmatically insists that *his* moral values must be the values of everyone else, and only a subjectivist with an egotistical cast of mind would ever make such an arrogant claim. The naturalist is, by comparison, far humbler. He does not believe that others ought to value what he values. He is content to let everybody worship God and pursue happiness in his or her own way. But although he believes values are *relative* to each individual, the naturalist does not, for this reason, conclude that all values are subjective and arbitrary. Since each individual has a definite character that cannot be altered by mere whim, it follows that some values will tend to express this definite character better than others. Hence, it is simply not true that one can adopt whatever values one pleases. Given the kind of person one is, some values will be more in harmony with one's inner nature than others. If, for example, an individual is fundamentally a good person, he will be doing a great wrong to himself were he to consider sadism a high moral value. But an individual who is congenitally evil and whose greatest joy is to cause pain in others will obviously be inclined to consider sadism a positive value.

My point in saying all this is not to justify the congenital sadist. On the contrary, I believe that all of us who detest sadism should do everything in our power to resist the sadist and, should he attempt to inflict harm on any of us, to imprison or exterminate him. I am only trying to point out that sadism is not necessarily immoral from the sadist's point of view, and that consequently it is useless to try to use rational arguments against any individual who is, for all intents and purposes, a *congenital* sadist. Such an individual can only be dealt with by force. This observation leads us to the final major conclusion of the naturalist view of ethics—namely, that some conflicts between men are rooted in their very natures and hence cannot be settled by rational persuasion. The notion that if everyone merely pursued their "real" or "true" or "higher" self-interest, then there would exist no genuine conflicts between men, is a pipe-dream which only someone who willfully blinds himself to the facts of human nature can possibly believe. Conflict is endemic to the human condition—as the annals of history demonstrate all too well. There will always be men who will hate each other and who will have no choice but to try to enslave or exterminate one another. Thus it has been, and thus will it always be.

Rand considered politics to be merely an application of ethics to society at large. To this extent I agree with her: if you are a naturalist in regards to human nature and ethics (as I am), then you have no excuse not to be a naturalist in politics as well. What does it mean to be a naturalist in politics? It merely means this: that perceiving politics as it *really* is, rather than how you may *wish* it to be, becomes the first principle. This does not mean that the naturalist can never have an opinion or express a preference; no, all it means is that he does everything in his power to keep his preferences from distorting his perception of political reality.

My own political preferences, as far as they go, may be summed up as follows: I am against any concentration of political or social power that is not absolutely necessary for the safety of the country. I believe in political decentralization, states' rights, and the reform of corporate law in favor of small businesses. I detest just about any concentration of power, whether it is centered in Washington, D.C. or in the boardroom of some gargantuan multinational corporation. Although I support the free enterprise system, I am not all that sympathetic with the form of "corporate capitalism" dominant today. I am for this reason not entirely sympathetic with Rand's unconditional support of laissez-faire capitalism; but I am not entirely antagonistic either.

My fiercest antagonism towards Rand is inspired by her views on aesthetics. None of Rand's views on human nature, epistemology, history, ethics, or politics bother me all that much. Even though I disagree with many of Rand's positions on these issues, I still respect her views on at least some of them. I cannot say the same about her aesthetic preferences, which seem to me shallow, uninformed, uncultivated, arrogant, and thoroughly appalling. Rand liked to pose as a champion of Western Civilization; but if her taste in literature, music, and painting is any indication, she seems to have held most of the artistic masterpieces of Western Civilization in utter contempt. She literally believed that no rational, psychologically healthy person could possibly enjoy the masterworks of Shakespeare, Beethoven, Rembrandt, or any other artist she considered "malevolent"—and she apparently considered nearly all the major artists of Western Civilization to fall within this ignominious category. In Chapter 7, I will criticize her aesthetic views and explain why my objection to them is so unyielding. In the meantime, let the reader be forewarned: on issues involving the Objectivist aesthetics, I cannot even pretend to be a detached or dispassionate critic.

Before concluding this introduction, I want to make a few general remarks about the hazards of attempting to criticize Rand's Objectivist philosophy. In the past, Rand's followers have generally sought to refute her critics by accusing them of intentionally distorting her views. I fear the same criticism may be essayed against this book as well. Before this happens, however, perhaps it would be a good idea to remember a few obvious facts about the nature of criticism. Any attempt to criticize a philosophy will necessarily involve an interpretation of that philosophy, since before any doctrine can be criticized, the critic must interpret it. In one respect at least, what follows is merely a criticism of the author's interpretation of Objectivism. The question then arises whether this interpretation is correct—which is to say, whether it actually corresponds to Objectivism as it was conceived in the mind of its originator, Ayn Rand.

Now obviously I have no direct access to Rand's mind. I have to judge her entirely by her writings—which is not always easy. In my opinion, the best way of circumventing some of the difficulties involved in interpreting Rand is to begin by focusing on her intentions as a philosopher, rather than on her actual doctrines. Her intentions at least are perfectly comprehensible—something not always the case with her philosophical doctrines, which are often riddled with non sequiturs and palpable distortions of reality. One of the greatest defects of her previous critics is that so many of them have no idea what it is that Rand is attempting to do in her philosophy. Every one of her doctrines is set up to achieve some predetermined goal. If you can find out what that goal is, it becomes that much easier to understand and interpret what Rand's philosophy is really all about.

Another defect of Rand's critics (and, incidentally, her defenders as well) has been the unfortunate tendency to get involved in merely verbal controversies over the meanings of words. In this book, I shall do everything in my power to avoid such futile disputes. I am content to allow Rand and her disciples to define their terms in any way they see fit, provided that I am granted the same liberty in my criticism of Objectivism. Philosophical criticism should not be about disputes over the definitions of words. What is important is not what this or that word means, but whether the word in question refers to anything existing in the real world of fact.

Another point I want to make has to do with the misunderstandings that can arise due to the piecemeal nature of philosophical criticism. For obvious reasons, it is impossible for me to criticize every doctrine in the Objectivist philosophy simultaneously. On the contrary, each doctrine must be examined one at a time. Now because of the interconnectedness of many doctrines in philosophy, sometimes it is impossible to thoroughly criticize one doctrine until many of its related doctrines have also been criticized. I make this point in order to warn any antagonistic readers from concluding that any criticism offered in the following pages is, in and of itself, completely exhaustive. This is not the case at all. I have taken great pains to, in effect, "structuralize" my criticism so that criticism of one doctrine will often reinforce criticisms of others—and *vice versa*. For this reason, I advise all my antagonistic readers *not* to make any assessment of the validity of any particular criticism offered in the ensuing pages until they have read the book in its entirety. I make this appeal because I would prefer criticism of this book to be as intelligent as possible. What I seek is not for my readers to agree with me—that would be an immense bore—but that they understand and criticize me intelligently. What is annoying is not criticism per se, but stupid and unenlightened criticism.

I will of course welcome any intelligent criticism made against this critique of Rand's Objectivist philosophy. Unlike Rand, I do not believe that anyone can be certain about purely theoretical knowledge. Only by allowing our theories, philosophical or otherwise, to be subjected to criticism can we ever hope to make progress towards the truth. And so if I have in fact made any errors during the course of this book, I would certainly appreciate having them pointed out to me. And if it turns out that I have unwittingly distorted any of Rand's doctrines, then I am certainly very sorry for that. Unlike many of her critics, I do not harbor any kind of personal animosity towards Rand's Objectivist philosophy. Nor do I consider Objectivism to be in any way dangerous, despite the quixotic efforts of Rand's followers to gain a wider following for their Objectivist creed. Compared to many other ideologies presently vying for attention on the contemporary scene, Objectivism strikes me as relatively benign and innocuous. If anything, it is not indignation or alarm that I feel towards Rand's followers, but merely pity, because they have placed their hopes in a philosophy which, to my mind, will never deliver what it promises.

CHAPTER 1:

————▼————

THEORY OF HUMAN NATURE

"Thus predetermination, a profound inveterate bias in will and effort, is the very condition of existence: a creature without it would be a nothing."

—George Santayana

Ayn Rand divided philosophy into five major branches: metaphysics, epistemology, ethics, politics, and aesthetics. One thing sticks out concerning this list: none of the five branches are exclusively devoted to the study of man's nature. Rand assigned the study of man's nature to metaphysics, which also studies the nature of the rest of the universe. Apparently, Rand did not regard the study of human nature to be important enough to warrant having its own branch.

Rand also held, curiously enough, that a philosopher's morality and politics are a mere "application" of his metaphysics and epistemology. In other words, a man's basic views of existence and human knowledge determine his views on how men should behave and what kind of political system they should live under. I do not altogether agree with this view. I believe that one's view of human nature plays a far more crucial role in determining one's ethical and political views than does one's views on metaphysics or epistemology. If, on the one hand, the individual entertains a largely sanguine view man's potential for moral and social development, he will be less inclined towards adopting a conservative politics and a traditional morality. But if, on the other hand, his view of man's moral and social potential is on the gloomy and pessimistic side, he will usually find himself drawn to a conservative politics and a traditional morality.

In the introduction I stated that there are two basic conceptions of human nature: the utopian and the naturalistic. Needless to say, it is the radical who reflects the utopian conception and the conservative who reflects the naturalistic one. Their diametrically opposed views of human nature stem from how they explain evil. The utopian blames evil, not on man, but on environmental factors, such as unjust social conditions, abusive parents, or an improper or pernicious education. By removing these malicious environmental influences, the utopian believes that most, if not all, of the evils of mankind can be removed. The naturalist, on the other hand, holds that evil is largely the product of corruptions intrinsic to human nature. And since human nature cannot be fundamentally changed, the naturalist concludes that there is no possible remedy for most, if not all, of the evils which beset and harass mankind. The most you can do, according to the naturalist, is to mitigate these evils; you cannot, nor should you even try, to eliminate them.

In this chapter, I will argue that Rand's view of human nature is utopian to the core. According to Rand, since man is "essentially" a rational creature, the evil he does must be a product, not of his nature, but of his ideas. By changing man's ideas, Rand believed she could, in effect, change man's nature.

*　　　　　*　　　　　*

(1) Although philosophers like to pretend that their primary goal is to discover the truth, this is rarely the case. Most philosophers are advocates and preachers who have made up their minds long before they attempt to systematize their views into a coherent philosophy. Ayn Rand is no exception to this general rule. She also had made up her mind long before she got around to systematizing her views. Her philosophy of Objectivism is largely a rationalization of her own preconceived, pet ideas. She nearly confesses as much in an interview with Alvin Toffler. In response to the question "Do you regard philosophy as the primary purpose of your writing?" Rand replied, "No. My primary purpose is the projection of an ideal man, of man 'as he might be and ought to be.' Philosophy is a necessary means to that end." (Rand, 1964a)

To admit, as Rand does here, that one's philosophy is merely a means to some end *other* than discovering the truth is tantamount to admitting that one's philosophy consists merely of an attempt to rationalize one's own personal convictions. And although this was certainly not Rand's intention when she made this statement, I do not think it is unfair to suggest that this is precisely what Objectivism is—a mere rationalization of man "as he might be and ought to be," as Rand was fond of putting it.

But what was so special about her concept of the ideal man that made her so eager to build an entire philosophy around it? I think the source of Rand's idolatry of man stems from her disgust with the mundane reality of everyday life. Rand was an incurable romantic. She found the reality of common life too insipid and unappetizing for her tastes. Life, she decided, ought to be exciting and glamorous. But life is rarely exciting and glamorous, and anyone who, like Rand, wishes it to be that way is only asking for trouble. Rand, unfortunately, was too stubborn and self-willed to accept this. To her way of thinking, life *had* to be as colorful, romantic, and exciting as an adventure novel. No other type of life would have been acceptable to her.

But how was Rand supposed to make her vision of life into a reality? Rand did not, in her own person, have the qualities necessary to lead the heroic, storybook existence she dreamed of. She was a short, stocky, unprepossessing intellectual who had so little mechanical sense that she could not even learn how to drive a car. Hardly the sort fit for high adventure and the like! Nor were the people around her all that adventuresome either. Her husband was a rather passive, mild-mannered gentleman who allowed himself to be ruled by his autocratic wife. Nothing heroic or "larger than life" about him! To tell the blunt truth, Rand was not the sort woman likely to attract the heroic type. Heroes prefer beautiful, fecund women who will not constantly be arguing with them about abstruse points of philosophy. Mere intellectuality and heroism rarely mix well together. Intellectuals tend to be sedentary in their mode of living. The rigors of a heroic existence rarely suit their effeminate, ultra-sensitive temperaments. Just look at the sort of people Rand attracted to her inner circle. You can say what you like for or against someone like Nathaniel Branden, but his behavior towards Rand can hardly be described as heroic. By his own admission, he was afraid to tell Rand that he had fallen in love with another woman. Some hero.

Despite all this, Rand would not have settled for anything less than a life of excitement, romance, and heroic achievement. But since she could not live such a life in her own person, how then was she to live it? Through her imagination, through her fiction—that is how she chose to live the heroic life she yearned for. Nor would there have been anything wrong with this if Rand had only been willing to admit that her fictions were based, not on reality and fact, as she kept insisting, but on the adolescent fantasies of her excessively romantic imagination.

Since the one thing necessary in order for life to be heroic and exciting and adventuresome was the existence of heroic, larger than life men, Rand built her fictional universe around the ideal man of her girlish fantasies. I suspect that, without this ideal man, Rand would have found life meaningless and empty. Most human beings, in order to find meaning and spiritual fulfillment in life, have to believe in something larger than themselves. For many people, God fills this need. For Rand, it was her heroic, ideal man. "[T]he difference between me and others," she once told a group of her disciples, "was my romantic sense of life, my more heroic sense of life. The heroic concept of man: that's what interested me." (Branden, Barbara, 1986, 34) If Objectivism really is, as Albert Ellis has argued, a religion, then its principle object of worship is not God, but Rand's ideal man. "I am an atheist and I have only one religion: the sublime in human nature," Rand once confessed. "There is nothing to approach the sanctity of the highest type of man possible and there is nothing that gives me the same reverent feeling, the feeling when one's spirit wants to kneel, bareheaded. Do not call it hero-worship, because it is more than that. It is a strange and improbable white heat where admiration becomes religion, and religion becomes philosophy, and philosophy—one's life." (1995, 15-16).

There is something very touching in Rand's attitude towards the "sublime in human nature," as she describes it. Far be it from me to ridicule or belittle such reverence as this! Living, as we do, in an age where so many individuals go out of their way to undermine or subvert or ridicule any symptom of greatness found in either their contemporaries or among eminent men of history, it is refreshing to run across someone who does not share the prevailing passion for dragging everything down to the lowest common denominator. However, in order to properly revere the sublime in human nature, this sublimity must have a basis in reality. If your conception of man's greatness is unrealistic, no man will ever be able to live up to it.

This is precisely what Rand is guilty of. Her standard of human greatness is so out of proportion with reality that no man could ever measure up to it. Only the purely fictional heroes of Rand's novels have ever managed to satisfy her exacting standards. Unfortunately, these fictional heroes are so extravagant and farfetched that it is difficult to take them seriously as projections of real men. They are all so pure and immaculate and even saintly in a peculiar, rationalistic sort of way that no one quite knows what to make of them. Although hardly ascetics in the traditional sense of the word, they nevertheless exhibit a kind of frigid single-mindedness one normally finds in religious enthusiasts of the most fanatical sort. And yet there is something strangely mellow and phlegmatic about them as well. The Randian hero does not allow himself to be consumed by his burning ambition to be perfect. In Rand's fictional universe, consuming ambition does not consume, nor does fanatical insistence on perfection lead to fanaticism. The Randian hero enjoys all the virtues of human nature without their corresponding defects. It is almost as if Rand has gathered up as many heroic virtues as she could find, separated them from their corresponding vices, and then glued them together to form a single mass. In the real world, men are never fashioned in this manner. The immutable laws of human nature, the most important of which is the absolute imperfectability of man, see to that. Rand's heroes might be possible in a better-constituted world; but in this world, they never can nor ever will draw breath.

Rand of course would never have accepted such a verdict. No amount of evidence, no matter how well collected or convincingly presented, would have ever forced her to admit that her fictional heroes were thoroughly unbelievable as human beings. Yet, outside Objectivist circles, this appears to be pretty much the consensus on the matter. How could anyone who is sensible of the limitations of human nature believe that John Galt, the hero of Rand's novel Atlas Shrugged, could ever be a real person? Rand portrays Galt as a completely flawless character, incapable of doing anything irrational or ill considered. As a young man, Galt, offended by the collectivist trends of society, decides that he will "stop the motor of the world" by organizing a strike of the "men of the mind" against the collectivist parasites of the ruling elite. Henceforth he travels around the country trying to convince all the non-parasitical industrialists in the land to give up everything they have worked for their entire lives—their businesses, their eminent social status, their homes, etc.—to go on strike against government exploitation of business. Eventually, he manages to persuade all the first-rate industrialists in the nation to join his strike, causing the economy, and the parasitical, socialistic government along with it, to collapse.

Yet this is not all he accomplishes. When he isn't running about convincing all the competent entrepreneurs and industrialists in the nation to give up businesses worth millions of dollars, he's working on what amounts to a perpetual motion machine, which he successfully builds and operates. Nor should we forget his romantic interest. Without even really trying, he easily manages to win the heart of his best friend's girl. In the real world, of course, his best friend would probably be just a bit teed off at having his girl snatched from him. But in the Randian universe such trivial laws of human psychology find themselves miraculously suspended. And so we find Galt's best friend demonstrating no resentment whatsoever over the filching of his girlfriend!

That both Rand's fictional characters and the stories which she builds around them should be so far removed from reality ought to make us pause and question Rand's pretensions to literary realism. Few of the incidents, and hardly any of the characters of her two major novels, *The Fountainhead* and *Atlas Shrugged*, could be considered realistic. Yet Rand never ceased insisting upon the realism of these novels. In a letter she wrote to the readers of *The Fountainhead*, Rand, responding to the assertion that the novel's hero, Howard Roark, "could not possibly be a human being," declared that, on the contrary, "Roark is the one genuine *human* being in the book—because he embodies precisely those qualities which constitute a human being [i.e., "rationality"], as distinguished from an animal." (1995, 671)

This is an especially revealing statement; for not only does it express, in the space of a single sentence, Rand's theory of human nature, but it also reveals one of her favorite epistemological tricks—i.e., that of assuming that the characteristic which distinguishes one object in a given class from all the others constitutes that object's "essential" characteristic. In this case, Rand has assumed that since rationality is (supposedly) the most important characteristic distinguishing man from all other animals, this means that rationality must be man's "essential" (i.e., most important) characteristic. Just because a certain characteristic is important in distinguishing one object from all others does not mean that it constitutes the "essential" characteristic from a practical point of view. Rationality is not necessarily man's most essential characteristic: there may be many others which he shares with animals that are just as important. To say that only the qualities that differentiate a species from a genus constitute the most essential qualities is to commit the *fallacy of difference.* Individuals guilty of this fallacy tend to exaggerate the importance of *distinguishing* characteristics at the expense of *generic* characteristics.

There is, to be sure, a great deal more to Rand's theory of human nature than simply a confusion about the relative importance of distinguishing and generic characteristics. In the next few sections, we will examine whether Rand's assertion that her fictional heroes are realistic has any merit at all.

           *   *   *

(2) Rand's theory of human nature is based on the idea that the human mind enjoys complete sovereignty over the body and the will. "Everything we do and are proceeds from the mind," Rand once declared. "Our mind can be made to control everything." (1995, 156) Man, we are told, is given his body, his mind, and the "mechanics of consciousness." The rest is up to him. "His *spirit*, that is, his own essential character, must be created by him," Rand averred. "In this sense, it is almost as if he was born as an abstraction, with the essence and rules of that abstraction (man) to serve as his guide and standard—but he must make himself concrete by his own effort, *he must create himself.* Specifically, he is born as an entity: man. But his field of action and emotion is open to his choice." (1997, 556)

This passage presents a fair example of Rand's method of reasoning. Notice the mixture of the banal and the incredible. Man, we are told, is not only capable of creating himself, he is *obligated* to do so: man *must* create himself! But how is it possible for an entity to create itself?

How can a man create his own character? Isn't the very notion of a man creating his own character a palpable contradiction? Doesn't a man have to be something (i.e., *have* a specific character) before he can create anything? To suggest that man must create his own character before he even has a specific identity is to imply that man begins as a sort of empty vacuum which through some mysterious process creates a specific character *ex nihilo*—out of nothing!

Mixed in with this absurdity is the utterance of one the most banal truisms ever invented: *man is born as an entity!* Isn't this wonderful? Think if man had been born a nonentity! How different his life would have been! Rand is very fond of placing such empirically vacuous truisms along side her more absurd declarations. It is almost as if she believes that the truisms will render the absurdities less glaring.

Even more provocative is her claim that man is born "almost as if" he were an abstraction and that he can only become a particular thing by his own effort. But what if he does not choose to make the effort? Does this mean he will remain "almost as if" he were *still* an abstraction? And what can it possibly mean to say than an individual is "almost as if" he were an abstraction? What would such an individual look like? All the individuals I know are particular and concrete. Indeed, to describe an individual as an abstraction involves an obvious contradiction. Individuals cannot be abstractions: the very fact of their individuality makes them by necessity particular. Nor does it help to qualify the statement with the phrase *almost as if.* Either individuals are concrete, or they are abstract. There is no *almost as if* about it.

The reason why Rand indulges in such blatant verbal legerdemain should be obvious: she has no empirical evidence to offer as corroboration for her theory. So she resorts to verbal trickery in order to carry a point that cannot be established on the basis of fact.

Rand's conviction that man creates himself is fundamental to her entire philosophy. It is not only crucial to her theories of history, epistemology, ethics, and aesthetics, but, more importantly, it serves as the philosophical underpinning of her "ideal" man. In order for a man to be genuinely ideal in Rand's eyes, he had to be able to take full credit for all his characteristics. He couldn't merely have been endowed with them at birth—no, he had to create them, *ex nihilo*, by his own unaided effort, like Baron Münchhausen pulling himself out of the mire by his own hair. None of this by-the-grace-of-God stuff for Rand. As far as she was concerned, man had to be his own God. Man's "essential entity," she wrote, "is his soul—and that he must create for himself. *There* is the god-like aspect of man." (1997, 564) Having rejected God, Rand sought to put man in His place.

Once Rand decided that man must create himself in order to become the ideal creature of her fantasies, she had to explain how this process of creation takes place. How exactly does a man "create" himself? According to Rand, man's "starting point, his tool for creating himself, [is his] mind. All the rest is only a development of it, a matter of remaining true to his rational mind." (1997, 564) And what, may we ask, does the rational mind develop in its effort to create its own character? What it develops is certain fundamental convictions about the nature of man and the universe. Over time, these convictions become integrated into the subconscious, where they help produce the emotions, desires, and motivations that make up each person's character.

Rand believed that a man's character is *always* the product of his fundamental convictions about himself and the world around him. She acknowledged no exceptions. All men, she insisted, are the product of their inner convictions. Even if the individual has no conscious convictions of his own, the world around him will provide a set of sub-conscious convictions as a replacement for the conscious ones. "You have no choice about the necessity to integrate your observations, your experiences, your knowledge into abstract ideas, i.e., into principles," Rand tells us. "Your only choice is whether these principles are true or false, whether they represent your conscious, rational convictions—or a grab-bag of notions snatched at random, whose sources, validity, context and consequences you do not know." (1982, 5)

Rand held that the quality of a man's character is determined by the quality of his fundamental convictions. "If they are honest but mistaken convictions (or, rather, limited), he will be an average good man. If they're honest and correct—he will be a great man." (1997, 556)

But if becoming a great man depends solely on choosing "honest and correct" convictions, then why aren't there more great men? If all men can create their own characters, why do so few men choose to be great? Objectivism explains this anomaly as follows. The initial formation of character takes place during childhood, before the individual can have any idea of what is at stake. The process goes like this: Each child self-programs his subconscious with various fundamental value-judgments or basic convictions about himself and the world around him—without, however, realizing that, by doing this, he is developing his personal character. Over time, these value-judgments become so ingrained into the psyche that it is nearly impossible to root them out and replace them with new ones. Like fixed habits, they resist all efforts to change them. But they are not completely implacable. If the individual is willing to work really hard at it, he can change the subconscious value-judgments at the base of his character, just as he can change his other bad habits. All he has to do is reprogram his subconscious with new value-judgments about himself and the world around him.

Note how this theory renders man completely responsible for what he becomes. Everything about his character, including his emotions, his impulses, his desires, his motivations, his passions, his sentiments, is the product of his own choices. If he had chosen differently, all these things would have been different. And so if a man feels improper emotions or experiences immoral desires, it is his responsibility, according to Rand, to make an effort to change them by reprogramming his subconscious. "Accept the fact that...nothing less than perfection will do," she declared. (1961, 224) Moral perfection, including the perfection of character, is the responsibility of every man.

But what constitutes perfection? How are we to distinguish a perfect man from an imperfect one? At this point we come across one of Rand's strangest fetishes: her obsession with harmonizing man's inner conflicts. The perfect man, we are told, is one who never (or rarely) experiences any conflicts between what he feels and what he thinks. He would be, as Rand herself puts it, "a fully integrated personality, a man whose mind and emotions are in harmony" and who, for this very reason, never experiences "inner conflicts." (1975, 29; 1964a)

Rand's belief in the possibility of doing away with all man's inner conflicts is fundamental to her theory of human nature and her vision of the ideal man. The principle motive behind it appears to be Rand's desire to prove that man can live exclusively by reason. Emotional conflicts pose a serious threat to human rationality, because passion predisposes man against reason. Rand could not accept the idea that man is innately predisposed against reason, because if this were true, then there would be no hope for man: his emotions would forever incline him against making the sort of "rational" choices she favored. Hence Rand's insistence that man's mind and his emotions could be integrated into a perfect harmony. Once a man achieved this perfect integration, there would exist no bias in his nature predisposing him against reason.

Rand had no intention of giving up her ideal of perfect rationality. Having convinced herself that human beings are not innately predisposed against rationality, she sought to convince others as well. Her basic argument strikes at the very notion of innate emotions: Man cannot be innately predisposed against reason because such predispositions would constitute innate emotions which, Rand declared, are impossible. "No person who understands the nature of emotions could entertain [the theory of innate emotions] for long," argues Rand's most faithful disciple and intellectual heir, Leonard Peikoff. "Innately set emotions, he would see, imply innate concepts and value judgments, i.e., innate ideas." (1991, 203-204)

This argument, like so many others used by Rand and her apologists, tries to prove one dubious assertion on the basis of another, while all along pretending that both assertions are so obvious that there is no need to prove either of them. The argument rests on the assumption that emotional predispositions are the product of ideas. But is this really true? Are a man's emotional predispositions really the product of his ideas? All the evidence at our disposal would appear to support the precise opposite conclusion. Emotional predispositions, far from being the product of ideas, are the precondition of having ideas in the first place. Now if this is true, then the Objectivist conclusion concerning the self-evident absurdity of innate ideas becomes irrelevant. Innate ideas may be as absurd as you like, but their absurdity does not rule out the existence of innate emotion.

I will explore this subject in more detail later in this chapter. In the meantime, let us finish this sketch of the Objectivist theory of human nature. So far, we have examined Rand's views on character formation and the relation between reason and emotion. The one other important component to her theory involves her view of motivation and choice. Rand's rejection of innate emotional predispositions placed her in the difficult position of trying to explain how human beings motivate themselves to make their very first choices. To declare that men are born without innate emotional predispositions is tantamount to claiming that they feel no emotions at birth. But if at birth, human beings are incapable of feeling anything one way or the other, then how can they ever be motivated to make their very first choices? An individual who felt no emotion would be completely indifferent to everything around him. Since he would not care about anything, he would have no motive to do anything; and if he had no motive to do anything, how could his conduct ever be explained? The answer is: it could not be explained. In the absence of motives, human behavior becomes completely inexplicable. Motives are to human conduct what causes are to events in nature. And just as we assume that every event in nature has a cause, so we assume that every human choice has a motive. These assumptions are essential to human knowledge. Any attempt to explain human behavior or natural events takes their validity for granted.

By the very fact that Rand has taken the trouble to formulate a theory of human nature implies her acceptance of the principle that every choice must have a motive; for if she had not accepted this principle, there would have been no point in devising her theory. The purpose of a theory of human nature is to explain the causes (i.e., the motives) of human behavior. Any theory of human nature which adopts the premise that certain human choices are intrinsically inexplicable—i.e., do not have identifiable causes or motives—subverts its very reason for being. If certain human choices are in fact inexplicable, then there can be no theory about them. The most you can do is confess your ignorance. A confession of ignorance, however, does not constitute a theory, because such a confession doesn't explain anything.

My contention is that Rand's denial of the existence of innate emotions leads her to be guilty of the very contradiction described above. This can be seen quite distinctly in her theory of choice, where, in a desperate effort to account for man's very first choice, she adopts principles that are contrary to the basic presuppositions of all human inquiry.

According to Objectivism, man's capacity to choose stems from a "primary choice" which, because it presupposes "all other choices and [is] itself irreducible," cannot "be explained by anything more fundamental." (1991, 57) What is this primary choice? Leonard Peikoff describes it as "the choice to *focus* one's consciousness." "Until a man is in focus," Peikoff goes on to explain, "his mental machinery is unable to function in the human sense—to think, judge, or evaluate. The choice to 'throw the switch' is thus the root choice, on which all others depend....By its nature, it is a first cause within a consciousness, not an effect produced by antecedent factors. It is not a product of parents or teachers, anatomy or conditioning, heredity or environment....In short it is invalid to ask: why did a man choose to focus? There is no such 'why.' There is only the fact that a man *chose*: he chose the effort of consciousness, or he chose non-effort and unconsciousness. In this regard, every man at every waking moment is a prime mover." (1991, 59-60)

There are so many questionable statements in this passage that I am not sure where to begin. Take, for instance, the assertion that man can choose between the "effort of consciousness" and the "non-effort" of unconsciousness. Where did Peikoff ever come up with the idea that consciousness requires effort? Or that a person can actually *choose* to be unconscious? The only time a person ever chooses to be unconscious is when he goes to sleep. Peikoff is here guilty of confusing the *fact of consciousness* with the *process of thought*. Thought requires effort and concentration. Consciousness requires simply being awake.

Yet this is not all that is wrong with Rand's theory from a psychological standpoint. The very notion that a man must first choose to be in focus before he can make any other choices is itself a psychological absurdity of the first order. No choice can be made unless the individual is capable of comparing the alternatives. But before he can make comparisons between the alternatives, he must already be in focus. Therefore, focus must exist *prior* to choice. To say that a man can *choose* to be in focus is as absurd as saying that he can choose to be born. Birth and focus are not matters of choice; on the contrary, they are *prerequisites* of choice!

What is most curious, however, about this theory, is not its dubious psychology, but its half-baked logic. When Peikoff describes man's primary choice as "a first cause within a consciousness, not an effect produced by antecedent factors," he unwittingly takes a detour into the miraculous. For what does it mean to say that something is a "first cause" not produced by any "antecedent factors"? Isn't the declaration that something is a "first cause" tantamount to saying that it arises *ex nihilo*, out of nothing? And isn't it just a little hypocritical for Objectivism, which prides itself on its rationalistic rejection of mysticism, to be resorting to this palpably mystical expedient? If some mystically inclined monotheist came along and attempted to defend the existence of God on the basis of a First Cause of the universe, Rand would have been the first to step forward and insist upon the fallacious logic behind the argument. Yet the very moment she finds herself in a logical bind, what does she do? She goes out and embraces the very same principle which, when used to prop up belief in monotheism, she would have unequivocally denounced as mystical and irrational! How are we supposed to explain such brazen hypocrisy? Is it possible that, unable to support her theory of human nature on the basis of reason alone, Rand had no choice but to adopt a frankly mystical, anti-reason approach? I do not believe there can be any doubt as to the answer to this question. As with most philosophers, Rand only follows reason when reason leads her where she wants to go. The minute reason turned on her, she turned on reason—as this whole primary cause argument shows only too clearly.

But what, precisely, is wrong with this primary cause twaddle? What is wrong with it is that is commits one of the most blatant self-contradictions in all of logic— namely, the notorious *causa sui*, which Nietzsche described as "the best contradiction that has been conceived so far...a sort of rape and perversion of logic." (1885, #21) A *causa sui* is something that causes itself. Usually it is applied by confused mystics to the Deity. In Rand's case, it is applied to the choice to focus or not. Since this choice is declared to be a "first cause" without any causal antecedents, then it must be a cause that originates in itself—or a *causa sui*. Why is the *causa sui* so objectionable? It is objectionable because it asserts that something can arise out of nothing—or, in other words, that something can happen for no reason. But this violates one of the very first premises of reason, according to which every action, whether mental or physical, must have a cause. To say that something causes itself is tantamount to saying that it has occurred outside the natural course of events. It is to say, in short, that a miracle has occurred.

Ayn Rand might have rejected the existence of most miracles, but the miracle of what she called man's "primary choice" she embraced with open arms. Nor should it surprise us that this should be the case. Despite her militant atheism and naive rationalism, Rand was, in her own unique way, an extremely religious person. Instead of worshiping God, Rand chose to worship the "heroic in man." As I have already pointed out, the ideal man portrayed in her novels constituted Rand's god, and in his honor she immolated what she considered man's highest virtue, his rationality. And how fitting that it should be so! For what more apposite tribute could she have offered to the idol of her deepest reverence than the sacrifice of what she regarded as man's highest virtue?

To be sure, the purpose of this "primary choice" construct goes well beyond giving homage to man. It also has a purely polemical *raison d'être*. Rand, in order to defend her theory of human nature, had to do everything in her power to prevent her followers from examining too closely the question of the fundamental basis of human choice. Hence Leonard Peikoff's admonishment against asking *why* a man chooses to be in focus. It is invalid to ask such a question, Peikoff declares, *because there is no why!* In other words, man chooses either to focus his mind or remain a gaping idiot for no reason at all! He simply chooses because he chooses, and from that choice spring all his other choices!

It is upon such absurdities that Rand attempts to justify the possibility of her ideal man. Because man can create his own character *ex nihilo*, she concludes that there is nothing in human nature to prevent man from becoming the fully integrated creature of her fantasies. The poor deluded woman! The immensity of her evasions beggars the imagination.

Later in this chapter I will explain what is wrong with Rand's ideal of a fully integrated human being. For now we will content ourselves with examining one other aspect of the Objectivist theory of choice: Rand's theory of free will. Like many other philosophers, Rand was confused about the issue of free will. She believed that man's freedom depended on the *liberum arbitrium indifferentiae*, that is, on the free decision of the will, immune from any influences outside one's control. Since man had to control every possible influence on the will, the existence of innate predispositions had to be rejected. The will, contended Rand, is completely *neutral* at birth: it contains no innate psychological tendencies whatsoever. Nor could it as long as men have free will. "A free will saddled with a tendency is like a game with loaded dice," insisted Rand. "It forces man to struggle through the effort of playing, to bear responsibility and pay for the game, but the decision is weighted in favor of a tendency that he had no power to escape. If the tendency is of his choice, he cannot possess it at birth; if it is not of his choice, his will is not free." (1961, 168-169)

This is about as unequivocal an expression of the *liberum arbitrium indifferentiae* as you are likely to find. The dice metaphor is especially revealing. To say that a free will saddled with an innate tendency would be like a "game with loaded dice" implies that a free will without such an innate tendency would be equivalent to a game played with *fair* dice. In other words, if the will is neutral at birth, as Rand contends, then one choice is just as likely as any other.

This view of free will is impossible to adhere to either in speculation or in practice. If all man's predispositions are the product of a "free" choice in the sense described above, then all human behavior must be regarded as purely arbitrary and contingent. One type of behavior becomes just as likely as any other type. Man's predispositions are merely the products of habits formed by chance. Under such a view, human behavior becomes inexplicable and unpredictable. Since it is obvious that no one, not even Rand herself, actually regards human beings as completely unpredictable, it is difficult to take the *liberum arbitrium indifferentiae* all that seriously. A handful of philosophers may pretend to adhere to it on paper, but no one consistently adheres to it anywhere else.

*　　　*　　　*

(3) A theory stands or falls on whether it can be corroborated by empirical reality. If evidence for a theory is lacking, the theory probably does not accord with reality. Without empirical evidence to serve as corroboration, theories are close to worthless.

Bearing this in mind, let us turn to the question of empirical evidence. Does there exist any viable corroborative evidence supporting Rand's theory of human nature? Or is this theory merely the product of wishful thinking and empirically vacuous speculation?

There are three main issues I want to focus on in this section. We will commence with an examination of Rand's claim that innate predispositions do not exist. Is it really true that human beings have absolutely no innate propensities of character at all? And what sort of evidence does Rand provide in defense of her claim? Next we will examine Rand's claim that man's emotions are the product of his ideas. Are emotions merely the manifestations of value judgments programmed by the mind into the subconscious? Again, our focus will be on factual evidence, not on mere argumentative innuendo. And finally, we will conclude with an examination of Rand's conviction that man can live by reason alone. Does this belief have a leg to stand on? Is there any evidence to suggest that a perfect, unbreached rationality is in fact possible? After examining the evidence relating to these three issues, we will be in a better position to determine whether Rand's theory of human nature accords with reality.

1. *Do innate predispositions exist?* Rand rejected the existence not only of innate emotional predispositions, but of innate behavioral and cognitive propensities as well. "Man is born with an emotional mechanism, just as he is born with a cognitive mechanism," she wrote; "but, at birth, *both* are 'tabula rasa.'" (1964b, 30)

Does Rand present any evidence for this view? No, she does not. You can go through all of her writings without finding so much as a shred of scientifically validated evidence supporting her contention that innate predispositions do not exist. There is a very good reason for this: no such evidence exists. The scientific evidence for innate, genetic determination of human behavior is enormous. As scientist and naturalist Edward O. Wilson has noted: "The question of interest is no longer whether human social behavior is genetically determined; it is to what extent. The accumulated evidence for a large hereditary component is more detailed and compelling than most persons, including even geneticists, realize. I will go further: it already is decisive." (1978, 19)

As one example, consider the phenomenon of incest taboos. Aversion to incest is one of the most widespread characteristics of the human race. Even in societies where incest occurs on a regular basis, it is nearly always regarded with shame and horror. How can we explain this aversion? Naive rationalists explain it as a means of preventing inbreeding, which leads to children of diminished body size, muscular coordination, and intelligence and carries with it an abnormally high rate of birth defects. (Wilson, 1978, 37) But this explanation assumes that knowledge of inbreeding is universally known, even among tribal savages. This assumption does not accord with reality. As Wilson points out: "Of the thousands of societies that have existed through human history, only several of the most recent have possessed any knowledge of genetics. Very few opportunities presented themselves to make rational calculations of the destructive effects of inbreeding. Tribal councils do not compute gene frequencies and mutational loads. The automatic exclusion of sexual bonding between individuals who have previously formed certain other kinds of relationships—the 'gut feeling' that promotes the ritual sanctions against incest—is largely unconscious and irrational." (1978, 38)

In other words, the aversion to incest is not a product of rational deliberation or choice. No one chooses to be averse to incest. That aversion is built into the very structure of human sentiments. It is a product of humanity's genetic endowment. (Pinker, 1997, 455-460)

Sexual selection is governed by many other innate propensities besides incest aversion. Young males nearly always prefer beautiful young women to wrinkled old hags as sexual partners. Is this aversion a product of their choosing? Of course not. How could it be? If males could choose to prefer wrinkled hags to beautiful young fecund wenches, why have nearly all of them chosen to prefer the young to the old? The fact that nearly all of them have chosen to prefer one over the other indicates the existence of some kind of innate bias.

Studies of identical twins provide further evidence that genetics influence human behavior. Such studies reveal a genetic component in a variety of traits affecting the emotional and cognitive development of human beings, including number ability, word fluency, memory, the rate of language acquisition, spelling, grammar, perceptual skills, psycho-motor skills, and extroversion-introversion. Even when the influence of environment has been factored in, identical twins nevertheless demonstrate a greater similarity in general abilities, personal traits, ideals, goals, and vocational interests then would be expected if genetic determination played no role whatsoever. (Wilson, 1978, 45-46; Pinker, 1997, 20-21) Genetic factors, which is to say *innate* factors, count for something very definite in human behavior. While they do not necessarily determine *everything*, they do determine quite a bit, especially in regards to the desires, sentiments, and emotions of human beings.

But what about the cognitive side of things? Is man's mind a "tabula rasa," a blank slate, at birth? The evidence would strongly suggest that the mind is not a blank slate at birth and that many learning propensities are built into the very structure of the mind. (Pinker, 1997, 34-36) A cardinal example is the propensity to learn language, which exists in all physiologically normal children. Children do not acquire language by choice, they acquire it on the basis of an overwhelming predisposition against which they are helpless to resist. That is why all physiologically normal children who are exposed to language learn to speak. There is no record of a child choosing *not* to learn how to speak. Only children with some sort of physical defect (e.g., deafness, mental retardation, disturbances of the brain) or who have never been exposed to human speech fail to develop the facility for communicating by means of language. (Pinker, 1997, 529) Choice has nothing to do with it. An infant child does not one day stop and reflect on whether he wants to learn how to speak. How could he? Since he cannot as yet use language, he is incapable of the sort of rational deliberation necessary to make such a choice.

Another important innate cognitive predisposition involves the propensity to expect environmental uniformities. When the infant has once burnt his fingers on the stove, he rarely, if ever, tries to touch the stove again. From the viewpoint of the tabula rasa theory of the mind, this behavior is entirely inexplicable. How could a completely blank mind conclude from one experience of touching a hot stove that all such experiences will prove equally painful? From one experience nothing can be rationally concluded. A blank mind would have no reason to assume that hot stoves will always burn fingers in the future. Yet this is precisely what the infant mind concludes. How can we explain this? Obviously, the only way to explain it is by assuming that human beings are born with an innate propensity to expect uniformities in their environment. If the stove burns the child's hand once, he instinctively expects it to burn his hand in the future and for this reason refrains from ever touching it again.

The most convincing evidence for the existence of innate predispositions resulting from inherited genetic structures is provided by the example of certain types of mutations. Turner's syndrome, which occurs when two X chromosomes are passed on during conception, impairs the ability to recall shapes and distinguish between right and left on maps and diagrams. Lesh-Nyhan syndrome, which results from a single recessive gene, inevitably brings about lowered intelligence and a compulsive propensity to pull and tear at the body, leading to self-mutilation. (Wilson, 1978, 44) If innate predispositions based on genetic determination do not exist, how do we explain these behavior propensities in mutants? If such tendencies do not provide conclusive evidence of innate, genetic-based predispositions, then there exists no such thing as conclusive evidence. One can hardly imagine more conclusive evidence than this.

Not all innate predispositions are general to the human race at large. Some are specific to certain individuals. Handedness is an example of this: although all men are predisposed towards handedness, they are not all predisposed to being either left-or right-handed. Most are predisposed toward being right-handed, but some are predisposed toward being left-handed. These predispositions are not chosen; they are innate. No one in his right mind would ever choose to be left-handed in a world dominated by right-handers. Those who are left-handed are born that way.

Another important point about predispositions is that not all of them are entirely compulsive. It is possible to act in defiance of them. Again, handedness is a case in point. In traditional Chinese societies, children are forced to use their right hand in writing and eating. This form of environmental conditioning works in nearly all instances. Nearly all left-handed children in China learn to write and eat with their right hands. Yet, curiously enough, in all other activities where conditioning is absent, their left-handedness reasserts itself. (Wilson, 1978, 57) When left alone, innate predispositions usually get their way.

Environmental factors also play a very important role in the development of predispositions. As we saw in the example of handedness, it is possible to condition people so that they will behave contrary to some of their predispositions. However, conditioning is only effective within certain parameters: human nature is not infinitely malleable. It will bend to a certain point, but beyond that point it will not budge. Moreover, the parameters of conditioning are not the same for all individuals. Some people can be more easily conditioned than others. Not everyone can be molded after the same pattern.

The general point made here is of great importance for understanding what is and what is not possible in human nature. Thinkers like Rand are eager to convince us that if a few human beings can act on the basis of this or that moral ideal, then most human beings can act on the basis of it as well. But this is a *non sequitur*. What is possible for the few is not necessarily possible for the many. If the majority of individuals are predisposed against acting in accordance with a given moral system, any attempt to make them act in accordance with it will probably fail. Forcing human beings to act against their innate predispositions is like swimming upstream: it can be attempted but it rarely gets you anywhere.

Not only are the parameters of conditioning different from individual to individual, but the effects of conditioning may also be different. One individual may develop one set of character traits as a result of environmental influences or conditioning, while another may develop an entirely different set of traits. It all depends on the nature of their innate predispositions. Some innate predispositions will remain dormant unless brought to life by specific environmental conditions. Others will fail to develop if conditions remain inauspicious. An individual born and raised among the Bushmen of the Kalahari Desert can never become a Nobel Prize winning scientist, because the social forces prevalent in Bushmen society would never allow him to develop the traits necessary for scientific activity. This would be true even if he is endowed with the innate predispositions which, under more propitious circumstances, would incline him towards a career in science. Just because a man is born with a specific innate predisposition does not mean this predisposition will cause him to behave in a specific way. Most (if not all) individuals of the male sex are born with a predisposition towards aggression, but not all of them behave aggressively. It often takes a specific environment to trigger the aggressive behavior. This fact, however, does not mean that men should be regarded as determined by their environment. If the predispositions which the environment triggers did not exist, the resulting behavior would most likely never occur. As Wilson puts it: "[I]nnateness refers to the measurable probability that a trait will develop in a specified set of environments." (1978, 100) *Probability* is the key concept here. If there were no measurable probabilities concerning the behavioral traits of human nature, it would be impossible to formulate realistic expectations concerning the conduct of human beings. If every human behavioral trait were the product of the *liberum arbitrium indifferentiae*, then knowledge of human nature would be impossible.

The fact that genetics and environment play a crucial role in human behavior does not mean that human beings are incapable of exercising volition or making choices: man is not an automaton. But the power of human choice is hemmed in on every side by the constraints provided by innate predispositions on the one side and social environment on the other. Failure to acknowledge the existence of these constraints can only lead to unrealistic expectations about human behavior. And this is precisely what is wrong with Rand's theory of man. In her eagerness to prescribe how man ought to be, she blinds herself to what he really is.

2. *Are emotions entirely the product of thinking?* Although many psychologists in recent decades have emphasized the role of thinking and ideas in the generation of emotions, few if any psychologists would accept Rand's theory that *all* emotions are generated by man's cognitive ideas. Anyone with extensive therapeutical experience understands that emotions are far more complicated than Rand makes them out to be. Even psychologists who believe that ideas play a crucial role in the development of emotions would never accept Rand's extreme version of the theory. Cognitive therapist Albert Ellis is a case in point. Ellis made a name for himself among psychologists for his advocacy of the view that emotional disturbances can be resolved through rational thinking. Although Ellis agrees with Rand about the important role of thinking and ideas in the generation of emotion, his experience as a psychotherapist prevents him from embracing the Objectivist assertion that *all* emotions are the product of cognition. "We would better face the fact that cognition itself (and its product, reason) is biased and restricted by our (also) limited powers of perceiving,

emoting, and acting," Ellis warns us. "Just *because* we are fallible humans *all* our behaving abilities—including sensation, perceiving, thinking, emoting, and acting—are imperfect and restricted. The virtually perfect, one-to-one relationship between our thought and emotions that objectivism posits is therefore nonexistent." (1968, 39)

Now considering the fact that no reputable psychologist believes that emotions are *solely* the product of our ideas, you would think that Rand would have been eager to back her theory with empirical data. This is usually what is expected of theorists who seek to challenge prevailing orthodoxies. To merely assert that these orthodoxies are mistaken is not enough. The theorist is expected to back his claims with scientific evidence. But Rand never once bothered to provide any such evidence. What we get instead is mere assertion occasionally supplemented with one or two irrelevant observations. (Rand, 1964b, 30-31; Peikoff, 1991, 153-158)

But even if man's emotions are not *entirely* the product of his ideas and his thinking, isn't it possible that at least *some* of man's emotions might be influenced by his thinking? Yes, it is possible, though only in a limited and indirect sense. Emotions are triggered by experiences relating to the frustration or satisfaction of bodily and spiritual desires. When our desires are satisfied—or we at least think they will be satisfied—we experience positive emotions. When our desires are frustrated—or we at least believe they will be frustrated—we feel negative emotions. The strength of the emotional experience, whether positive or negative in content, is roughly proportional to the strength of the desire. When we are on the verge of attaining something we desire very badly, we feel ecstatic with joy. But when it appears that we will not get what we badly want, we feel bitterly disappointed.

The emotions brought about by the frustration or satisfaction of desires are *never* determined by thinking. In this respect, man's emotional mechanism is *not* empty at birth. Men always feel positive emotions when their desires are satisfied and negative emotions when their desires are frustrated. They do not choose to feel this way by thinking, as Rand implies. No man could program his emotional mechanism to generate positive emotions when his desires are frustrated and negative emotions when his desires are satisfied. This is obvious from common experience.

But although man's thinking cannot affect *how* he will react emotionally to the satisfaction or frustration of his desires, it can influence his emotions in other ways. The principle function of human thought is to develop strategies of desire-satisfaction. If the mind can develop effective strategies of desire-satisfaction, more desires will be satisfied and the individual will experience more positive emotions as a result. But if the mind fails to develop effective strategies for desire-satisfaction, fewer desires will be satisfied and the individual will experience more negative emotions as a result. Emotional trouble is often caused by the development of poor strategies for desire-satisfaction. Over time, these strategies become habituated into the psyche, so that the individual follows them without realizing it. One of the duties of the psychotherapist is to identify these bad strategies and help the patient replace them with better ones—something that is not always easy to do, since there are often very powerful emotional compulsions at the base of these ineffective strategies. But if the patient can learn to think about these strategies in rational terms, it is possible for him to change the type of emotions he experiences. But the change does not take place by any sort of "reprogramming" of the emotional mechanism, as Objectivism suggests. The individual still feels happy when his desires are satisfied and depressed when they are not. What is changed is the efficiency of desire-satisfaction: more desires are satisfied and the individual enjoys the illusion of happiness to a greater extent.

Another way thinking can affect our emotions is through its influence on how we interpret our prospects for desire-satisfaction. Emotions do not only occur when our desires are either frustrated or satisfied: they also occur as a result of our assessment of our prospects for desire-satisfaction. If we think that our prospects are good, we will feel happy; if we think that they are bad, we will feel depressed.

Many psychological problems result from adopting presuppositions about the world and ourselves, which cause us to misinterpret our prospects for desire-satisfaction. The most common misinterpretation stems from the presupposition that desire-satisfaction is an extremely precarious business and will fail under most circumstances. Because the individual is pessimistic about his prospects for desire-satisfaction, he tends to assume that he will never be able to get what he wants, which leads to feelings of distress and unhappiness.

In her theory of the emotions, Rand contended that *all* man's emotions stem from his basic presuppositions about himself and the world. While there is an element of truth in this contention, Rand is clearly guilty of exaggeration. Man's presuppositions about himself and the world exercise, at best, merely an indirect and limited effect on the emotions. Such presuppositions, through their influence on a man's assessment of his prospects for desire-satisfaction, can help determine whether the individual experiences one type of emotion rather than another, but the emotion itself is always determined in the context of a man's desires. These desires may be purely physical, such as hunger or sexual lust, or they may be "spiritual," such as the desire to maintain the integrity of some custom or ritual or the desire for the admiration of others (i.e., vanity).

The truth of this can be established by a very simple psychological experiment. Ask yourself why you experience any emotion. Always you will find at the bottom of it the satisfaction or frustration of some desire. If you are angry, it is because you believe someone is responsible for causing you an injury—i.e., of thwarting one of your precious desires. If you feel jealous, it is because the possession of something you desire—i.e., friendship, love, honor—is threatened by a rival. If you feel gratitude, it is because someone has prevented one of your desires from being frustrated (i.e., saved you from misery and pain). Although presuppositions, ideas, thoughts, etc. may influence your emotional experiences in one way or another, the one constant is desire. Therefore, desire must be regarded as the *primary* cause of emotion. Thinking, at best, is merely a *secondary* cause.

Further evidence for the secondary role of thinking is provided by empirical studies of the effect of physiological changes on emotional experience. Hormonal changes precipitated by pregnancy and birth, menstruation and menopause are known to have a profound impact on the emotional experiences of women. One study demonstrated that the mood cycles of a sample of college women can be predicted from the menstrual cycle. (Konner, 1982, 118) Other studies have shown that the risk of psychotic and other mental breakdown in women is five times greater in the three months postpartum than during the last trimester of pregnancy. (Konner, 1982, 342) What has become known as the "postpartum blues" is an established scientific fact.

If thinking is the sole or primary cause of emotions, how can we account for the profound effect of hormonal changes on the emotional experiences of women? Is it merely a coincidence that many women experience depression after giving birth? Or is there some other factor at work here?

Studies of the emotional life of infants have proven the existence of emotional experiences which cannot possibly be caused by either thinking or environmental influences. Melvin Konner, the author of *The Tangled Wing*, relates that in "every sample of infants, in widely separated social classes and cultures around the world, the percentage of infants who fret, cry, or show other signs of distress when the mother leaves or when a strange person appears rises markedly after the age of six months. In each sample, some or even many infants do not show obvious fear at all, and some respond positively to strangers. But the growth change is universal in this sense: Before the age of six months, and especially between birth and four months of age, signs of fear are for all intents and purposes nonexistent, whereas after seven or eight months of age, they are quite common, and in some samples predominate." (1982, 222)

To suppose that the emergence of fearfulness among infants is caused by thinking would be ludicrous. Yet this is precisely what Rand's theory of emotions would have us suppose. Since Rand believed that all man's emotions are the product of his thinking, it follows that the emotion of fearfulness in infants would also have to be the product of thinking! No wonder Rand failed to provide evidence for her theory. The fact of the matter is, all the scientifically relevant evidence points to a very different theory.

As absurd and contrary to fact as Rand's theory of emotions undoubtedly is, her theory of human desire is, if anything, even more ludicrous. Consider the following passage from Rand's philosophical journal: "The basic process of man's life goes like this: his thinking determines his desires, his desires determine his actions. (Thinking, of course, is present all along the line, at every step and stage. His desires are a combination of thought and emotion (the 'production' and the 'consumption' sides being involved), and all his emotions are determined by his thinking, most particularly by his basic premises.)" (1997, 475)

Those who regard Rand as a great thinker ought to ponder some of the assertions made in this passage. How can anyone in his right mind seriously believe that man's thinking determines his desires? The desire for food exists whenever a man has not eaten all day. What he thinks has nothing to do with it. The same goes for many other desires. Thinking does not cause thirst—deprivation of water causes thirst. Thinking does not cause the increase of sexual desire during puberty—no, the physical and hormonal changes brought about by puberty are the cause of increased sexual desire. Thinking does not cause the desire for personal affection—how could it? We find evidence of this desire in infants and animals, neither of which knows how to think on a human level.

3. *Is it possible for men to subject every aspect of their lives to the dominion of reason?* Rand believed so. "If one recognizes the supremacy of reason and applies it consistently, all the rest follows," she wrote. "This—the supremacy of reason—was, is and will be the primary concern of my work, and the essence of Objectivism." (Binswanger, 1986, 410)

Rand is here guilty of the old error of confounding the instrumental with the teleological, the means with the end. Rand describes reason as "man's *tool* of knowledge, the faculty that enables him to perceive the facts of reality." (1964b, 20) But if reason is a tool, how can it be regarded as a leading principle of human life? The function of a tool is to serve, not to command. To try to subject every aspect of human life to what is merely instrumental is to confuse the means with the ends.

No one can live for the sake of reason, any more than they can live for the sake of a hammer or a broom. These are all instruments meant to serve something higher than themselves. The purpose of reason is to develop strategies for desire-satisfaction. Reason, being a mere tool, can never, on its own initiative, originate the desires which it serves.

The truth of this was established by the British philosopher David Hume. "Reason, being cool and disengaged, is no motive for action," argued Hume, "and directs only the impulse received from appetite or inclination, by showing us the means of attaining happiness or avoiding misery." (1751, 88) Hume, in order to prove this thesis, suggested the following experiment:

"Ask a man, *why he uses exercise*; he will answer, *because he desires to keep his health*. If you then enquire, *why he desires health*, he will readily reply, *because sickness is painful*. If you push your enquiries further, and desire a reason, *why he hates pain*, it is impossible he can ever give any. This is an ultimate end, and is never referred to any other object.

"Perhaps, to your second question, *why he desires health*, he may also reply, that *it is necessary for the exercise of his calling*. If you ask, *why he is anxious on that head*, he will answer, *because he desires to get money*. If you demand *why? It is the instrument of pleasure*, says he. And beyond this it is an absurdity to ask for a reason. It is impossible there can be a progress *in infinitum*; and that one thing can always be a reason, why another is desired. Something must be desirable on its own account, and because of its immediate accord with human sentiment or affection." (1751, 87)

What is here demonstrated is that human beings require some sort of desire or sentiment or passion—call it what you will—to motivate their conduct. Reason is merely an instrument of this motivation. It is not, nor can it ever be, the *cause* of the motives it serves. As Hume put it: "Reason is...the slave of the passions, and can never pretend to any other office than to serve and obey them." (1739-40, 462) I believe that anyone who honestly reflects on his own motives will have to agree with Hume's conclusion.

Now if reason is incapable of originating the motives of the will, then Rand's desire to subjugate every aspect of human life to reason must be regarded as a futile undertaking. Man's motives are determined, not by his reason, but by his desires. You take away a man's reason, and he is still capable of acting; but if you take away his capacity to desire, then you have irretrievably paralyzed his will. The satisfaction of desire (i.e., pleasure) and the avoidance of pain are the only possible motives for action.

Closely related to Rand's desire to make reason supreme in human nature is her belief in the possibility of disposing of all man's inner conflicts. "There is no necessary clash, no dichotomy between man's reason and emotions—provided he observes their proper relationship," Rand insisted. "A rational man knows—or makes it a point to discover—the source of his emotions, the basic premises from which they come; if his premises are wrong, he corrects them....In appraising a situation, he knows why he acts as he does and whether he is right. He has no inner conflicts, his mind and emotions are integrated, his consciousness is in perfect harmony." (Binswanger, 1986, 142)

Sounds wonderful—but is it true? Of course it isn't! How could it be? Man's inner conflicts are caused, not by a clash between feeling and thought, but by clashes between rival desires. (Pinker, 1997, 419-421) And since a man's desires stem from innate, genetically determined components in human nature, it is futile to think that they can be gotten rid of through some sort of psychological trick. Such conflicts constitute an essential part of the human condition. No man is entirely free from them.

Rand's conviction that it is possible to do away with inner conflicts, like her concomitant conviction that it is possible to live by reason alone, has no foundation in anything other than her own wishful thinking. Every day of our lives we find ourselves being forced to choose between conflicting desires. Should I have cereal for breakfast, or ham and eggs? Should I vacation in Europe or Hawaii? Should I spend the evening watching television or go to a concert? So many of our decisions involve choosing between two or more things which we desire but which we cannot enjoy at the same time. Some of these decisions are trivial, but others can be very difficult. Should a woman seek fulfillment in a career or in having a family? Should a man pursue a career that he enjoys or one that makes him a lot of money? Should a politician seek to do what is honorable or what increases his chances of getting elected? All these conflicts involve clashes between rival desires, whether it is the desire for material success, for procreation, for vocational fulfillment, for honor, or for power. Such clashes of desires cannot be eliminated merely by "harmonizing" one's consciousness—whatever that means! As long as human desire remains unlimited— which is to say, as long as human beings continue to exist and suffer—men will experience inner conflicts. To think otherwise is to evade the obvious.

$$*\qquad\qquad *\qquad\qquad *$$

(4) *Conclusion.* The great difficulty in analyzing Rand's philosophy arises out of the complexity of its confusions. Objectivism is hardly the coherent system of philosophy its creator believed it to be. At best, it is merely a haphazard collection of facile rationalizations thrown together for polemical purposes. Rand sought to convince herself and

others that man "is a being of self-made soul." (1961, 160) Her principle argument consists of nothing more than the assertion that man must be the creator of his own soul, because if he is not, then his soul is the helpless product of forces outside its control.

In the previous two sections, I have tried to explain as clearly as possible why I believe this theory of human nature is false. In this section, I want to examine what might happen were this theory accepted as gospel truth. Suppose it were possible to convince people that man's character is the product of his fundamental convictions? What effect would this belief have on their lives? How would their view of man and society be changed? What impact would it have on their expectations regarding the behavior of other people?

The most significant aspect of Rand's theory of human nature involves her denial that human beings have innate predispositions. If it were possible to convince people to behave as if this premise were true, the consequences would be tremendous. In the absence of innate predispositions, the behavior of human beings would be largely unpredictable. Under such a premise, human nature would be entirely fluid. No type of behavior would be any more likely than any other type. Consequently, we would not be able to form expectations about strangers, because no single type of behavior would be any more likely than any other. Nor could we form very secure expectations about our intimate acquaintances, since at any time they could choose to alter their personalities. Even judgments made about society at large—as, for example, those found in the various theories of the social sciences—would all have to be rejected as so much sophistry and superstition.

The disciplines of economics, politics, sociology, and psychology are all based on the assumption that some forms of human behavior are more likely than others. Economics, for instance, assumes that there exists an innate predisposition in human beings to buy cheap and sell dear. It is from this predisposition that most of the laws of free market economics are founded, including the law of supply and demand. Imagine trying to run a business without being able to rely on the validity of the basic principles of economics! Yet this is just one of the many radically subversive consequences that would inevitably follow if Rand's doctrine of human nature were universally accepted and taken to heart.

Of course, in real life, it would be impossible to follow such a doctrine in practice. The necessity of believing that some forms of behavior are more likely than others is so great that no theory could ever overturn it. Even Rand herself, despite her denials to the contrary, believed in certain innate predispositions—as we shall shortly see. Nor could it have been any other way. As Rand herself admits, everything must have a nature, including man. Rand would have us believe that man's nature is not to have a nature; but this is absurd. To have a nature means to have a predisposition to act in a certain way. The predisposition of a bowling ball is to roll when pushed. Although the predispositions of man are greatly more complex than those of a bowling ball, nonetheless the same principle must hold. One factor contributing to the greater complexity of man's predispositions over those of inanimate objects is man's capacity to choose between various alternatives. But before he can exercise his faculty of choice, there must exist a basis for choice. The basis of choice is preference, which must precede choice and cannot, for this reason, be a product of choice. Where, then, does this preference come from? It can come from only one source: from innate factors built into each one of us. It is from this innate, genetic endowment that human beings are able to form intuitive or rational expectations concerning the probable behavior of other members of the species.

Although Rand did not always adhere to her conviction that man is born without innate preferences, on those occasions when she did allow herself to be influenced by it, she inevitably got herself into trouble. According to Leonard Peikoff, Rand was repeatedly taken in by many of the young people who sought access to her inner circle. Yet no matter how often this happened, she refused to make, as Peikoff puts it, "collective judgments." "Each time she unmasked one of these individuals she struggled to learn from her mistake," Peikoff tells us. "But then she would only be deceived by some new variant." (Rand, 1990a, 350)

In her unwillingness to make "collective judgments"— or, as I would put it, *to discover uniformities in the behavior of those around her*—Rand at least was consistent to her philosophy of human nature. If no form of behavior is any more likely than any other, then of course collective judgments are out of the question. But in that case we would be pretty much at a loss to know how to deal with other people. If none of us had any idea of what to expect from others, our lives would be virtually unlivable. Success in life depends on having at least some sort of idea how the people around us are likely to behave. Expectations concerning human behavior are formed on the basis of various uniformities discovered in both individual men and the human race in general. People who are ignorant of them will tend to make bad decisions in their dealings with others. Indeed, an argument could be made that knowledge of the uniformities of human nature constitutes the most important knowledge there is. Without it, we are pretty much at the mercy of others. Ayn Rand herself is an eloquent example. It is hardly surprising that a woman whose philosophy discourages making collective judgments about people should have repeatedly found herself taken advantage of by individuals eager to cash in on her fame. Anyone with any kind of insight into human nature would know that there will always be a great many people eager to profit from an association with famous writers and philosophers. An individual has to be willfully naive not to understand this.

It is my contention that Rand's theory of human nature constitutes Objectivism's most serious flaw. Although Rand liked to pose as an uncompromising realist who never allowed her emotions to compromise her grasp of reality, she can hardly be regarded as a realist in regards to human nature. Her theory is utopian to the core. Human beings are free, she declares, to adopt any sort of nature they please. The only possible limitation to this freedom is *external* reality: man, Rand admits, cannot choose to develop a moral and social nature inimical to his survival unless he is prepared to suffer the consequences. But as long as the character chosen by the individual in question is in harmony with the requirements of his survival, the sky is the limit.

From this theory of man's nature it is possible to construct a concomitant theory of man's secular salvation. It goes without saying that Rand, good rationalist that she was, did not believe in any kind of religious or other-worldly salvation for man. But like so many other secular thinkers eager to replace traditional religion with some sort of puerile rationalistic ideology, Rand could not bring herself to reject the fundamental impulses at the base of religion, especially those dealing with the question of man's spiritual salvation. She, too, wanted to save man's soul, but instead of looking to God for help, she believed she could save him all by herself. She sought to justify this extravagant *hubris* by developing a theory of human nature which vindicated her belief that man could achieve a state of moral and spiritual perfection in *this* life, here on earth. The magic formula through which man could perfect himself was philosophy. With the right ideas, a man could secure the secular equivalent of religious salvation. And what was true of man as an individual was also true of society as a whole. Although Rand adamantly denied advocating a utopian vision of society, she nevertheless believed in what, for all practical purposes, amounts to the same thing—namely, the "ideal" society of free and rational individuals living under a social system of perfect *laissez-faire* capitalism; a society where, in the words of Rand scholar Chris Sciabarra: "People would not act on the basis of an uncritical acceptance of traditions and/or of tacit rules of behavior. They would understand the nature of their actions and the implications of their beliefs...Accepting their own uniqueness and potential, such people would have a benevolent attitude toward one another. Human communications, sexual relations, spiritual commitments, and material exchanges would not be masked by strategic lying and deceit, but by mutual trust and respect." (1995, 367-368)

Anyone who, like myself, is sympathetic to the naturalist view of human nature must regard this particular manifestation of wishful thinking as clearly falling under the utopian standard. How could it be anything but utopian? According to the naturalist view, before a theory of what is possible in human nature can be considered plausible, there must exist at least some historical evidence for it. Where, then, might I ask, is the historical evidence for this view? The answer is: there is no historical evidence—*none* exists. Throughout the entire history of mankind, there has never been a society in which human relations, whether sexual, spiritual, or economic in nature, have not been, to at least some degree, marked by "strategic lying and deceit." Nor has a society ever existed in which individuals could dispense with "uncritically accepted traditions." For this reason alone, if not for a multitude of others, it would appear that Rand's ideal society is nothing more than the puerile fabrication of a mind that has lost all connection with reality.

In the next chapter, we will examine some of the arguments Rand put forward to justify her conviction that the ideal society presented in her philosophy is not merely possible, but, given the laws of history, nearly inevitable.

CHAPTER 2:

THEORY OF HISTORY

"In place of all these [factors], so numerous, so varying, so compli-
cated, worshipers of the goddess Reason see only one, the state of
knowledge and the logical consequences of knowledge, thence going
on to imagine that the modes and forms of society are determined by
reasoning. That notion is highly pleasing to 'intellectuals,' for they
are manufacturers of reasonings, and every manufacturer sings the
praises of his wares."

—Vilfredo Pareto

One of the most characteristic assumptions of Rand's
Objectivist philosophy is that reality is far less complicated
than most educated people are inclined to believe. To her
way of thinking, most of the phenomena of reality can be
reduced to a single, monistic, "primary" cause. The idea
that an effect might have more than one cause struck
Rand as intellectually perverse—a product of what she

called the "anti-conceptual mentality." Reality, as far as she was concerned, had to be simple. Otherwise, how could it be knowable?

Rand's theory of history represents a perfect example of her monistic inclinations. According to this theory, the course of history is primarily determined by one major factor: *philosophy*. "Philosophy is the factor that moves a nation, shaping every realm and aspect of men's existence, including their values, their psychology, and, in the end, the headlines of their daily newspapers," explains her faithful protégé, Leonard Peikoff. (1991, 339) But what about other possible causes of historical change? What about economic, political, and psychological factors? Don't these other factors also play a role in the historical farce? While Peikoff is willing to admit that "philosophy is not the only cause of the course of the centuries," he nevertheless insists that "it is the *ultimate* cause," which means: "the cause of all the other causes....If there is to be an explanation of so vast a sum as human history, which involves all men in all fields, only the science dealing with the widest abstractions can provide it. The reason is that only the widest abstractions can integrate all those fields." (1991, 452)

This passage positively reeks with monism. In effect, Peikoff is saying that it is the very complexity of history which justifies reducing it to a single, fundamental, "ultimate" cause, since, as he tells us, "only the science dealing with the widest abstractions" can explain "so vast a sum as human history." But let us interject a little common sense into the subject. To argue, as Peikoff does, that something as complicated as history can only be explained by reducing it to a single "ultimate" cause is as absurd as it would be to argue that a simple fact requires a complicated, multi-causal explanation. If simple good sense is to be our guide in such matters, we would expect the exact opposite to be the case: if the subject matter is vast and complex, we would expect the explanation also to be vast and complex; while if the subject matter is relatively simple, we would expect that a simple explanation would suffice.

Peikoff's second conclusion is even more debatable. Because history is "so vast a sum," Peikoff would have us believe that "only the science dealing with the widest abstractions" (i.e., philosophy) can handle it. It is arguments of this sort that give philosophy a bad name. There are at least two fallacies embedded in it. To begin with, it does not follow that just because a subject constitutes "so vast a sum as human history" that it can only be explained by "the science dealing with the widest abstractions." There are many subjects that are every bit as vast as history yet which cannot be explained by philosophy. Take quantum mechanics, for instance. One can imagine few subjects constituting so vast a sum as this one (the whole sub-molecular universe). Yet if any philosopher ever dared to suggest that so vast a sum as quantum physics can only be explained by philosophy, because *only* philosophy can explain something so complex, he would be regarded as a charlatan trying to sneak his way into a field of study that he knows nothing about. Quantum physics is the province, not of those who deal with the widest abstractions, but of those who know something about the subject itself—i.e., of physicists. The same goes for history. It is the historian, not the philosopher, who must determine the factors behind historical change.

Those who claim that philosophy is the only science that can provide "primary" or "ultimate" explanations for historical developments are usually motivated by a desire to replace conclusions based on historical evidence with conclusions based on mere philosophical speculation. This is precisely what I suspect Rand and Peikoff are trying to accomplish with their Objectivist theory of history: to replace historical evidence with philosophical speculation. I am not suggesting that they seek to replace *all* conclusions based on historical evidence with philosophical speculation; not at all, they are perfectly willing to accept any historical evidence that can be construed, by fair means or foul, as proof of Rand's philosophical opinions. But as for that portion of the historical record which contradicts her philosophy, especially her philosophy of human nature— she preferred to have that portion explained away. This is where her theory of history comes in. Its purpose is to explain how a supposedly rational being capable of moral perfection could have behaved so irrationally throughout most of human history.

In this chapter, we will examine Rand's attempt to account for man's historical irrationality. We will also examine the practical upshot of the Objectivist theory of history, giving special emphasis to its probable effects on those who believe it and on its value as an instrument of prognosis.

*　　　　*　　　　*

(1) A utopian view of human nature will inevitably lead to a utopian theory of history. The reason for this should be obvious: history does not support the utopian

view of man. For this reason, utopians, in order to justify their theory of man, have to explain why the historical evidence is irrelevant. Out of such explanations a utopian theory of history emerges.

Utopian historical theory usually goes as follows. First, the assumption is made that most, if not all men, are fundamentally good. Since this assumption will tend to clash with the facts of history, which paint a much darker view of man's nature, a second assumption is introduced to explain this disparity. Men, it is conceded, have behaved deplorably in the past. But this is not because they are, by nature, wicked. They have behaved deplorably because of external factors over which they had no control. When men learn how to control these external factors, things will be different. Man's natural goodness will reassert itself and evil will disappear from human existence and a good time will be had by all.

Utopians differ as to the nature of the external factors that have prevented man from reaching his full moral potential. Rousseau believed that these factors were embedded into the very nature of modern society and could only be removed by returning to a more natural form of existence. Marx, on the other hand, believed that it was an unjust economic system which prevented man from reaching his potential; Marx's remedy, as is well known, was to save man by changing his economic conditions.

Most utopians embrace some form of Marx's solution to the problem of history. The evil that men do is blamed on unjust economic or social conditions. Remove or attenuate these unjust conditions, and you will be able to prevent (or at least mitigate) the wickedness of men.

President Johnson's infamous "war on poverty" was largely based on this utopian premise. The partisans of this war blamed crime and other social problems on the poverty created by the prevailing economic system. An attempt was made to cure the ills of society by eliminating poverty. Unfortunately, things didn't turn out the way the liberal utopians expected. But then, they never do. That is why individuals who advocate such policies deserve to be called utopians. Their view of man and society fails to accord with the facts of reality.

Rand's own particular brand of utopianism rejects the versions endorsed by Marx and Rousseau. Instead of blaming the horrors of history on pernicious social conditions, Rand blames them on bad philosophy. Too often man has lived under the sway of irrational ideas. It is these irrational ideas that have made the horrors of history possible. If man had lived under the guidance of rational ideas, none of these horrors could have taken place.

But why has man failed to live under the guidance of rational ideas? If only rational ideas can prevent horrors from occurring, why haven't men chosen to follow rational ideas? Doesn't the fact that men have *not* chosen to follow rational ideas indicate a congenital bias *against* rationality? After all, if it is really true, as Rand contends, that irrational ideas are the cause of most, if not all, the horrors of human history, then why would anyone voluntarily choose to follow irrational ideas? *Because*, answers Rand, *most people don't know any better.* They have been taught that, because reason is somehow flawed or incomplete, no one can live by reason alone. If they had been taught differently, if their intellectual leaders had made a point of insisting upon the supremacy of reason, then most of

them would not have succumbed to the influence of irrational ideas.

It only remains to discover why mankind's intellectual
leaders have failed to preach the supremacy of reason.
Rand places the ultimate blame on philosophy. Because
philosophers have been unable to formulate a convincing
defense of man's reason, most intellectuals have wound up
concluding that reason must somehow be flawed or impotent. And why not? If even the greatest philosophers cannot validate the supremacy of reason, isn't this proof
enough of reason's limitations?

Having reached this point in her argument, Rand steps
in and declares herself reason's champion and defender.
The inability of philosophers to validate the supremacy of
reason is not, she insists, the fault of reason itself, but
merely the fault of those philosophers who, though they
tried to defend reason, only made things worse by advancing confused and misleading arguments. Their failure was
caused, not by any flaw in reason, but simply by their own
philosophical incompetence. They were unable to solve
the "problem of universals." This gave the enemies of reason the opening they needed. By attacking this weak
point, irrationalists like Hume, Kant, and Hegel were able
to carry the day. But have no fear: all is not lost. Rand herself has formulated a solution to this very problem of universals upon which the ship of reason has so lamentably
foundered! Henceforth, reason will no longer be at the
mercy of its enemies: rather, its enemies will be at *its*
mercy. Once the supremacy of reason is validated, it will
be possible to refute all the irrational ideas which are
destroying Western Civilization. And once these irrational
ideas are shown to be false, it is only a matter of time

before most people begin to realize that reason is the supreme principle of human existence.

Rand bases this theory of history on her view of man. She begins by assuming that human beings really are the product of their ideas. But if this is so, then society itself, which is merely an aggregation of individual human beings, must also be the product of ideas. The only question is: what exactly is meant by claiming that society is the product of ideas? What kind of ideas are we talking about? Just any sort of ideas? Or is there a specific kind of idea that Rand has in mind?

Rand believed that *philosophical* ideas were the most influential in determining the character of man and society. Why philosophical ideas? Because only philosophical ideas are broad enough to include every aspect of man's life, including his emotions, his desires, and his motivations. Man requires some kind of direction in his life, some principle that he can use to meet every challenge which comes his way. This direction, this principle can only come from an abstraction broad enough to cover every situation confronting the individual. Such principles, such abstractions, such *ideas*—call them what you will—are precisely what Rand and her followers mean by the term *philosophy*. "Philosophy is concerned with those fundamental issues that everyone has to deal with one way or the other," writes Leonard Peikoff. (1985, 4)

According to Objectivism, the most important, most fundamental issue in human existence is the issue of how man should use his consciousness. "[Man's] conclusions in every field depend on his method of using his consciousness, [that is, on] his epistemology," declares Peikoff. "How a man uses his consciousness determines his metaphysics, which in turn determines his morality and politics. In the life of man, epistemological, metaphysical, and moral ideas—which means: philosophical ideas—are the ruling power." (1991, 451)

One obvious objection to this theory is that, since most people are totally ignorant of philosophy and have little if any understanding of philosophical concepts, it would appear absurd to suggest that philosophy constitutes the ruling power in human life. How can something that a man knows nothing about be the ruling power in his existence?

The Objectivist response to this objection is as follows. According to Rand, every decision a man makes reflects a certain fundamental view of existence. This being the case, before a man can act he must have arrived at certain conclusions regarding the fundamental nature of himself and the universe at large. The fact that he is unaware of this has no relevance one way or another. Without fundamental ideas, a man simply cannot function, because he has no method by which to direct his efforts. Either he thinks up these fundamental ideas on his own, or he absorbs them unwittingly from others. It must be one or the other: because the ideas have to get into his head *somehow*. "As a human being," Rand tells us, "you have no choice about the fact that you need a philosophy. Your only choice is whether you define your philosophy by a conscious, rational, disciplined process of thought and scrupulous logical deliberation—or let your subconscious accumulate a junk heap of unwarranted conclusions, false generalizations, undefined contradictions, undigested slogans, unidentified wishes, doubts, and fears, thrown together by chance, but integrated by your subconscious into a kind of mongrel philosophy." (1982, 5)

Now implicit in this Objectivist view of human psychology is the unacknowledged premise that the subconscious mind is incapable of forming its own ideas. Only the conscious mind can do that. The subconscious can only integrate ideas which it has absorbed from sources outside itself. In practical terms this means: either we get our philosophical ideas from our own conscious mind, or from the conscious minds of others.

Now if this is true, several interesting conclusions necessarily follow. In the first place, if a philosophy of life can only be formulated by a conscious mind, it follows that anyone who refuses to consciously define his basic philosophy of life must find himself dependent on somebody else who does. This conclusion has enormous ramifications for Rand's theory of history. Since Rand believes that ideas determine how a man will act, it follows that those who depend on other people for their ideas will, *ipso facto*, no longer be in complete control of themselves. If you allow other people to formulate the principles which will end up guiding your life, you will, in effect, have surrendered your autonomy as an individual into their hands.

Since, according to Rand, only a small proportion of the total population actually takes the trouble to define their ideas through a process of conscious deliberation, it follows that this small group must necessarily exercise an enormous influence on the rest of society: for it is this small group which will, in the final analysis, chose the guiding philosophical principles for the rest of society. Rand refers to this group as "the intellectuals," whom she describes as "guides, as trend-setters, as the transmission

belts or middlemen between philosophy and culture."
(Binswanger, 1986, 234) It is the intellectuals who decide
which philosophical ideas will dominate a given age.
However, since intellectuals are not themselves capable of
originating philosophical ideas, their decision as to which
ideas will likely dominate a nation's culture will depend on
the alternatives available to choose from. But where do
these alternatives ultimately come from? Rand's answer is:
from the great philosophical system builders—i.e., from
mankind's "most abstract minds." (1985, 13) It is these
philosophers—the "great" philosophers of history, Plato,
Aristotle, Kant, etc.—who determine the alternatives from
which to choose from. Consequently, it is these philosophers who, in the final analysis, end up determining the
course of history. (Rand, 1961, 25, 27, 40-42; 1971a, 4;
1982, 4; Peikoff, 1982, 97)

Now let us suppose that an intellectual has the opportunity to choose between several rival philosophical systems. Which one is he most likely to choose? Although
neither Rand nor any of her followers have ever discussed
this question in detail, an answer can be extracted from
several remarks scattered throughout the Objectivist literature relating to it. Rand appears to have believed that
most men, when given the opportunity to choose between
a philosophy of reason and a philosophy of unreason, will
tend to choose the philosophy of reason. I say *tend* because
Rand did not believe, as she put it, that there is any "guarantee that [men] will choose to be rational." However,
even if there exists "no predetermined necessity about it,"
Rand nonetheless believed that "In any historical period
when men were free, it has always been the most rational
philosophy that won." (1964a)

This statement, I suspect, needs to be taken with a grain or two of salt. It is unlikely that Rand meant it to be taken literally—because if she did, she would have a lot of explaining to do. The statement is explicitly contradicted by remarks she made elsewhere pertaining to the unhappy plight of the modern world. Rand held that most of the problems of the twentieth century are the result of Immanuel Kant's attack on the human mind. It was Kant who, more than any other philosopher, "closed the door of philosophy to reason." (1961, 31) "If one finds the present state of the world unintelligible and inexplicable, one can begin to understand it by realizing that the dominant intellectual influence today is still Kant's—and that all the leading modern schools of philosophy are derived from a Kantian base." (1961, 33)

In another place, Rand came right out and called Kant "the most evil man in mankind's history." (1971a, 4) Now if Kant were as evil and irrational as Rand makes him out to be, how come his philosophy has managed to become the "dominant intellectual influence" of the last one hundred years? If it is really true that in "any historical period when men were free, it has always been the most rational philosophy which has won," how is it that Kant's philosophy, which, as Rand puts it, "closed the door of philosophy to reason," ended up winning the battle of ideas during the very period of history (i.e., the Nineteenth Century) which Rand considered to be the freest? (1982, 65)

Obviously, Rand's statement that the most rational philosophy "always" wins was not meant to be taken as a literal statement of historical fact. It was meant, rather, as a prediction of what will happen in the future. In the future,

Rand is assuring us, the most rational philosophy *will* win. As for the past—well, that is an entirely different matter. The reason why the most rational philosophy failed to defeat Kant's philosophy of unreason during the politically free Nineteenth Century is because—as I explained above—the partisans of reason did a bad job of defending reason against Kant's subversive epistemological doctrines. It was the failure of the pro-reason philosophers to offer a convincing defense of man's mind that made Kant possible in the first place. "Most philosophers," Rand acknowledges, "did not intend to invalidate conceptual knowledge, but its defenders did more to destroy it than did its enemies. They were unable to offer a solution to the 'problem of universals,' that is: to determine the relationship of concepts to perceptual data—and to prove the validity of scientific induction. Ignoring the lead of Aristotle, who had shown the direction and the method by which the answer could be found, the philosophers were unable to refute the [mystic's] claim that their concepts were as arbitrary as his whims and that their scientific knowledge had no greater metaphysical validity than his revelations." (1961, 30)

Because pre-Kantian philosophers were unable to come up with a convincing defense of human rationality, Kant was able to get away with his great assault upon the human mind. If the pre-Kantian philosophers had only been able to discover a convincing validation of man's conceptual knowledge, Kant would never have been able to become the "dominant intellectual influence" of our times. Kant's philosophy won, not on its own merits, but because of the errors and mishaps of the opposing camp.

The victory of Kant's pernicious ideas had enormous consequences on the course of history. All the horrors of the modern world, including the Soviet Gulags and the Nazi death camps, occurred as a result of Kant's influence. Yet Kant's ideas could never have exercised such a deleterious influence if it had not been for the egregious mistakes of philosophers like Bacon, Descartes, and Locke.

Note how adeptly this theory manages to take human nature off the hook. The horrors of the modern world are not the result of man's moral imperfectability and the corruption embedded in his very nature. No, they are merely the result of the failure of philosophers to solve the problem of universals. Once mankind's philosophers find a solution to the problem of universals, none of these horrors will ever happen again.

Since Rand believed that she had actually discovered a solution to this problem of universals, she concluded that it was only a matter of time before Objectivism would save the world (or, if not the world, at least America). Only the American universities stood in Objectivism's way. The university is where intellectuals get their ideas. But since most universities only teach irrational, Kantian ideas, their students are never exposed to rational ideas and are thus not even aware that a rational alternative exists. If Objectivists want to change the world, all they need to do is infiltrate American universities and introduce Objectivism into the curriculum. "I have said all my life, let there be one-hundred socialists for every one pro-capitalist [at the universities], and we would win the battle," declared Leonard Peikoff on his radio show in Los Angeles. By "pro-capitalist," Peikoff means "pro-Objectivist," and by "socialist" he means any brand of academic irrationalism. The fact that he believes it will only take one Objectivist for every one-hundred irrationalists testifies to Peikoff's immense faith in human nature. In effect, he is saying: If there is just *one* voice of reason on campus for every *one-hundred* voices of *un*reason, your average college student will choose to follow the voice of reason. But is this really true?

Suppose every university in America had at least one Objectivist professor who did nothing but teach classes on Rand's ideas. Would this lead to a mass conversion of university students to the doctrines of Objectivism? I hardly think so. If I had to guess, I would say that introducing Objectivism into the curriculum would only slightly increase the number of students who become interested in Rand's ideas. Most students would continue to be indifferent to philosophical ideas, choosing instead to follow whatever ideology or religion most appealed to their congenital sentiments.

Rand and her followers tend to assume that intellectuals are naturally inclined towards reason. I regard this view as completely at odds with the facts. I would contend that intellectuals tend to be even more irrational than non-intellectuals. Nor is it surprising that it should be so. The development of intellectual interests often depends on the failure to develop in other areas—most notably, in the areas of physical strength and athletic puissance. Few adolescents who excel at sports and who have the courage to beat up other kids ever become intellectuals. Why should they? They can satisfy their vanity through physical excellence alone. The development of intellectual skills is thus not terribly important for such individuals. But it is different with those adolescents who do not excel at sports and are deathly afraid of getting into fights. Since they cannot satisfy their vanity through sports or physical intimidation, they must find something else to excel at. If they happen to be intelligent, they are likely to be drawn toward some type of intellectual pursuit, for it is only in such endeavors that they can ever hope to distinguish themselves in comparison with others. But note their motives in the whole business: it is their athletic incompetence and intransigent cowardice that cause them to become intellectuals, not respect for reason or truth.

Now I'm not trying to suggest that *all* intellectuals are motivated solely by cowardice and athletic incompetence. I am speaking here only in terms of statistical probabilities. Most of the intellectuals that I am familiar with lack both the purity of motive and the moral courage necessary to distinguish facts from wishes. This leads me to conclude that what most intellectuals are interested in is not facts, which usually leave them cold, but ideas, which they can manipulate to conform to their wishes and needs. The modern intellectual, in a great many respects, is a mere hedonist of ideas. He gets his thrills, not from grasping the cold hard facts, but from creating systems of thought that soothe and comfort his hurt feelings or gratify the malice of his envy. Peikoff's belief that such individuals would likely choose Objectivism if they were exposed to Rand's ideas in college strikes me as astonishingly naive.

On the face of it, Rand's theory of history appears absurd. But how does it appear upon closer examination? In the next section, we will attempt to answer this question.

$$* \qquad * \qquad *$$

(2) Rand's theory of history is built upon a number of extremely questionable premises, many of which Rand failed to support with either factual evidence or logical argumentation. Instead, what we get is one dogmatic assertion after another, supported, if at all, by over simplified generalizations of history and distorted interpretations of Hume, Kant, Russell and other important modern philosophers.

I have identified at least three questionable premises at the base of Rand's theory of history. In this section, we will examine each one.

1. The first and perhaps most important premise of Rand's theory of history is her belief that man's character is the product of ideas. Having already refuted this premise in the previous chapter, there is no need to say anything more about it here beyond noting that without this premise, Rand's view of history becomes logically untenable. For if human beings are *not* in fact the product of their ideas, then there is no reason to suppose that history can be the product of ideas. Since history is the product of human action, whatever causes human action must be regarded as the primary cause of history. And if men are not primarily motivated by ideas, as I argued in Chapter 1, then history itself cannot be primarily caused by ideas.

2. Another important premise behind Rand's theory of history is her assumption that human beings (and history as well) are the product, not of ideas in general, but only of *philosophical* ideas. Why only philosophical ideas? As I explained in the previous section, Rand considered philosophical ideas the ultimate determinants of human behavior because they were the only ideas abstract enough to apply to all the basic issues of human existence. Note the

underlying logic of this position: it is precisely because philosophical ideas are the most abstract ideas that they can exercise so great an influence. Had they been any less abstract, they would not have been so influential.

Is there any reason for believing this to be true? Are abstract ideas really more influential *because* they are abstract? No, of course not. There is absolutely no reason to believe that ideas become more influential as their degree of abstractness increases. If anything, they probably become less influential. The greater the degree of abstraction, the greater the vagueness. Philosophical principles, which, according to Objectivism, are the broadest and most abstract ideas of all, must also, for this very reason, be among the most vague and indefinite of all principles. The question then arises: how can principles so vague and indefinite possibly guide man's concrete actions? From vague principles nothing definite can be logically deduced. Every individual interprets such principles in his own unique way. To one man they mean one thing, to someone else they mean something else altogether. And since they lead to nothing definite, they cannot be regarded as the causes of anything definite.

Rand's belief in the indomitable influence of high-level abstractions commits a very serious fallacy—*the fallacy of reductivism*. This fallacy occurs whenever an attempt is made to determine matters of fact on the basis of vague, empirically empty generalizations. It is a very common fallacy among intellectuals of all ideological stripes, especially of those who specialize in ideological polemics. Instead of trying to master a given subject through an immersion in the relevant facts, such ideologues prefer to establish their doctrines on the basis of dubious generalizations and principles so indistinct that they can deduce anything they please from them. The result is conclusions which over-simplify reality to the point of serious distortion.

Nearly all of Objectivism commits this fallacy to at least some degree. I have already noted the monistic implications of her theory history, but the same criticism could be leveled at her theory of human nature, which reduces human beings to mere abstractions. In later chapters we will find even more examples of this appalling tendency in Rand's philosophy.

3. The last faulty premise we will examine involves the assumption that man must formulate the abstract ideas which (supposedly) rule his life through a process of *deliberate conscious reasoning*. According to Rand, principles formed through a process of conscious reasoning are necessary to his very existence. He cannot survive without them. The only question is whether these principles are formulated by his own conscious mind or by the conscious mind of someone else.

I regard this view of the matter as palpably false. It rests on an egregious misunderstanding of the sources of man's knowledge. Rand tended to assume that all man's knowledge has to be produced through the medium of the conscious mind. Human knowledge, she declared, is conceptual in nature, which means it consists of abstract ideas. Human beings can only attain knowledge by reducing the perceptual data of their senses to abstract ideas in the form of conceptual generalizations. But such conceptual generalizations can only be produced by a process of deliberate, conscious thought. Rand defined this process as "reason," which she insisted was man's only valid means of knowledge.

This view of knowledge fails to take into account the vast amount of human knowledge that is not conceptual in nature. Many human skills, for example, are developed without the aid of conceptual knowledge. Skills learned by infants (e.g., walking, language skills, manipulation of adults through tantrums, etc.) are all acquired before the capacity for conceptual thought even exists. Indeed, the skill of conceptual thinking must itself be the product of something other than conceptual thinking, since no skill can be the product of itself. To assert as much would be to commit the fallacy of *causa sui*.

I would go even farther. I would argue that no human skill can be learned exclusively on the basis of concepts or deliberate conscious reasoning. This can easily be demonstrated by experiment. Take any complex human skill, such as swimming or playing the piano or driving a car and try to master it by merely thinking or talking about it in conceptual terms. It cannot be done. You can think or talk about it all you like: you will never learn how to swim or play the piano or drive a car in this way. The only way to master any of these skills is by actually going out and trying to perform them. Through the method of trial and error, the brain develops the capacity to direct the motions necessary to perform the skill in question. Conceptual thinking may assist in this process, but it cannot develop the skill on its own resources alone. Only the method of trial and error can do this.

By claiming that abstract ideas are the primary source of man's knowledge, especially of his knowledge of skills, Rand is guilty of committing the old fallacy of reversing cause and effect. In nearly all cases, it is not the abstract idea or concept which determines the skill, but the skill which determines the abstract idea. Men originally learn how to do something through trial and error. Later, after they have acquired the skill, they attempt to explain it in terms of concepts. This is where man's principles come from. A principle is nothing more than a short hand description of how something is (or ought) to be done. But note: knowledge of the principle of how to do something is not the same as actually knowing how to do it. No one, for example, could ever know how to fly an airplane merely because someone had related to him the principles of flying. On the contrary, knowledge of how to fly a plane can only be attained by actually getting into a plane and trying to fly it.

I contend that the greater portion of human knowledge is acquired through this experiential process of trial and error. This type of knowledge I call *intuitive* knowledge. It is based, not on rational deliberation or speculative thought, but on practical experience. (Oakeshott, 1991, 11-17; Popper, 1983, 40-43)

Now if a good portion of man's knowledge is developed through this process of trial and error, then Rand's contention that philosophical ideas are the ultimate determinants of human action simply cannot be true. Man is not completely dependent on his conscious mind for direction. He is also blessed with the capacity to develop intuitive knowledge based directly on practical experience.

*   *   *

(3) Having examined some of the premises upon which Rand's theory of history is based, we can now turn to the question of empirical evidence. Is Rand's theory supported by the *facts* of history? Or do these facts suggest a very different theory?

In order to come to any sort of definite conclusion on a subject as vast and multifaceted as this one would require several volumes. Each period of history would have to be subjected to an intensively detailed examination in order to determine the causal factors predominant in that era. Then the causal factors of each era would have to be compared with those of other eras in order to discover possible uniformities operative in all periods of history. Finally, these uniformities would have to be carefully analyzed on the basis of the best interpretive tools developed by the social sciences in order to determine the extent of their validity and whether they can be counted on to persist in the future. Causal uniformities about history can be discovered in no other way. Those who believe that the causal uniformities of social change can be grasped simply through a cursory glance at history demonstrate a complete ignorance of how causal uniformities are discovered. It is only through hard work and intense self-criticism that anything of substance can be learned about a subject as complex as history and the evolution of society over time.

Since it is beyond the scope of this book to empirically verify the causal factors prevalent in every period of history, I will confine my critical analysis of the Objectivist theory of history to three specific evidentiary claims that Rand and her followers have made on behalf of their theory. The first claim argues that Christianity is responsible for the all the poverty, superstition, fanatical asceticism and other horrors of the Dark Ages; the second, that the growth of statism in America is the byproduct of the altruist morality; and the third, that German philosophy is responsible for Hitler's rise to power and the subsequent Nazi death camps.

1. *Is Christianity responsible for the Dark Ages?* In their zeal to prove that Christianity is contrary to human well-being, Rand and her followers have tried to blame the squalor and poverty of the Dark and Middle Ages on the ideas propagated in the gospels. "In the ancient world, after centuries of gradual decline, the choice was the ideas of classical civilization or the ideas of Christianity," asserts Leonard Peikoff. "Men chose Christianity. The result was the Dark Ages." (Peikoff, 1982, 338)

Peikoff gives very little viable evidence for his thesis. The following is the most extensive passage on the subject to be found in the Objectivist literature: "Unlike many Americans today,...the medievals took religion seriously," Peikoff informs us. "They preceded to create a society that was antimaterialistic *and* anti-intellectual. I do not have to remind you of the lives of the saints, who were the heroes of the period, including the men who ate only sheep's gall and ashes, quenched their thirst with laundry water, and slept with a rock for a pillow. These men were resolutely defying nature, the body, sex, pleasure, all the snares of this life—and they were canonized for it, as, by the essence of religion, they should have been. The economic and social results of this kind of code were inevitable: mass stagnation and abject poverty, ignorance and mass illiteracy, waves of insanity that swept whole towns, a life expectancy in the teens. 'Woe unto ye who laugh now,' the Sermon of the Mount had said. Well, they were pretty safe

on that account. They had precious little to laugh about."
(Rand, 1990a, 71)

If Mr. Peikoff regards *this* as evidence, then it is obvious he has no idea of what constitutes genuine, scientific
evidence. The causes of the prevailing economic and social
conditions of a given historical era cannot be judged on so
broad a basis. The causes of history can only be grasped
through a laborious study of detailed facts. History will
not yield up its secrets to those who try to understand it
on the basis of vague generalizations.

I must comment on at least a few of the factual claims
made by Mr. Peikoff. Peikoff begins by asserting that the
medievals, unlike people today, took religion very
seriously. The problem with this statement is that it is
intolerably vague. What *precisely* does it mean to take
religion seriously? If the rest of the passage is anything to
judge by, taking religion seriously means, according
Peikoff, being antimaterialist, anti-intellectual, and
insanely ascetic. But is this a fair characterization? Of
course not. What Peikoff is trying to do is evade certain
facts about religion that do not accord with his theory. He
wants to prove that religion, by its very "essence," must
lead to poverty, illiteracy, mass insanity, and so on. But
there have been many periods of history when religion
clearly did not lead to so deplorable a result. And so, in
order to avoid having his thesis refuted by this fact, Peikoff
makes a distinction between religions that are taken
seriously and religions that are not taken seriously. It is
only when religion is taken seriously, contends Peikoff,
that it leads to universal horror and misery. But how are
we supposed to distinguish between a religion that is taken
seriously and one that is not? Why, it is very simple. If a

given society experiences mass destitution, cultural ruin, ascetic fanaticism, political tyranny, and waves of insanity, then chances are, this society is guilty of taking religion seriously. If a society, on the other hand, is guilty of none of these morbid excesses, then it is assumed that religion is not being taken seriously, even if religious belief happens to be widespread.

The only problem with this method of distinguishing between the two types of religion is that it fails to prove anything. Peikoff will always regard any society characterized by mass illiteracy and appalling poverty as guilty of taking religion seriously. His method of distinguishing societies which take religion seriously from those that don't is a mere rationalization allowing him to blame religion for society's ills.

But what about Peikoff's overall argument? Is it really true, as he asserts, that the medieval period was an age of terrible poverty and ascetic fanaticism? Not entirely. Peikoff, as usual, exaggerates. While there certainly was a great deal of poverty and illiteracy during the Middle Ages, it is misleading to describe the period as dominated by ascetic mores. The literature of the age does not substantiate such a description. Chaucer and Boccaccio, the troubadour romances, the Arthurian legends, and the Chroniclers all provide a far more ambiguous account of medieval mores. Although medieval society had more than its fair share of religious zealots and extreme ascetics, it would be a grave error to assume that everyone who lived during the Middle Ages—or even a majority of the people—was either a religious fanatic or an uncompromising ascetic. They were nothing of the sort. Very few people practiced asceticism and most wavered in their religious devotion, swinging from periods of intense religiosity to periods of forgetfulness and backsliding.

I must note one other glaring error in Peikoff's argument. Peikoff asserts at one point that the medievals, in effect, "created" the social conditions of the Middle Ages. This implies that the social conditions of medieval society were intentional and that the people of that era brought about just the sort of society they most wanted. Nothing can be further from the truth. Medieval society was not the product of design or intent. It came about, not from anyone's express will, but from the accidental concatenation of an immense number of individual intentions, many of them working at cross-purposes. Very few human beings ever make an effort to bring about a specific type of society. They are too busy earning a living to waste their time with such futile undertakings. Human society is not the product of human intention or design.

The historical evidence concerning the collapse of the Western Roman Empire and the subsequent abject poverty and cultural stagnation of the eight, ninth, and tenth centuries suggests that the intentions of the medievals had little, if anything, to do with the abysmal condition of society. Nor did the doctrine of Christianity play much of a role in the business. What did have a great deal to do with it was the expansion of Islam into the Mediterranean. In 638, Syria, the center of export trade to the East, fell to the Arabs; next fell Egypt (in 642), the breadbasket of Western Europe. By 689, the Arabs controlled all of North Africa. Spain fell next, and by 711, the Arabs had advanced to the Pyrenees. The soldiers of Charles Martel kept them from advancing further into the West, just as the walls of Constantinople, the world's greatest city at the time, prevented further advance in the East. But from that point on, the Mediterranean became, as the Belgian historian Henri Pirenne aptly put it, "a Moslem lake." (1925, 25) The economic effect of this state of affairs on the West was nothing short of devastating. Consider, as evidence of this statement, the fate of Marseilles, the most important trading port in the Frankish kingdom. "The trade of Marseilles...waned gradually as the Moslems advanced in the Mediterranean," Pirenne tells us. "Syria, conquered by them in 633-638, no longer kept it thriving with her ships and her merchandise....The importation of spices kept up for a while, for the monks of Corbie, in 716....A half century later, solitude reigned in the port of Marseilles. Her foster-mother, the sea, was shut off from her and the economic life of the inland regions which had been nourished through her intermediary was definitely extinguished. By the ninth century Provence, once the richest country of Gaul [i.e., what is today France], had become the poorest." (1925, 29-30)

During the ninth century (the period of the greatest economic stagnation in Western Europe), the Moslems consolidated their stranglehold over the Western and Southern Mediterranean. They seized the Balearic Isles, Corsica, Sardinia, and Sicily. They established ports in Tunis, Mehdia, and Cairo. Palermo, in Sicily, became their principle base in the Tyrrhennian Sea (between Sardinia and Italy). Pirate fleets were allowed to devastate the coasts of Provence and Italy. In 889, a Moslem garrison was established not far from the roads connecting France with Italy. (Pirenne, 1925, 30-31)

While all this was going on in southern Europe, Danish and Norwegian barbarians were mercilessly pillaging and devastating regions in the North and West. "The devastation was so complete that, in many cases indeed, the population itself disappeared," noted Pirenne. "Such conditions were incompatible with the existence of a commerce of first-rate importance." (1925, 31-32)

From all this, we can easily conclude that it was the stifling of trade, and not Christianity, that brought about the so-called "dark ages." But what if Peikoff were to argue that the Moslem advances in the Mediterranean were only possible because Christianity had so demoralized and weakened Western Europe that it could no longer defend itself? If this were true, Christianity could still be regarded as the prime culprit of the economic devastation of Western Europe in the early Medieval period.

The problem with this argument is that it fails to explain certain other facts which run directly against it. If Christianity is to blame for the Moslem advances during the seventh, eight, and ninth centuries, then how are we to explain the advances of Western Europe during the eleventh and subsequent centuries? By 1096, the date of the first crusade, the Islamic world had already been retreating little by little in the wake of the expanding commercial empires of Venice, Pisa, and Genoa. The Crusades finished what the Italian city-states had begun. "A mystic enthusiasm of which [the Christian Church] was the inspiration animated her congregation and launched them upon the heroic and grandiose enterprise of the Crusades which brought Western Christianity to grips with Islam," Pirenne informs us. (1925, 79) "All shipping in the ports of the Levant came gradually under [European] control.

Their commercial establishments multiplied with surprising rapidity in the parts of Syria, Egypt, and the isle of the Ionian Sea. The conquest of Corsica (1091), of Sardinia (1022) and of Sicily (1058-1090) took away from the Saracens the bases of operation which, since the ninth century, had enabled them to keep the West in a state of blockade." (1925, 90-91)

By the twelfth century, Western Europe had undergone a tremendous economic and social transformation. Cities were repopulated and took on a new life. The tyranny of the old feudal system slowly began to erode as serfs fled their seigners to become tradesmen or skilled workmen in various handicrafts. Trade stimulated industry, which in turn stimulated the growth of cities and an increase in the overall population. Western Civilization was well on its way to recovering its former glory. Yet all this took place during the centuries when the Catholic Church enjoyed its greatest power and influence over Western Europe.

Peikoff would have us believe that the recovery of Western Civilization was due to the influence of St. Thomas Aquinas. "What—or who—ended the Middle Ages?" he asks. "My answer is: Thomas Aquinas, who introduced Aristotle, and thereby *reason*, into medieval culture." (Rand, 1990a, 72) Unfortunately, Peikoff does not provide any viable historical evidence to support this conclusion. And since nearly all the evidence compiled by historians and scholars specializing in the study of medieval history yields a very different conclusion, this must be regarded as a serious omission.

The historical evidence strongly suggests that it was the revival of trade which ultimately led to the cultural reemergence of Western Europe. In the ninth century, Charlemagne had attempted to revive culture and humane letters by executive fiat, but the abject poverty of his kingdom doomed his efforts to failure. Only when trade began to revive in the eleventh and twelfth centuries was culture able to come to life again, as it did during twelfth and thirteenth centuries, well before the so-called Renaissance. St. Thomas Aquinas, far from being the man who ended the Middle Ages, was one of the age's most representative figures. Aquinas sought to harmonize the unworldly sentiments of the Christian faith with the worldly impulses of the rising civilization in his midst. Like Dante, the great poet of the High Middle Ages, Aquinas was very much a man of his time. In his philosophy, he attempted to supplement faith with Aristotelian "reason." This is why Peikoff gives him credit for reintroducing "reason" into medieval culture. But this "reason" which Aquinas reintroduced must not be confused with either the scientific method or the practical reason of everyday life. Aquinas' "reason" is a purely scholastic method of determining matters of truth. It is based almost entirely on an uncritical acceptance of Aristotle's scientific and logical treatises.

Peikoff's distortion of history demonstrates an obvious bias against Christianity. He is eager to prove that Christianity is incompatible with capitalism and freedom. That is why in his brief account of the Middle Ages he places so much emphasis on asceticism. The ascetics, he tells us, were the "heroes of the period"; it was their code of value that led to all the stagnation and poverty of the era. Nothing, however, could be more misleading. The ascetics might have provoked admiration among the populace, but they were hardly the only heroes of the period.

The Middle Ages was also the period of the great feudal
knights, many of whom were famous throughout all of
Europe. It must also be kept in mind that, despite the
popularity of the ascetics, they nevertheless exercised little,
if any influence on the conduct of the masses. Throughout
the Middle Ages, ascetic practice remained confined to a
small minority of religious fanatics. Even the church did
not adhere strictly to ascetic ideals. As sociologist William
Graham Sumner has noted: "It was well understood, and
not disputed, that celibacy was a rule of the church....It
was an ascetic practice enjoined and enforced on the
clergy. *They never obeyed it*....Yet the notion of celibacy for
the clergy had been so established by discipline in the
usage of priests and the mores of Christendom that a married priest was a disgusting and intolerable idea. At the
same time usage had familiarized everybody with the con-
cubinage of priests and prelates, and all Christendom
knew that popes had their bastards living with them in the
Vatican, where they were married and dowered by their
fathers as openly as might be done by princes in their
palaces." (1906, 519, italics added.) In other words, most
medievals praised asceticism in theory but did not follow
it in practice. Such is human nature. Moral ideals are often
praised for purely aesthetic rather than for practical reasons. Such moral ideals tickle the sentiments of their
admirers without, however, exercising much influence on
actual conduct.

Peikoff makes the unwarranted assumption that if a
theory is admired, individuals will be compelled to follow
it in practice. "I do not believe that hypocrisy is a factor in
history," he once declared. "[The] motives that operate on
a historical scale are open, stated, avowed." (1985, 8-9)

But history does not support this conclusion. In history we find countless examples of individuals worshiping moral ideals which they never followed in practice. This is particularly true of ideals espoused by religions. Such ideals often conflict with the most prominent impulses in human nature. If a religion advocating high moral ideals is ever to attain a wide following in this world, it must be willing to make certain compromises with human nature. As the Italian sociologist Vilfredo Pareto aptly pointed out: "Religions are idealistic....They overstep realities, yet they have to live and develop in a real world. So they are obliged perforce to find some way to bring idealism and reality into harmony....Of such situations one could give examples without end from all countries and religions. Here we will mention just a few from our Western countries and the Christian religion. As everybody knows, as Christianity gradually won converts in the Roman world, it had to relax its primitive strictness and tolerate failings that at first it had fiercely condemned. Many conversions, furthermore, were largely superficial, more changes in form rather than substance. That was the case especially with conversions of Barbarians in the days when the Roman Empire was falling. One may see from St. Gregory of Tours how thin the Christian varnish lay over Frankish kings and Barbarian chieftains who were adapting the new religion to their fierce warlike natures....Christian [doctrine] in no way enfeebled their bellicose instincts, but merely tempered excessive manifestations of them that might have proved disastrous." (1916, §1799)

If the ascetic ideals of Christianity were really as potent and as destructive as Peikoff contends, we would expect every society dominated by Christianity to be economically destitute and culturally stagnant. But this is not what we find in history. Those who, like Peikoff, regard Christianity as responsible for the collapse of Roman Civilization fail to realize that only the Western half of the empire fell. The Eastern half, which was every bit, if not more, Christian then the West, remained a viable political force during the entire period of the Middle Ages. While Western Europe suffered through centuries of abject poverty and feudal anarchy, Byzantium persevered amid a veritable sea of enemies. Byzantium might not have created a great civilization, but it did manage to keep the Moslems at bay in Asia Minor. Without Byzantium, it is unlikely that Venice could have developed into a great commercial city during the economically stagnant centuries of the Dark Ages. (Pirenne, 1925, 83-88) Nor would Western Europe have regained control of the Mediterranean as early as did if it had not been for Byzantium's naval presence in the waters around Asia Minor and the Greek archipelago.

But the most conclusive evidence against Peikoff's thesis is provided by Max Weber in his famous essay *The Protestant Ethic and the Spirit of Capitalism*. While Weber's thesis about the role of Calvinism in producing the psychology necessary for the development of the free enterprise system is debatable, what is not debatable is Weber's documentation of the historical compatibility of extreme religious doctrines on the one side and the spirit of capitalist enterprise on the other. "Even more striking...is the connection of a religious way of life with the most intensive development of business acumen among those sects whose otherworldliness is as proverbial as their wealth, especially the Quakers and Mennonites," wrote Weber.

"The part which the former have played in England and North America fell to the latter in Germany and the Netherlands. That in East Prussia Frederick William I tolerated the Mennonites as indispensable to industry, in spite of their absolute refusal to perform military service, is only one of the numerous well-known cases which illustrates the fact....Finally, that this combination of intense piety with just as strong a development of business acumen, was also characteristic of the Pietists, is common knowledge." (1904-5, 44)

When Weber describes these facts as "common knowledge," he means that they were common knowledge among scholars and educated persons at the turn of the century. They are obviously not common knowledge today, even among the so-called educated. But they are nevertheless true for all that. Thus we must conclude that Christianity, even in some of its most fanatical and otherworldly manifestations, can hardly be regarded as contrary to economic growth and capitalist enterprise.

2. *Is the expansion of government power and state control in America caused by the predominance of altruistic morality in American society?* "It was the morality of altruism that undercut America and is destroying her," Rand insisted. (1961, 62) "Altruism is incompatible with freedom, with capitalism and with individual rights. One cannot combine the pursuit of happiness with the moral status of a sacrificial animal." (1964b, 95)

According to Rand, it was the influence of altruism which prompted the government to assume more and more control over the economy. Laissez-faire capitalism, which depends on the profit-motive, cannot exist for long in a society dominated by a morality that preaches self-sacrifice of the individual to society. Sooner or later, the contradiction between altruism and the profit-motive will be noticed, and the government will be asked to step in to rectify the situation. This is precisely what has happened in America, contend Rand and her Objectivist cohorts. The predominance of the altruistic morality has made it impossible for anyone in business or government to defend the right of individuals to pursue their self-interest in a free and unregulated market.

Rand's account of the rise of statism in America indicates that she knew virtually nothing about how political institutions change and develop over time. She took it for granted that such institutions are determined by moral theory. Yet this is hardly the case. Moral theories rarely play a significant role in the evolution of political institutions. Like language, etiquette, and jurisprudence, political institutions nearly always develop independently of the intentions, moral or otherwise, of those who created them. Even on those rare occasions when political institutions are founded on the basis of a rationally deliberated plan (e.g., like the political institutions of the United States), they always lead to developments not anticipated by their originators. These developments carry in their wake new institutional mechanisms which determine who advances to positions of power and who doesn't. More often than not, political institutions develop in such a way that only individuals interested in increasing their personal power thrive within them. When this happens, then the power of the state will inevitably increase. It will increase regardless of the moral convictions predominant in society. Those individuals who are unwilling to compromise with state power will simply never attain positions of influence and control, since their moral convictions make it impossible for them to take the steps necessary to advance their political careers. This leaves the field wide open to those who are much less scrupulous about the question of power and the aggrandizement of the state.

Something like this has happened here in the United States. The expansion of state power in America was largely brought about by unintended developments in the institutions of the Federal government, especially in the institutions of Congress. The most important of these developments involves the gradual emergence of the political practice known as "logrolling." This practice created institutional incentives within the House of Representatives that favored the expansion of government power. The process works like this. Each member of the House, in order to increase the probability that he will be reelected, must do everything in his power to see that the most influential voters in his district are well satisfied. One of the best ways of accomplishing this goal is to secure for his district special privileges in the form of political pork and government jobs. But since every other representative in the House will want to do the same thing, a conflict arises over the distribution of government favors. Any Congressman who wants to pass a bill that distributes pork to his district must persuade at least half of his colleagues to go along with him in order to get the bill approved. But since half of Congress is not going to pass a bill solely for the benefit of one member, incentives have to be provided in order to drum up support for the bill. The most effective way for providing incentives for other members is to simply agree to give everybody pork. And so a situation arises in which everyone agrees to vote for everyone else's pork. This is what is called "logrolling." (Buchanan & Tullock, 1960 ch. 10)

It does not take a great deal of insight to figure out what will be the inevitable consequence of logrolling. Over time, as the House distributes more and more pork, the federal government must grow bigger and bigger. This will happen despite the intentions of individual Congressmen, who are only trying to please their constituencies to secure votes on election day. Note how no philosophical ideas are required to explain this process. Institutional forces are the primary culprits. Any Congressman who attempted to resist these forces would probably find himself voted out of office for not having secured enough pork for his own district. For those interested in maintaining a career in politics, there is no way to get around it. Unless the ambitious politician plays the logrolling game like everyone else, he will probably have to quit politics altogether.

Because of Rand's emphasis on the role of philosophical ideas in history, she is unable to understand the concept of logrolling and its importance in explaining the rise of statism in America. Believing that altruism is the primary cause of American statism, she concludes that all you have to do in order to overturn statism is to refute altruism. The naiveté of this view can hardly be overstated. None of the politicians who find themselves compelled by the institutional forces prevailing in the House of Representatives to participate in the practices of logrolling give a damn about the moral validity of altruism. As far as they are concerned, Miss Rand can go on refuting altruism until she is blue in the face: the outcome of such abstruse exercises matters little, if at all, to these politicians. For they are primarily motivated, not by vague moral ideals, but by the need to secure reelection; and this involves, among other things, dishing out pork to their constituents and to their most important campaign donors. Whether such unsavory practices can be defended on moral grounds does not greatly concern them. Human beings are primarily motivated, not by abstruse moral ideals, but by the day-to-day effort to meet the pressing challenges of the moment.

3. *Is German philosophy responsible for the rise of Hitler and the subsequent Nazi death camps?* Leonard Peikoff, in his book *The Ominous Parallels*, attempts to prove that German philosophy is the primary cause of both Hitler and the Holocaust. "Modern German culture, including its Nazi climax, is the result of a complex development in the history of philosophy, involving dozens of figures stretching back to the beginnings of Western thought," states Peikoff. (1982, 17) The three most important contributors to this development are Plato, Kant, and Hegel. "These three, more than any others, are the intellectual builders of Auschwitz," Peikoff avers. (1982, 37)

How precisely did Plato, Kant, and Hegel "build" Auschwitz? Peikoff claims they built Auschwitz by advocating a universe of non-identity. "The essence of the [Nazi death] camp method was the attempt to achieve the effects of a certain theoretical viewpoint without mentioning the viewpoint or any other abstraction....In essence, what the Nazis wanted for themselves from the camp was the same unlimited unreason that they imposed on the prisoners. They expected it to wreck the prisoners, while making the rulers omnipotent. For both purposes, what they needed was a certain kind of universe: a universe of non-fact, non-thing, *non-identity*.

"It was a universe that had been hinted at, elaborated, cherished, fought for, and made respectable by a long line of champions. It was the theory and the dream created by all the anti-Aristotelians of Western history." (1982, 273-275)

In other words, the Nazi death camps were a deliberate attempt to use the philosophical ideas of anti-Aristotelian philosophers like Plato, Kant and Hegel to attain complete power over the individual. "The Nazis preached a certain philosophy," we are told, "and they carried it out in action." (1982, 273) Peikoff attempts to prove this curious thesis by quoting first-hand accounts of the horrors perpetrated in these camps. Such first-hand accounts, however, do not constitute proof that Nazi's were motivated by Plato, Kant, and Hegel. All they prove is that the Nazis deployed extremely dehumanizing and brutal methods of incarceration and, ultimately, mass extermination. They fail to prove *why* the Nazis employed such methods. Peikoff's thesis is purely speculative in character. He does not offer any viable evidence in support of it.

But this is not all that is wrong with Peikoff's thesis. Peikoff's attempt to demonstrate a logical connection between the death camps and the philosophical ideas of Plato, Kant, and Hegel is itself deeply flawed. Peikoff is simply mistaken in his belief that these philosophers advocated "non-identity." Nor were they advocates of irrationality. Some of their ideas might have been irrational, but this is not the same thing as advocating irrationality. Peikoff, apparently, is incapable of understanding this distinction.

Another thing he apparently is incapable of grasping is the scandalous vagueness of philosophical ideas, especially the ideas of philosophers like Plato, Kant, and Hegel, all of whom are guilty of setting forth some of the vaguest speculations on record. Since vague ideas can be made to mean anything one pleases, it is possible to use them to justify nearly anything, no matter how outrageous. Yet if this is true, then it follows that such ideas can never be regarded as the cause of anything specific, because the ideas themselves have no specific meaning. One could just as easily prove that the ideas of Plato, Kant and Hegel led to the liberation of the camps at the end of the war as one could that they led to the camps themselves.

Peikoff is on even shakier ground when he blames Kant, Hegel, and other German philosophers for the rise of Nazism. "The Nazis could not have won the support of the German masses but for the systematic preaching of a complex array of theories, doctrines, opinions, notions, beliefs," Peikoff avers. "And not one of their central beliefs was original. They found these beliefs, widespread and waiting, in the culture; they seized upon them and broadcast them at top volume, thrusting them with new intensity back into the streets of Germany. And the men in the streets heard and recognized and sympathized with and embraced these beliefs, and voted for their exponents." (1982, 13)

And what were these beliefs that the Nazis preached and the public embraced? Peikoff cites three major ones: irrationalism, altruism, and collectivism. "These three theories together constitute the essence of the Nazi philosophy, which never changed from the start of the movement to its end," he declares. (1982, 97)

Is it really true, as Peikoff here contends, that the Nazis won the support of the German masses by preaching irrationalism, altruism, and collectivism? The relevant historical evidence suggests otherwise. The Nazis' rise to power depended largely on Hitler's astute political judgment and on the blunders of Germany's reigning political leaders, especially Hindenburg and Papen. The Nazis certainly did not owe their success to preaching irrationalism, altruism, and collectivism. If they had done nothing but preach such abstruse doctrines, they would never have won a plurality of delegates in the Sixth and Seventh Reichstag. The Nazis electoral successes in the early thirties were founded on pure demagoguery. Like politicians in democracies everywhere, they went out of their way to tell the masses what the masses wanted to hear. As historian Samuel W. Mitcham, jr. relates: "Many of the Nazis' appeals were similar to the Communists—'Freedom, Work and Bread!' was a slogan used extensively by both—but Hitler aimed his appeals at all classes except the Jews; the Reds targeted only the workers. Hitler courted the farmers by advocating a concrete program...[which] called for state credits, higher tariffs on foreign produce, cheaper fertilizer, cheaper power, and reduction and remission of taxes. To the voelkisch groups, he used the anti-Semitic approach. To the workers he also offered the hope of employment. When speaking to audiences from the educated classes, he clearly avoided anti-Jewish comments but instead offered them hope for a better future." (1996, 134-135)

No wonder Hindenburg called Hitler "the greatest demagogue in world history." (Turner, 1996, 180) Hitler helped the Nazis win the Reichstag elections of July and November, 1932 by appealing to the interests and sentiments of the German masses. Yet despite this, the Nazis failed to win a majority of the electorate, acquiring only 37.3% of the vote in July and only 33.1% in November. (Mitcham, 1996, 163, 168) By itself, this was not enough to secure power for Hitler. Before the Nazi regime could be established, it was necessary for Hitler to become chancellor. This would never have occurred had not the reigning government split apart due to political intrigues hatched by former chancellor Franz von Papen against his replacement, Chancellor Kurt von Schleicher. "Only through the political blindness and blunders of others did Adolph Hitler gain the opportunity to put his criminal intentions into effect between 1933 and 1945," writes historian Henry Turner. (1996, 182) Hitler owed his success, not to German philosophy, but to this own political savvy and the ineptitude of Germany's political leaders.

*   *   *

(4) *Conclusion.* Objectivism has always appealed more to the young than to the old. Conversions to the Objectivist creed usually occur in high school or college; rarely do they occur in middle or old age. The reason for this is not hard to fathom. Rand's philosophy is far too shallow and factually inaccurate to appeal to those who have lived long enough to develop insight into the nature of the world. Ignorance stemming from inexperience is a necessary prerequisite for appreciating Rand's ideas. Anyone who has taken the trouble to acquaint himself with the relevant facts concerning human nature and the history of mankind will have no choice but to conclude

that, however gifted Rand might have been as a contriver of intellectual romances and polemical rants, she nevertheless knew very little about man or his long and lamentable history. Nor is the man of the world, whose knowledge of human nature comes, not from books, but from actual experience of men in the real world of fact, likely to entertain any higher opinion of Rand than the conscientious scholar: for there is nothing like the day-to-day experience of real men to inoculate oneself against the vapid charms of Rand's ideal hero. Experience and knowledge—these, in the final analysis, are the best antidotes to Objectivism. And since it is precisely the young who are most lacking in both experience and knowledge, they are the ones who are most likely to be seduced by Rand's ideas.

Rand's supporters would like to ascribe her popularity among the young to the greater idealism and moral purity of youth. Yet this is a mere rationalization. It is the ignorance and inexperience of youth that allows them to fall prey to Rand's Objectivist philosophy. The young have no idea how different the world is from Rand's abstruse speculations about it. They believe it is perfectly acceptable to determine matters of fact on the basis of logical or moral constructions. In their youthful enthusiasm and naiveté, they fail to understand that reality—especially the reality of human nature—is far too complex to be summed up in a few vague generalizations masquerading as "fundamental ideas." To understand a subject *thoroughly*, it is not enough to merely reduce it to the "science of the widest abstractions." On the contrary, one has to take the complexity head-on and grapple with it the best one can. There are no short-cuts to knowledge. If you want to understand human nature and the history of man, you have to put in a lot of work. It is not enough just to read a dozen or so works by Rand and her disciples. To attain so much as even a general understanding of man and his history can take years—nay, even decades—of study and observation.

Nowhere in Rand's writings do I find any evidence of a grasp of the real problems at issue in the study of either man or history. All the great minds who have grappled with these problems she either dismisses with contempt or ignores completely. No where in the Objectivist literature will you find an intelligent discussion of Machiavelli's sociopolitical methodology, or Burke's theory of tradition, or Tocqueville's insights into the social institutions of democracy, or Sumner's ethical relativism, or Weber's sociology of religion, or Pareto's theory of elites, or Michel's iron law of oligarchy, or Sorel's political myths and the role of violence in society, or Schumpeter's arguments for the intrinsic instability of capitalism. In my opinion, no theory of history can consider itself competent to make sweeping generalizations about the destiny of man unless it has first come to terms with the problems raised by these men.

Rand would have us believe that philosophy determines the course of history. But what evidence does she offer in support of her view? Very little. Most of her theory is supported with purely verbal arguments—that is, with words, words, and more words. In the final analysis, we must regard Rand's entire theory as nothing more than an inept and feeble ideological construct. Indeed, it tells us far more about Rand and her followers than it does about history.

I have already mentioned what I consider to be this theory's primary motive. Rand needed to explain why the facts of history fail to support her utopian view of man. But in addition to this, Rand also wanted to convince herself that she could exercise a profound influence on the course of history. This is where her touching faith in the power of philosophy comes in. Like most intellectuals, Rand was utterly powerless to change social conditions through political or military means. After all, there was no chance that anyone would appoint her dictator for life. Nor could she have raised an army and imposed her will on the nation through brute force. The only way she could ever hope to change the world was through the medium of ideas. Only by persuading other people to accept her ideas could she ever hope to alter the course of history. This being the case, she simply took it for granted that the only power that determines the course of history is "the power of ideas." (1967, 165)

Rand is not, alas, the only powerless intellectual who has embraced this fallacy of the power of ideas. It is a very popular fallacy among those intellectuals whose knowledge is almost entirely confined to the sterile theories they have read in (usually) worthless books. Regrettably, it would seem that the typical intellectual has no other purpose in life but to engage in futile polemical controversies with other intellectuals. If it were possible for the intellectual to reflect upon his existence with the sober, detached realism characteristic of successful men of action, he would be forced to admit that he is one of the most useless of all human beings—a mere dilettante who likes to play with big words but who never really understands what these words are supposed to mean in terms of concrete facts. But since there exists no creature more conceited than your typical intellectual, he is loath to see himself in so unflattering a light. He a useless creature? "No!" he shouts in defiance. "Far from being the most useless of creatures, we intellectuals are in fact the most essential! We are, to quote Shelley, 'the unacknowledged legislators of the world.' Without us, you would be quite unable to function. Your heads would be empty and your hard-headed practicality impotent. Only through *us* can *you* exist!"

Although they are reluctant to come right out and say it, nonetheless I suspect that such sentiments are at the bottom of the intellectual's faith in the power of ideas. When he talks about the power of ideas, he usually means the power of *his* ideas. The megalomania implicit in such a view hardly needs comment. Unfortunately, most people, when they hear intellectuals gabbling about the power of ideas, do not appear to understand how self-serving and immodest such talk really is. Instead, they regard the notion that ideas have power as a harmless truism. What, after all, is wrong with insisting upon the power of ideas? Examples of this power can be found throughout our modern world: in the advancement of science technology; in the spread of ideological systems, good and bad, across the globe; and in the influence of the mass media. Nor would I ever think of denying that, in the sense described above, ideas have power. Yet this is not what intellectuals like Rand mean when they claim that ideas have power. No, they mean something else altogether. Indeed, the very phrase *the power of ideas* is nothing more than a code word for one of the most naive and dubious fallacies of them all. When Rand or anyone else begins expounding upon the glorious power of ideas, what they really are trying to convey by this ostentatious phrase is their conviction that social conditions can be changed by refuting the ideas that (allegedly) brought them about in the first place.

The reason I regard this view of the matter so objectionable is because it encourages the sort of ignorance and naiveté about social phenomenon that I find most deplorable. Those who operate under the delusion that social conditions can be changed by persuading those who support the status quo to change their ideas are guilty of entertaining several dubious assumptions, none of which can stand the light of critical scrutiny. The two most important of these assumptions is: (1) the conviction that social conditions are the product of abstract ideas constructed by a conscious mind; and (2) the conviction that most men are amenable to rational persuasion. I contend that both of these assumptions are false and that the belief in either of them blinds the individual to the real forces responsible for the way things are.

Let us begin with the first of these assumptions. Is it really true that prevailing social conditions are caused by abstract ideas constructed by a conscious, reasoning mind? No, of course not. Rand is here guilty of what Friedrich Hayek has called "constructivism," which he defined as the contention "that all… useful human institutions were and ought to be deliberate creations of conscious reason." Hayek described this view as "a relapse into an earlier naive way of thinking, into a view which habitually assumed a personal inventor for all human institutions, be it language or writing, laws or morals." (1967, 85) The problem with constructivism is that it fails to take account of the fact that many human institutions, as Adam Ferguson put it, "are indeed the result of human action, but not the execution of human design." (1767) Man's customs and social institutions are largely the product, not of rational deliberation, but of the unintended consequences of his attempt to solve the mundane problems of everyday life. Take the institution of monetary exchange, for example. No one sat down one day and thought up the idea of money. The monetary system is something that gradually evolved out of the barter system. Men discovered that there were certain goods which were much easier to trade than others, because even if they did not need that good, they were sure to find someone else who did. Salt was such a good. Even if you did not need any salt, you always knew that, if you took it as recompense for your own goods, you could always trade the salt later for something you really did need. Salt then became a medium of exchange—that is, an incipient form of money.

Most human institutions and customs developed in just this way. The institutions of man are produced, not by following any sort of definite blueprint or philosophical theory, but by the minute efforts of a large number of individuals each of whom is seeking solutions to specific problems. Those solutions which prove most useful over time tend to be imitated by others and soon spread throughout the entire social order. Those solutions which, on the other hand, lead to further problems will, over time, become less and less used. Thus a process analogous to Darwinian natural selection is found behind the formation of social institutions.

Rand's constructivist bias blinds her to the evolutionary, spontaneous origin of most human institutions. Yet this is not her only blindness. She is also guilty of allowing her rationalistic prejudices to blind her to the profound influence that human sentiments play in the determination of the social order. Rand was eager to believe that human beings were essentially rational in orientation. The essence of man, she repeatedly avowed, is his rationality. This view of man, however, does not square with the facts. Reason plays a much smaller role in human life than rationalists like Rand are willing to admit. Part of this is due to reason's instrumental function. As an instrument, reason assumes, at best, only a subsidiary role in human life. And often, its role is even less than that. One merely has to examine the history of human thought to find plenty of evidence supporting this assertion. *Prima facie*, you would expect that reason would at least play a predominant role in the thought processes of most human beings. But this is clearly not the case. A few exceptions notwithstanding, the thinking of most individuals is permeated through and through with sentiment. That is why it is often very difficult to persuade individuals to change their minds in regard to any issue they feel strongly about. No matter how overwhelming the evidence or irrefragable the logic of your arguments, they will prove useless in the face of rooted convictions. Rand herself is an example of someone impermeable to rational persuasion. Nothing any of her critics might have said would have ever caused her to admit that she might have been wrong about one of the central tenets of Objectivism.

Now if most human beings are not amenable to rational persuasion, it follows that reason cannot be regarded as a major determinant of either human behavior or the concomitant social order. But if reason is not the major determinant of human behavior, than what is? I believe that the primary determinants of the social order are the desires and sentiments that motivate the conduct of individuals.

The Italian sociologist Vilfredo Pareto constructed an entire theory of society around the idea that desires and sentiments are the primary determinants of the social order. In opposition to the Objectivist view, he denied that philosophical theories exercise much of an influence on society. Such theories he regarded as mere "derivations"— that is, as rationalizations *derived* from sentiment. At one point in his massive sociological treatise, *The Mind and Society*, Pareto commented upon those who, like Rand, erroneously regard derivations as the primary cause of social activity: "The person who is influenced by a derivation imagines that he accepts or rejects it on logico-experimental [i.e., scientific] grounds," explained Pareto. "He does not notice that he ordinarily makes up his mind in deference to sentiments and that the accord (or conflict) of the two derivations is an accord (or conflict) of [sentiments]. When, then, a person sets out to study social phenomenon, he halts at manifestations of social activity, that is to say, at derivations, and does not carry his inquiry into the causes of that activity, that is to say, into [sentiments]." (1916, §1402)

This is precisely what is wrong with Rand's theory of history: it fails to carry its inquiry into the *real* causes of historical and social change, opting instead to confine itself to mere superficial manifestations of the causes. At the same time, because of her failure to realize that it is not reason, but sentiment which guides most men, Rand ends up entertaining the delusion that she can convince people to adopt her philosophy of Objectivism by appealing to their reason. "It took decades of collectivist philosophy to bring this country to its present state," she wrote to one of her correspondents in March of 1962. "And it is only the right philosophy that can save us. Ideas take time to spread, but we will only have to wait decades—because reason and reality are on our side." (1995, 596)

Nearly four decades have passed since Rand wrote these words, and yet the country has become, if anything, even more collectivist. But how can this be? If Objectivism really is, as Rand always insisted it was, the philosophy of reason and reality, how is it that it has made no progress in stopping the statist trends of the country? Could it be that the ideas of Objectivism are largely impotent against these statist trends, because such trends are primarily caused, not by abstract ideas constructed by the mind, but by the unintentional consequences of actions motivated largely by sentiment and desire?

I am content to let this question be answered by the future course of history. If Objectivism goes on to become the dominant philosophy of America, then my criticisms of Rand's theory of history will have to be regarded as erroneous. If, on the other hand, Objectivism does not go on to become the dominant philosophy of the future, then my criticisms will have been vindicated.

CHAPTER 3:

▼

THEORY OF KNOWLEDGE

"No one in the world feels the weakness of generalizing more than I. If you depict an entire people, age, or region, what have you depicted? If you group together peoples and periods that succeed one another in perpetual flux like waves of the sea, what have you described? ...If you then summarize all this in nothing but a generality whereby everybody probably thinks and feels whatever they please, what an imperfect means of description! How easily can you be misunderstood!"

—Johann Gottfried Herder

There are few subjects in philosophy more abstruse and difficult than epistemology, the study of how man's mind assimilates and validates knowledge. Since most people are not accustomed to reflecting upon how their minds work, they find the subject of epistemology hard to relate to. It seems to them nothing more than a mass of irrelevant technicalities.

There is, it must be confessed, an element of truth in this assessment. Much that passes for epistemology these days is just that: a mass of irrelevant technicalities. Moreover, these technicalities are, in the majority of cases, conveyed in a jargon so viciously recondite that no one, not even the perpetrator of it, has any idea what it means.

Although I will do everything in my power to avoid being excessively technical or abstruse, it will not be possible to ignore entirely some of the thornier problems of epistemology in this chapter devoted to Rand's theory of knowledge. Those readers who have no stomach for complex epistemological analysis would be well advised to skip this chapter (especially the first two sections, which are the most difficult of all) and proceed to the less abstract regions of philosophy explored in the last five chapters of the book. The rest of us meanwhile will boldly march forward into the abstruse swamps of the Objectivist epistemology.

In order to make my critique of Rand's theory of knowledge as accessible as possible, I will continue emphasizing, as I have throughout this book, the practical side of Rand's theories. As I have already mentioned several times in these pages, Rand's theories were formulated to achieve distinct practical ends. Her primary end, as Rand herself confessed, was the rationalization of her fictional projection of the "ideal man." In her theory of human nature, Rand sought to explain how this ideal man was possible in the real world of fact. In her theory of history, she sought to explain why her theory of human nature does not accord with the facts of history. In her theory of knowledge, Rand sought to tie up some of the loose ends in her theory of history.

In the previous chapter I explained why Rand considered modern philosophy to be responsible for man's failure to conform to her view of human nature. Modern philosophy was unable to solve the problem of universals, thus opening the door to philosophers like Kant and Hegel, who were bent on destroying man's mind and turning him into a helpless victim of mysticism and state power. Rand believed that if a solution to this problem of universals could be found, philosophers like Kant and Hegel would lose their enormously pernicious influence over human civilization and man's potential for greatness would finally be set free from the bonds of superstition, irrationality, and arbitrary force. Men would embrace the ideals of rational self-interest and laissez-faire capitalism, and freedom and prosperity would sweep over the world. Ideal men would become as common as houseflies.

The purpose of Rand's epistemology is to bring this Objectivist utopia into existence by providing a solution to that old philosophical choke-pear, the problem of universals. "The issue of concepts (known as 'the problem of universals') is philosophy's central issue," she wrote in the forward of her book on epistemology. "Since man's knowledge is gained and held in conceptual form, the validity of man's knowledge depends on the validity of concepts. But concepts are abstractions or universals, and everything man perceives is particular, concrete. What is the relationship between abstractions and concretes? To what precisely do concepts refer in reality? Do they refer to something real, something that exists—or are they merely inventions of man's mind, arbitrary constructs or loose approximations that cannot claim to represent knowledge?" (1990b, 1)

Through the course of her modest treatise on epistemology, Rand attempts to answer these questions with her theory of concept-formation. In the first section of this chapter we will investigate whether Rand's theory of concept-formation does in fact solve the problem of universals. Rand claimed that it does, but I believe this claim is easily refuted.

Another crucial premise of Rand's theory of knowledge involves her assumption that all "man's knowledge is gained or held in conceptual form." (1990b, 1) This identification of knowledge with man's "conceptual faculty" is fundamental to Objectivism. After Rand's theory of the ideal man, it is the most important doctrine in her whole philosophy. It constitutes the major premise behind her theory of history, and is crucial to her view of man as well. Objectivism, as a coherent system, is almost unthinkable without it.

Because of its importance, I will devote an entire section towards refuting it. When this has been accomplished, we will turn to some of the less purely theoretical elements in the Objectivist epistemology—those, in other words, that have the clearest relation to the *practice* of Objectivist epistemology. The Objectivist theory of knowledge, beside providing an alleged solution to the problem of universals, also serves as a kind of apologia for a method of validating facts which I consider highly dubious but which figures prominently in Objectivist arguments. Some comments will be made concerning this aspect of the Objectivist epistemology in the third section of this chapter.

Finally, we will conclude by examining one of Rand's most outrageous epistemological claims: namely, her conviction that certainty is possible. We will analyze both her motives for embracing such a dubious conviction and the arguments she advanced in its defense.

There is one thing that I must needs emphasize before commencing this critique of Rand's theory of knowledge. There is a tendency in Objectivism to assume that anyone who dares to attack Rand's theory of concepts must be an irrationalist bent on undermining man's confidence in the efficacy of his mind. It goes without saying that this is not what I'm about. What I'm attacking in the chapter is not man's mind, but only Rand's *conception* of man's mind, which I regard as deeply flawed. If Rand's typical mode of argumentation is anything to go by, she apparently believed that matters of fact can be determined by subjecting highly abstruse and, I suspect, cognitively vague and empty conceptions to logical analysis and speculative manipulation. I consider such a procedure of arriving at the truth to be cognitively perverse and thoroughly invalid. If you want to know what the truth is, you have to immerse yourself in facts and develop an intuitive sensibility about their practical significance to the concerns of everyday life. To believe that high-level abstractions can serve as a substitute for an intuitive knowledge of concrete facts is a delusion of the first magnitude.

* * *

(1) The problem of universals can be summed up as follows. Everything that we perceive is a concrete manifestation of some particular object or quality or process or

relation existing outside our consciousness. The tree I see outside the window, its green leaves, and the way its branches shake in the wind—these are all particular manifestations stemming from the observation of a single tree. Yet the terms by which I describe these manifestations— i.e., *tree, green leaves, shaking branches*, etc.—are general terms that could refer to *any* tree with green leaves and branches shaking in the wind. Ever since Plato, philosophers have been puzzled by the allegedly paradoxical relationship between conceptual terms like *tree, green*, and *wind* and the particular manifestations in reality which such terms are supposed to represent. The terms themselves are universal, because they refer to all such particular manifestations regardless of time and place; but the actual manifestations are concrete. How then can something universal refer to something concrete?

I must confess from the outset that I don't see any problem here at all. As far as I'm concerned, the problem of universals is not really a problem at all. It is simply one of those manufactured problems that philosophers have created to give themselves something to cavil about. (Popper, 1979, 123n) No one outside philosophy really gives a damn one way or another about the allegedly "problematical" nature of universals. Ordinary people whose brains have not been muddled by too much bad philosophy use universal terms all the time without having the foggiest notion that there is anything paradoxical or problematical in them. They see no difficulties in the relation between universal terms and the particulars symbolized by such terms. Nor are they interested in such purely technical problems such as *What is more real—the universal or the particular?* They are too busy getting important work done to bother with such nonsense.

Ayn Rand, as we have seen, holds an entirely different view regarding the importance of this question. For her, the problem of universals constitutes one of the fundamental issues facing mankind. "If...the problem might appear to be esoteric, let me remind you that the fate of human societies, of knowledge, of science, of progress and of every human life, depends upon it," we find her declaring in the *Introduction to Objectivist Epistemology*. "What is at stake here is the cognitive efficacy of man's mind." (1990b, 3)

These are pretty strong words. Not only the fate of human societies in general, but even the fate of every individual human being—including, presumably, the fates of you and I—depends upon whether this problem of universals can be solved. But how can this be so? How can some obscure epistemological problem which hardly anyone understands and which, according to Rand, has remained unsolved for most of human history possibly have any bearing on our own personal lives? Peikoff attempts to shed some light on the question in a passage from his treatise on Objectivism. "As long as men remain ignorant of their basic mental process, they have no answer to the charge, leveled by mysticism and skepticism alike, that their mental content is some form of revelation or invention detached from reality," alleges Mr. Peikoff. "This kind of viewpoint can go into remission for a while,...however if it is not burned out of men's souls completely by an explicit philosophical theory, it becomes the most virulent of cancers; it metastasizes to every branch of philosophy and every department of culture, as is now evident throughout the world. Then the best among men become paralyzed by doubt; while the others turn into mindless hordes that march in any irrationalist era looking for someone to rule them." (1991, 88)

Peikoff is here arguing that we cannot be sure we know anything unless we can explain *how* we know. In other words, if I cannot explain *how* I know that there is a tree outside my window, then, according to Mr. Peikoff, there is nothing to prevent a mystic or skeptic from undermining my confidence in my knowledge of the tree. But is it really true, as Peikoff so blithely assumes, that man's confidence in his own knowledge can be so easily undermined? I hardly think so. If someone were to tell me, in all seriousness, that I had no right to believe that there was a tree outside my window unless I could explain the mental processes leading to this belief, I would regard him as an intellectual nuisance trying to impress me with his facile cleverness. "This man is speaking the sort of drivel only an intellectual would think up," I would say to myself. And this would be the verdict, I suspect, of nearly all men, regardless of how ignorant they were of their basic mental operations. There are many things men can do despite not being able to explain *how* they do them. Indeed, many skills have to be learned and mastered *before* any attempt is made to explain how they work. This is true even of the skill of thinking. No man can understand *how* he thinks unless he has already developed the skill of thinking. The development of most skills usually *precedes* the ability to explain them.

The absurdity of the Objectivist claim that knowledge of *how* we know is necessary to prevent mystics and skeptics from undermining our confidence in *what* we do know can easily be illustrated by applying the same logic to the skill of swimming. Most people who know how to swim could not, if asked, explain the physical process that makes swimming possible. True enough, they might try to explain it by saying that swimming is made possible by paddling their arms and kicking their legs, but as anyone who has ever attempted to learn how to swim by taking such advice knows, there is more to swimming than just paddling one's arms and kicking one's legs. If that is all you do, you will sink to the bottom very quickly. How, then, is swimming made possible? What is it that every swimmer does to prevent himself from helplessly sinking in the water?

Swimmers stay afloat by regulating their breathing so the lungs are never entirely empty. This allows the body to retain enough air so that it will remain buoyant in the water. Although most swimmers are unaware of this fact, this does not prevent them from knowing how to swim. The process of breath-regulation during swimming is something they have absorbed intuitively, without consciously knowing that they have done so. Through the practical effort of trying to develop the skill of swimming, they have unwittingly hit upon the practice of breath-regulation without ever having spent a moment's thought on it. (Polanyi, 1958, 49) There are many skills, including purely intellectual skills, which are developed in just this fashion.

Now according to the underlying logic of the Objectivist theory of knowledge, the fact that a swimmer does not know *how* he keeps his body afloat in the water would make him vulnerable to any mystic or skeptic claiming that swimming is a purely illusory activity detached from reality. We would therefore presumably need to develop an explicit philosophy of swimming in order to defend the skill of swimming against those who claim swimming is impossible, because without such a theory, the best swimmers would become paralyzed with doubt, while everyone else would turn into swimmingless hordes that march around looking for someone to tell them what sport to pursue.

The absurdity of the Objectivist position should be obvious. Mystics and skeptics could rail all they like against the skill of swimming—yet none of their blather would ever cause any swimmer to doubt whether he could swim. The same is true of the process of knowledge acquisition. No amount of subversive criticism against human knowledge will ever cause men to doubt their ability to know, any more than subversive criticism against swimming would ever cause men to doubt the fact that they can swim. Men *know* that swimming is possible because they *experience* its possibility whenever they go into the water. The same is true of knowledge. Men *know* that at least some knowledge is valid because they experience the effects of successful knowing in their everyday lives. Valid knowledge leads to successful action; invalid knowledge leads to failure. Nothing said by the mystic or skeptic will ever blind men to this all too obvious fact.

I will have more to say of this in the next section. I only brought it up in this section to prevent Rand's diehard followers from losing heart after I have finished demolishing her theory of concepts. The survival of Western Civilization does not depend—despite Rand's self-serving asseverations to the contrary—on the validity of Rand's solution to the problem of universals. If it did, then we would have no choice but to regard Western Civilization as doomed, because Rand's "solution" to the problem of universals is nothing more than an inaccurate description of some of the more superficial processes involved in the development of universal terms of thought.

Rand attempts to solve the problem of universals by formulating a theory of concept-formation. A concept is merely a mental classification of the objects of experience. The concept *knife*, for example, classifies under one universal term all small objects with a handle and a sharp blade used for cutting foods and stabbing people. Concepts are necessary in order to reduce the enormous number of perceptual concretes which exist in the real world to a manageable level. "Man forms concepts, as a system of classification, whenever the scope of the perceptual data becomes too great for his mind to handle," noted Rand. (1990b, 65) In order to make clear the point Rand is trying making here, just imagine how confusing the world would be if each individual existent in reality had to have a separate name, so that just as every man now goes by a particular name, so would every tree, house, event, relation, etc. Thinking under such conditions would become impossible. There are simply too many trees, houses, relations, and events out there for each of them to go by a separate name. Hence the need for classifying the existents of reality under various words which symbolize our conceptions of those existents.

The question arises whether our conceptual classifications of the individual existents of reality are made arbitrarily, on the basis of convenience, or if there is something existing in the very nature of reality which, in effect, renders certain conceptual classifications mandatory. Does the concept *elephant*, for example, refer to an entity that really constitutes a distinct species of its own? Or is this concept a purely arbitrary classification that does not in any way reflect the basic nature of what we mean when we use the concept *elephant*?

Rand seeks to demonstrate the validity of the former, rather than the latter view. As far as she is concerned, man's conceptual classifications are the product, not of arbitrary choice, but of the nature of reality itself. Concepts like *cat, yellow, fact, justice, universe* refer to actual *types*. The concept *man*, for instance, refers to an animal that really does have its own unique nature distinct from that of any other living creature. The concept *man* is not, then, a mere arbitrary construct invented for purposes of convenience. Even if men did not have the capacity to classify the data of consciousness under various conceptual headings, they would still exist as a separate, unique, *natural* species.

Rand equates any theory of knowledge that denies the objective reality of man's conceptual classifications with the denial of the *referential* validity of man's conceptual knowledge. In other words, Rand regards any theory that holds that man's conceptual classifications are arbitrary as tantamount to a denial that man's concepts refer to anything in reality. Here, however, she is obviously confused. Even if man's concepts were arbitrary, this would not necessarily mean that his conceptual knowledge must be regarded as invalid. Arbitrary concepts can, and often do, refer to things in reality. Suppose, for example, I were to classify all pets existing in houses owned by individuals whose Christian names begin with the letter X under the concept *pliffer*. Now there is absolutely no justifiable reason for forming such a concept. No purpose at all can be served by classifying pets in so willful and subjective a manner. Yet, as arbitrary as this concept undoubtedly is, it nevertheless does in fact refer to something existing in reality—namely, to every household pet owned by an individual whose Christian name begins with the letter X. The trouble with the concept *pliffer* is not that it doesn't refer to anything in reality, but that it is irrelevant. There exists no practical reason for forming it.

Rand seems to have forgotten that there is a difference between an invalid concept (i.e., a concept that does not refer to anything in reality) and an arbitrary concept. Those philosophers who claim that man's concepts are "social constructs" or who believe that concepts are formed for reasons of convenience or utility do not necessarily hold, as Rand claims, that man's conceptual knowledge must therefore be invalid. Rand has an egregious tendency of over-dramatizing the philosophical questions at issue by making it seem as if the very existence of man's mind depended on the outcome of the debate. This, however, only serves to introduce a great deal of recriminatory passion into the subject.

Rand's theory of concepts seeks to demonstrate the referential validity of man's conceptual knowledge by explaining precisely how man *forms* his concepts. In fact, Rand's theory of concepts should really be called a *theory of concept-formation*, because that is the primary focus of the theory. Other problems relating to concepts, such as the notorious "problem of induction," she more or less ignores.

According to Rand, concepts are formed by a process of *abstraction*, which Rand defined as "a selective mental focus that *takes out* or separates a certain aspect of reality from all others (e.g., isolates a certain attribute from the entities possessing it, or a certain action from the entities performing it, etc.)." (1990b, 10) The concept *book*, for instance, is formed by focusing upon those characteristics that all books share in common and abstracting away all those characteristics that they do not share in common.

Now in order to give at least a semblance of originality to this rather conventional abstraction theory of concept-formation, Rand adds a new wrinkle to it. Abstraction, she claims, involves a process of "measurement-omission." "Ayn Rand's seminal observation," notes Leonard Peikoff, "is that the similar concretes integrated by a concept differ from one another only quantitatively, only in the measurements of their characteristics. When we form a concept, therefore, *our mental process consists in retaining the characteristics, but omitting their measurements.*" (1991, 83)

I suspect that most readers will be scratching their heads at this, wondering how any of it could possibly have a bearing on the issue of the validity of man's concepts. Not to worry: it doesn't. But since hardly anyone can relate Rand's theory of abstraction via measurement-omission to the concerns of everyday life, the tendency will be either to reject the theory out of hand or to accept it without ever taking the trouble to figure out what it means. I suspect that even Rand's diehard followers do not really understand the theory. But because it *sounds* good, they unthinkingly regard it as a "momentous discovery" worthy of the ages. (Peikoff, 1991, 82)

Perhaps a concrete example taken from the Objectivist literature will give us a somewhat less amorphous idea of what this measurement-omission principle is all about. The following is a description of how a child uses measurement-omission to form the concept *table*: "The child differentiates tables from other objects on the basis of a distinctive perceptual shape. All tables have a flat, level surface and support(s)....In order to reach the concept, the child's mind must retain this characteristic, while omitting '*all* particular measurements, not only the measurements of shape, but of all the other characteristics of tables (many of which he is not aware of at the time).'" (Peikoff, 1991, 84)

What Rand seems to be getting at with this measurement-omission principle is something which really should have been quite obvious without it—namely, the fact that many general concepts do not refer to specific measurements. When I use the concept *dog* in a general sense, I am not referring to a dog of any particular size. In this sense, you could say that the size of the dog, or its measurements, has been omitted in the concept *dog*. Rand merely attempts to extend this principle to *all* the attributes shared universally by referents of a concept, even those that do not have anything to do with physical size. This may seem like an unwarranted extension: for it should be obvious that it is not merely considerations of size that are omitted in a general conception, but other considerations as well. Dogs, for instance, differ not just in terms of size, but also in terms of personality and temperament. Some dogs are very gentle and friendly; others are mean and will bite people merely for the fun of it. In our general conception of *dog*, these characteristics must also be "omitted."

This would seem to indicate that general conceptions omit more than just considerations of size.

Rand answers this objection by insisting that such other considerations, regardless of their nature, will always be quantifiable, which is to say—measurable. The personality and temperament of a dog, Rand would argue, are *quantifiable* in the sense that they can be measured in terms of more or less. Thus, one dog can be regarded as meaner or less friendly than another. It is the relative intensities of a dog's personal characteristics that are measurable—and it these intensities that are omitted in the general conception of a dog.

Is the measurement-omission theory as universally valid as Rand claims it is? Is it really true that the particular referents of a concept only differ from one another quantitatively, and not qualitatively? To test this claim, let us use Rand's favorite epistemological example, the concept *table*. This concept, we are told, "omits every measurement which…one would have to specify in order to reproduce any particular table." This includes, curiously enough, "measurements of weight, *color*, temperature, and the like." (Peikoff, 1991, 84) I've italicized the word *color* because it is the key term here: it is what gives the game away. Properly speaking, there is no such thing as a "measurement of color." Weight, temperature, size—these, admittedly, can be measured. But how is color to be measured? Sure, individual colors have degrees or intensities of color, so that you can describe an object as being of various shades of blue, green, or red. But how are you supposed to measure different colors? Do we arbitrarily assign a number to each color and say that *that* is its measurement? If so, then Rand has surrendered all claims to being non-arbitrary in her theory of concepts.

Yet it is much more serious than that. Color is not the only characteristic that all tables have in common but which cannot be retained by omitting its measurements. All tables share the characteristic of materiality; that is, they all have to be made out of something (though they may be made out of anything, as long as it is solid). But how do you measure materiality? Suppose you have two tables of exactly the same size, temperature, and weight except that one is made from redwood and the other from an alloy of metal that has the same density as redwood. If we attempted to form the concept table from these two tables alone, what measurements would we be omitting? None. And yet these two tables are in fact different, so we would have to, according to the Objectivist theory, be omitting *something*. That *something* of course would be the specific materiality of the tables. Measurement-omission would not apply in this situation.

Some might argue that this example is so artificial as to be misleading. Fine. Let us take, as another example, the concept *motherhood*. The characteristic which defines the state of motherhood is that of having given birth. There are no measurements involved in this characteristic. Either a woman has given birth or she hasn't. If this concept is formed by abstraction, measurement-omission plays no part in the process.

Examples such as this could be thought up *ad nauseum*. It is simply not true that the referents of a general concept only differ quantitatively: they differ qualitatively as well. Human beings differ not merely in their weight, size, and degree of rationality, but also in the skill which they use words, the profundity of their thoughts, and the expressiveness of their features. Yet these latter characteristics are immeasurable. Oh, sure, you can describe one person as more articulate or more profound or more expressive than another, but such talk is purely metaphorical and imprecise. Literally speaking, no one can measure the profundity of a thought or the beauty of a woman. These are nebulous qualities that defy measurement. You can say that this thought is more profound than that one or this woman more beautiful than another one, but you can never prove your assertions. Someone else may have an entirely different opinion. How then can your differences of opinion by resolved? Lacking any objective standard of measurement, there is no way to resolve a dispute of this nature.

Yet this is not the worst of it. The invalidity of Rand's theory of concepts goes well beyond her fallacious principle of measurement-omission. It lies at the very heart of her theory, in the premise that *all* concepts are formed by a process of abstraction. I don't believe that this is the case at all. On the contrary, I strongly suspect that very few, if any, concepts are formed by a process of abstraction.

Now it is important to understand that, even if abstraction plays no role whatsoever in the *formation* of concepts, this does not mean that concepts cannot be *considered* as abstractions. I will admit that this may sound somewhat paradoxical. If concepts are in fact abstractions, how else can they be formed but by a process of abstraction? But the mistake here is to assume that, merely because X has attribute a, then X must be caused by a. When we say that concepts are abstract, we are merely noting that they have the attribute of abstractness. Yet this does not mean that concepts must for this reason be caused by abstraction. Abstractness is a purely secondary phenomenon of conception—something that is noticed only after a concept has been formed. Moreover, its status is largely fortuitous and relative. What one man considers abstract another may consider perfectly concrete. It all depends on the individual's point of view. As the philosopher George Santayana has aptly pointed out: "The whole distinction between sense-data, percepts, and concepts is psychological and historical. The abstract is what is less familiar to the speaker than something less simple which includes it; the general is whatever does not contain discriminations we are accustomed to make. The taste of water is abstract, if you expect whiskey with it; and my near-sighted vision of this mere bird is general, if you can plainly see it is a swallow; but even yours is general, if you cannot tell me whether it is a female swallow or a male....The straight line for our experience is no abstraction from seeing the actual sinuosities of rulers and rails; these look straight from the beginning. The ideally straight line is one of the first essences [i.e. datum of consciousness] yielded by the inspection of many a thing in motion, and it is precisely the same essence in them all. It is a constituent in our descriptions, not an abstraction from our objects. When a child has not yet learned to distinguish 'father' from 'strange gentleman,' his simple notion of man is no abstraction from more detailed [observation]; nor do we ever call generic our notion of an individual person, say ourselves, because it covers rather vaguely a changing and complex fact." (1969, 98)

The most glaring flaw in the abstraction view of concept-formation is its inability to explain how anyone can know which attributes should be abstracted and which ignored as irrelevant to the general conception. According to the theory of abstraction, concepts are formed only on the basis of those attributes universally shared by all the particular objects subsumed under the concept. The concept man, for example, is formed by focusing only on those characteristics which all men share in common. Characteristics which only some men share have no part in the concept. For example, not all men enjoy classical music or collecting stamps. Hence, listening to classical music and stamp collecting are not included as attributes of the concept *man*. All men, however, require food and water to survive. This necessity, therefore, is included in our conception of *Homo sapiens*.

Now according to the abstraction theory of concept-formation, a concept can only be formed on the basis of the common attributes shared by all the concept's referents. A child forms the concept *man* by isolating the characteristics which men have in common and ignoring the characteristics which men do not share in common. But how is a child supposed to know which characteristics are common to all men and which are not? Presumably, when the child forms his conception of man, his knowledge of individual men will be extremely limited. If he happens, for example, to live in a secluded place, he might have perceived only a dozen or so men in his entire life. How is he supposed to know which characteristics *all* men have in common if he has only perceived a dozen or so men? If all the men of his acquaintance enjoyed listening to classical music and collecting stamps, he might end up believing that these two characteristics form an essential part of the concept *man*.

The fact that a child might have integrated certain errors into his concept of men may not seem like that big a deal. Nor would it be for any philosopher who accepted the inveterate fallibility of human conceptualization. But Rand is not one of those philosophers. She wants to validate man's conceptual knowledge beyond all doubt. But until someone explains how anyone can know for certain what attributes a given class of objects share in common, her validation of conceptual knowledge will remain inadequate.

Neither Ayn Rand nor any of her disciples appear to have realized this shortcoming in their abstraction view of concept-formation. They assume that there is nothing easier than identifying the characteristics which a given class of objects has in common. Rand even goes so far as to imply that all you need in order to form a concept is just "two or more" observations. This can be gathered from her definition of a concept, which she defines as "a mental integration of *two or more* units possessing the same distinguishing characteristic(s), with their particular measurements omitted." (Rand, 1990b, 13, emphasis added) Presumably, this means that what is needed to form the concept man is the observation of two men. But this would appear to be, on the face of it, absurd. How could anyone determine which distinguishing characteristics are shared by all men if they have never observed more than *two* such objects?

In order to give Rand's theory a little more plausibility, let us suppose that a concept requires more than just two observations. Very well. How many are enough? Twenty? One-hundred? Three million? No matter how many were suggested, we could never be certain that there did not exist some man whom we as yet had not observed who did not share some of the characteristics which, in our ignorance, we fallaciously attributed to all men. In order to be absolutely certain, we would have to observe all men; yet this would be impossible.

Our inability to determine how many observations would be enough to establish the universality of an attribute arises from what philosophers have called "the problem of induction." An induction is any attempt to reason from the particular to the general. From our observation of *some* men we notice that none of them have eyes in the middle of their foreheads. We therefore infer that *all* men lack an eye in the middle of their forehead. From a strictly logical point of view, this inference is invalid. The fact that *some X* is *A* does not mean that *all X* is *A*.

Many philosophers have tried to get around this difficulty by concocting various theories of induction. To date, no philosopher has succeeded in showing how we can know anything to be universally true on the basis of only a finite number of observations. How can anyone say for certain that all swans are white, or that all wood floats, if no one has ever observed every swan or tested every piece of wood? For it is quite possible that there may exist swans that are not white or sinkable types of wood which, in our limited experience, we have not yet come across.

Since the validity of the abstraction theory of concept-formation depends on the validity of induction, Rand and her followers have no right to consider the Objectivist theory of concepts valid until they have provided us with a solution to the problem of induction. Alas, no solution has been forthcoming. Yet Rand has the arrogance to consider her theory of concepts as proved! (Peikoff, 1991, 109)

Unfortunately, this is not all that is wrong with the abstraction theory of concept-formation. Another objection can be made to it which, from a purely empirical point of view, may be even more serious than the objection indicated above.

Let us return for a moment to Rand's definition of a concept. Rand defines a concept as "a mental integration of *two or more* units possessing the same distinguishing characteristic(s), with their particular measurements omitted." If this definition is correct, this would mean that no concept could ever be formed on the basis of one observation alone. In other words, there would have to be at least two observations of two separate objects before any process of abstraction could begin. If, during the course of my life, I had observed only one palm tree, it would be impossible, according to the abstraction view advocated by Rand, for me to form the concept *palm tree*. Even if I had been extremely impressed by the one palm tree I observed and its image had remained with me for the rest of my life, I could still not take credit for conceptualizing it. The palm tree would always remain for me a *sui generis* object, a particular rather than a universal. Only when I had at last seen a second palm tree and could compare the second tree with the first and isolate their common characteristics would I be able to form the concept *palm tree*.

The trouble with this view of the matter is that it does not accord with experience. Concepts are formed on the basis of single observations all the time. As a matter of fact, there is reason to believe that most concepts are formed in this manner.

Let me give a concrete example that illustrates the point I am trying to make. Two children go to the zoo and are taken to see the hippopotamus. Neither child has ever before seen this animal nor been exposed to the term *hippopotamus*. When the first child arrives at the cage, there is only one hippopotamus in view. Seeing the animal, he points at the creature and asks: "What is that?" He is told it is a hippopotamus. Later the second child arrives at the hippo cage. This time, several such beasts are now on view blundering about their cage. The child points and asks: "What are those things?" He is told they are hippopotami. Now according to Rand's abstraction theory of concept-formation, only the second child will be able to form the concept *hippopotamus*, because only the second child had the opportunity to observe more than one example of the beast. The first child, meanwhile, would know of the hippopotamus only as an *individual* thing, but would not understand it as a *universal*, that is, as a concept. In his mind the word *hippopotamus* would be a mere proper name, applicable only to the hippo he had observed at the zoo.

Such are the practical implications of the abstraction theory of concept-formation advocated by Rand. Obviously, it is absurd to believe that only the child who had seen two or more hippos in the cage is capable of forming a concept of the animal. Plenty of examples can be found from everyday life of concepts formed on the basis of a single observation. Take our conceptions of the beasts of mythology, for instance. Such concepts as *unicorn, centaur, faun, minotaur, griffin*, etc. are often learned at our first exposure to them. We either come across them in books or in drawings, or maybe they are explained to us by a teacher: but however we first come across them, one exposure is usually all that is needed to form the concept of each one of these mythical beasts.

If concepts can be formed on the basis of a single observation, then Rand's claim that a concept involves the "mental integration of *two or more* units" must be dismissed as invalid. A mental integration of just one unit is enough to form a concept. The child who observes a single hippo for the first time simply takes it for granted that there might be other hippos like this one. Nor does he have to see another hippo to formulate this conjecture. It comes to him naturally, just as the absorption of language comes to him naturally. And also note: having seen one such beast, no process of abstraction is necessary for him to identify other instances of the beast. One perception is enough to know what all such beasts look like and how to identify them.

What is true of hippos is probably true of all perceptual data. Once a particular datum has been identified and given a name, it can be used to identify another datum that is similar to it. Abstraction has nothing to do with the process. What enables a child to recognize light yellow and bright yellow as two instances of the same color is not any process of abstraction whereby the intensities of the color are omitted. Not at all. When a child comes across a new shade of yellow, rather than abstracting the shade of color away (whatever *that* means!), he instead makes every effort to relate the new experience with what he already knows. Since he has already familiarized himself with a darker shade of yellow, he merely interprets this new experience of light yellow on the basis of the old experience of dark yellow. Thus does he use the known to grasp the unknown.

The intellectual skills involved in using the known to grasp and understand the unknown are crucial to concept-formation. Like all skills, it is purely intuitive in nature and is developed through a process of trial and error. The reason why children just learning to speak make so many hilarious errors in their fumbling attempts to classify the objects around them into the appropriate conceptual categories is because their skill of interpreting the unknown by relating it to the known has not been sufficiently developed. For this reason, they are unable to make the sort of intuitive discriminations that adults take for granted. A good example of this is the toddler who, upon seeing an ape for the first time, points at the creature and says: "Look! A hairy man!" Adults find such errors amusing, but if we look more closely, we will find that errors of this sort can be very instructive about what is going on in the child's mind. Here the child is obviously trying to understand the unknown (i.e., an ape) by relating it to something that he does know (i.e., *hairy* and *man*). The reason for the child's error is that his intuitive judgment has not yet developed to the point where he can distinguish an ape from a man. Later, after years of practical experience, he will not only be able to distinguish men from apes, but wolves from dogs, crocodiles from alligators, and any number of other similar but distinct categories of objects.

Rand would not have accepted this account of concept-formation, because it violates her inveterate prejudice against any method of knowledge or human skill that cannot be described in terms of formalized rules. The knowledge that allows us to group similar but different objects under the same conceptual heading is intuitive, rather than conceptual, in nature. It is the product, not of conscious thinking, but of the unconscious integrations performed during our haphazard efforts in childhood to learn how to use mental conceptions to describe and interpret experience. (Lakoff & Johnson, 1999, 13, 18) Because of the intuitive nature of this form of knowledge, any attempt to explain it in terms of words will likely prove inadequate. This is why Rand's endeavor to validate man's conceptual knowledge is so ill advised. Such validation must of course be expressed in terms of concepts. But concept-formation is an intuitive process that defies translation into conceptual terms. Any attempt to articulate conceptually the intuitive nature of concept-formation will only serve to make the process seem even more recondite and mysterious than it really is.

In the next section, we will examine in more detail why Rand and her followers believe so firmly in the necessity of reducing all of man's most crucial mental processes to a system of formalized, articulable rules.

*   *   *

(2) Rand's most serious epistemological error is her assumption that all human knowledge is ultimately conceptual in nature and can only be formulated through a process of deliberate conscious reasoning. Implicit in this view is the rejection of any kind of knowledge formulated without the aid of concepts. According to the Randian paradigm of knowledge, man must think before he can know. This means that his concepts must

be formulated consciously, through a deliberate effort of focused awareness.

This view of knowledge leads to several difficulties, not the least of which is its inability to explain the existence of *tacit* knowledge. As I noted in the previous section, there are many things that people know how to do even though they cannot explain or articulate this knowledge. I gave swimming as an example, but there are many others. How many people, for instance, can explain how to ride a bike, or create an exciting story, or solve a difficult philosophical problem? All attempts to explain such things have always been dismal failures. Try to teach a child how to ride a bike through concepts and just see how far he gets! Not until the child actually gets on the bike and attempts to ride it can he ever master the skill of bike riding. There is something nebulous in the process of learning how to ride a bike that defies conceptual articulation. The same is true of writing a story and solving philosophical problems. These activities cannot be taught merely by talking about them. This being the case, how can Rand justify her claim that all knowledge is conceptual in nature?

Rand tries to circumvent this difficulty by introducing what she called "automatized knowledge," which she described as knowledge that has been stored in the subconscious and which can be immediately accessed to serve as the basis of intellectual judgments. "A mind's cognitive development involves a continual process of automatization," she insisted. "For example, you cannot perceive a table as an infant perceives it—as a mysterious object with four legs. You perceive it as a table, i.e., a man-made piece of furniture, serving a certain purpose belonging to a human habitation, etc.; you cannot separate these attributes from your sight of the table, you experience it as a single, indivisible percept—yet all you see is a four-legged object; the rest is an automatized integration of a vast amount of conceptual knowledge which, at one time, you had to learn bit by bit. The same is true of everything you see and experience; as an adult, you cannot perceive or experience in a vacuum, you do it in a certain automatized *context*—and the efficiency of your mental operations depends on the kind of context your subconscious has automatized." (1971b, 192-193)

At first blush, this theory may seem to come pretty close to what I have called intuition. There is, however, at least one important difference. Rand believes that this "automatized" knowledge is the product of concepts that have been "programmed" into the subconscious. "The status of automatized knowledge in his mind is experienced by man as if it had a direct, effortless, self-evident quality (and certainty) of perceptual awareness," she wrote. "But it is *conceptual* knowledge, and its validity depends on the precision of his concepts, which require as strict a precision of meaning...as the definitions of mathematical terms." (1990b, 86)

Any empirical investigation of human knowledge will demonstrate the falsity of this view. In fact, it is so insupportable that not even Rand and her followers can stick to it consistently. In several places, we find them guilty of contradicting it. Consider the following passage, taken from Peikoff's treatise on Objectivism: "The process of measurement-omission is performed by us by the nature of our mental faculty, whether anyone identifies it or not. To form a concept, one does not have to know that a form of measurement is involved [i.e., it can be formed unconsciously, without the subject knowing anything about it]....On the conscious level, one need merely observe similarities." (1991, 85)

Here we find Peikoff advocating a type of automatized knowledge that is *not* conceptual in nature. For it is admitted here (at least by implication) that the measurement-omission process, which Rand considered so crucial in the formation of concepts, takes place whether the individual knows anything about it or not.

This is a somewhat subtle point, so perhaps I should explain in more detail. Rand holds that automatized knowledge is ultimately conceptual in origin. Man's knowledge, she claims, is the product of concepts that have been programmed by the conscious mind into the subconscious. Such concepts can only be formed through a volitional process of conscious thinking. If a man does not form the concepts which he programs into his mind, he must get them ready-made from the mind of someone else. This view of the matter, however, is directly contradicted by Peikoff's assertion that individuals omit measurements when they form concepts, "whether anyone identifies it or not." Presumably, this means that measurement-omission constitutes a type of automatized knowledge. But here we run into a problem. If measurement-omission constitutes a type of automatized knowledge, then ultimately it must be the product of concepts consciously programmed into the subconscious. The problem is: what concepts? Where did they come from? Let us not forget that before Rand came along, the concept of measurement-omission was completely unknown. As far as we know, no man's mind had ever entertained it. If this is so, it would be impossible to account, on the basis of Objectivist principles alone, for how anyone could have programmed their minds with the concept of measurement omission *before* anyone had any conscious knowledge of it. The only way to account for such a thing would be to acknowledge the existence of some form of automatized knowledge that is not a product of conscious thinking or of concepts.

Now if a mental skill as crucial to mankind as concept-formation can be developed without the aid of concepts, why can't other intellectual skills be formed without the aid of concepts? And if concepts are not needed to form mental skills, why should we assume that they are needed for the development of moral or political skills as well? Indeed, there is no reason to believe they are necessary in any branch of knowledge. Yet if human knowledge is not dependent on conceptual principles, as Rand believed, then the Objectivist view of man as a "conceptual being" who is determined by his broadest conceptual integrations must be dismissed as unwarranted.

To extricate herself from this logical quagmire, Rand introduced yet another epistemological principle which she called an "implicit" concept and which she defined as knowledge "which is available to your consciousness but which you have not conceptualized." Measurement-omission, we are told, is an example of such an "implicit" concept. (1990b, 159-160) Before an individual has explicitly identified measurement-omission as the process that enables him to form concepts, it exists in his mind as an implicit concept. Therefore measurement-omission, even though it existed for centuries prior to Rand's explicit conceptualization of it, is still a form of conceptual knowledge, since it is ultimately derived from an "implicit" concept.

The trouble with the notion of an "implicit" concept is that it is a contradiction in terms. If an implicit concept is knowledge that has not been conceptualized, how can it be regarded as a concept, implicit or otherwise? Curiously enough, Rand was confronted with this contradiction in one of her workshops on epistemology. "Why do you identify this type of awareness as an implicit concept?" one of the professors attending the workshop wanted to know. "There seems to be an obvious objection that the notion of an 'implicit concept' is a contradiction in terms. For you to have a concept, there must be some form of integration, and you are speaking here of an awareness which is avowedly not integrated." To this very sensible objection, one of Rand's disciples replied by suggesting that the idea of an "implicit concept" is no more self-contradictory than the idea of a "potential man." (1990b, 161) This, however, is pure sophistry. The analogy suggested between the concepts *implicit* and *potential* is not a valid one. There exists a crucial difference between something which is implicit and something which is potential. The implicit exists in the here and now. Rand's notion of an implicit concept constitutes knowledge which the individual can use at any time. Though unarticulated, it is nonetheless something tangible and real. Now if, on the other hand, a man's knowledge were merely *potential*, rather than implicit, it is difficult to understand how he could possibly use it. What is potential belongs to the future; it cannot exist in the present (if it did, it would be *actual*, rather than potential, in nature).

To assume a strict logical analogy between the concepts *implicit* and *potential* is to commit a palpable fallacy.

But even if it were not a fallacy, it would still fail to extricate Rand from the logical quagmire she fell into when she declared that man's knowledge is conceptual in nature. By merely acknowledging the existence of implicit concepts, Rand has admitted that not all man's knowledge is conceptual. Since an implicit concept, by her own admission, is knowledge that has not been conceptualized, it follows that such concepts are not really concepts at all. By calling them "implicit concepts," Rand is engaging in what can only be described as a form of philosophical deceit. She was well aware that some of man's knowledge is not conceptual. But rather than come out and admit it, she decided to invent this entirely fictitious notion of an "implicit" concept.

The principle motive behind all this philosophical leg-erdemain is Rand's prejudice against the tacit, inarticula-ble element in human knowledge. Her entire philosophical enterprise rests on the premise that articula-tion is critical to human survival. That is why philosophy, to her mind, is so important: because philosophy articu-lates what would otherwise remain merely tacit and inse-cure. In order for men to have confidence in their reason, she believed they must be able to *validate* the process of reason; and in order to validate the process of reason, they must be able to *articulate* the principles of reason. In her attempt to justify this view, she was driven to adopt the premise that all man's knowledge is conceptual and is ulti-mately the product of deliberate conscious reasoning.

That this premise is false can easily be demonstrated by testing it against the relevant empirical facts. I have already given the examples of swimming and concept-formation as knowledge-skills that do not depend on concepts developed through conscious deliberation. Before concluding this section, I want to provide one more, in order to drive my point home even further.

The formation of grammatical structures in language is about as clear an example of an intellectual development that depends, not on concepts developed through conscious deliberation, but on intuitive knowledge developed unconsciously. As Pareto aptly observed: "It would be absurd to claim that the theory of grammar [i.e., the *concepts* of grammar] preceded the practice of speech. It certainly followed, and human beings have created the most subtle grammatical structures without any knowledge [i.e. without being conscious] of it." As usual with Pareto, he is not content to merely utter a general observation, but he also feels obliged to give at least some concrete evidence to back it up. "Take the Greek language as an example," he continues. "We cannot imagine that the Greeks one day got together and decided what their system of conjugation was to be. Usage alone made such a masterpiece of the Greek verb. In Attic Greek there is the augment, which is the sign of the past in historical tenses; and, for a very subtle nuance, besides the syllabic augment, there is the temporal augment, which consists in a lengthening of the initial vowel. The conception of aorist, and its functions in syntax, are inventions that would do credit to the most expert logician. The large number of verbal forms and the exactness of their functions in syntax constitute a marvelous whole." (1916, §158)

What is true of grammar is also true of morality, jurisprudence, aesthetic appreciation and scores of other behavioral and reactive phenomena found in human societies and cultures. Can anyone seriously believe that the theory of morality preceded the practice of morality? Or that the theory of jurisprudence or the theory of aesthetic appreciation preceded the practice of law or the practice of aesthetics? The practice, the conduct, comes first; a theory is then devised to explain or describe the conduct. And since the practice precedes the theory, the practice cannot be regarded as the product of concepts discovered through a process of conscious deliberation. The factual evidence would appear to suggest that moral conduct, legal conduct, linguistic conduct, and aesthetic appreciation are all governed, to a very appreciable extent, by an intuitive form of knowledge developed unconsciously. Now this does not mean that concepts play no role whatsoever. They may, in certain circumstances, play a very important role. But, generally speaking, their importance has been greatly exaggerated, especially by rationalistic thinkers like Ayn Rand.

In closing, I wish to make a few comments about Rand's theory of the subconscious. Several of the propositions which make up her theory are clearly not in accord with the facts. Her leading expositor, Leonard Peikoff, went so far as to declare that "There is nothing in the subconscious besides what you acquired by conscious means. The subconscious does perform certain important integrations (sometimes these are correct, sometimes not), but the conscious mind is always able to know what these are (and to correct them, if necessary). The subconscious has no purposes or values of its own, and it does not engage in diabolical manipulations behind the scenes. In that sense, it is certainly not dynamic." (Binswanger, 1986, 484)

There are at least three dubious assertions in this paragraph. Let us examine them one by one.

1. *That there is nothing in the subconscious besides what you acquired by conscious means.* This constitutes one of the most inveterate prejudices in all Rand's philosophy. It is easily falsified empirically. Just return for a moment to our example of grammar and language. Does anyone seriously believe that children, when they learn how to speak, stop and reflect about the grammatical structure of the language they are learning? Certainly not! Children learn how to speak largely through an unconscious imitation of the speech of those around them. If a child is exposed to speech which observes the rules of "correct" grammar, he will learn to speak "correctly." If not, he will learn to speak "incorrectly." Conscious reflection has nothing to do with the process. When children imitate the speech patterns of those around them, they have no idea of the grammatical significance of those patterns. Yet this does not mean that they have not learned them. A child who has learned how to speak grammatically does know and understand, in a tacit sort of way, the rules of grammar: he simply has not consciously formalized these rules. His knowledge of the rules of grammar is thoroughly intuitive and unconscious.

Now it could be argued, in response to this, that, even if the child's knowledge of grammar is unconscious—or "subconscious," as Rand would say—the manner in which he imbibed this knowledge (i.e., through the imitation of the speech patterns of others) *was* conscious. How could it not be conscious? Before a child can imitate something, he must be consciously exposed to it. However, there is a rather subtle error in this reasoning that needs to be pointed out. It is quite true that the child is consciously aware of the speech from which he imbibes the unconscious knowledge of how to speak grammatically. But it is not from the speech per se that this knowledge is derived, but from the grammatical structures embedded within that speech; and it is precisely these structures which the child, when listening to those around him, is not conscious of in any significant sense of the term. Knowledge of grammar is therefore not only unconscious in the child, but is absorbed unconsciously as well.

2. *The conscious mind is always able to know about subconscious integrations.* This would appear to be false just from our example of a child learning how to speak grammatically. The child has no idea that, by simply learning how to speak through a process of imitation, he is *ipso facto* learning how to speak according to the rules of grammar.

3. *The subconscious has no purposes or values of its own.* Although it may not seem so at first blush, this statement expresses the inveterate tendency of Objectivism to hypostatize consciousness into an active agent. The point of the statement is to affirm the dependence of the subconscious on the conscious mind. Consciousness, according to Objectivism, is an "active process…maintained by continuous action." (Rand, 1990b, 37) This is a very misleading description of consciousness. Strictly speaking, consciousness never "acts"—it merely passively reports the data that is fed into it either by the mind or the senses. Once again, Rand has committed the error of confusing the datum with the medium in which the datum is revealed. Man's consciousness, we are told, is an active agent whose "function is…to look outward" and "perceive that which exists." (Peikoff, 1991, 47) Yet it is not consciousness per

se which "looks outward" and perceives "that which exists," it is the *mind* that does these things. Consciousness is simply the medium through which the mind perceives the external world. It does not control or direct or cause anything. Consciousness is like a movie screen: it docilely receives whatever images are projected upon it. It neither thinks nor perceives nor acts upon any knowledge within the mind. It merely *experiences* such thoughts or perceptions of the mind. And while it is true that man's subconscious has no purposes or values of its own, the same is true of his consciousness. It is not his consciousness, but his innermost self, which has values and purposes. His consciousness merely experiences these purposes and values. It does not, nor can it, have purposes and values of its own.

Thus ends our examination of Rand's implacable tendency to exaggerate the importance of conceptual principles formed solely by a process of conscious deliberation. While the conscious human mind certainly plays a significant role in human existence, its role is nowhere near as significant as Rand claims it to be. A large portion of human knowledge is absorbed unconsciously, without the guidance of conscious deliberation. Such knowledge is intuitive, rather than conceptual, in nature. Rand, in her zeal to reduce every element of life to conceptual reason, constructed a theory of the subconscious that has, at best, only a tenuous accordance with reality. In her attempt to rationalize this theory, she was led into all sorts of silly errors, the most ridiculous being the confusion, manifested in her view of consciousness, between the *medium* of experience and the *object* of experience. The medium, however, is not the same as its object. Failure to realize this blinded Rand to many of the errors she committed in formulating her theory of knowledge.

            *   *   *

(3) In the first chapter of this book, I argued that the philosophy of Objectivism can be regarded as a mere rationalization of Rand's personal sentiments, especially her sentiments about what she chose to call the "ideal man." Rand, I have argued, was primarily concerned with providing verbal justifications for her beliefs. She had only a slight interest in determining whether such beliefs are in accord with empirical reality. That is why she and her followers are so niggardly when it comes to providing supporting evidence for Objectivist doctrines.

Rand and her followers are not alone in their reluctance to provide empirical evidence in support of their beliefs. This sort of reluctance is very common among philosophers and ideologues of all stripes. Most people who have any opinion at all about ethics or politics or the nature of man are inclined to consider their views as so obvious that there is no need to test them against experience. If you call upon them to prove their opinions, instead of giving you factual evidence, they will give you all sorts of purely verbal proofs based on misleading general observations and on definitions that assume the very point at issue. This method of proof I call *verbalism*. Verbalism involves the attempt to determine matters of fact on the basis of logical or rhetorical constructions rather than on the basis of empirical observation or scientific investigation. The verbalist substitutes words for facts, vague generalizations for specific descriptions, and introspection for experience of external reality. Complex facts are simplified to the point of serious distortion and then combined with principles destitute of empirical content to bring forth conclusions that have only a meager resemblance to empirical facts. The verbalist, in brief, seeks to establish the truth of his convictions through mere patter. For that is really all that verbalism adds up to in the end: worthless patter.

If we were to classify and describe the various modes or argumentation adopted by verbalist thinkers, the process would probably require several large volumes. Since we have neither the time nor the inclination to discuss every single type of verbalist fallacy ever committed on behalf of the congenital mendacity of man, we will confine our dissertation to some of the more prominent ones found in the Objectivist literature. The four most prominent types of verbalist fallacies committed by Rand and her followers could be classified as follows:

I. *The fallacy of the unsubstantiated assertion.*

II. *The fallacy of restating the assertion in different terms.*

III. *The fallacy of reasoning on the basis of indefinite terms.*

IV. *The fallacy of reasoning on the basis of an over-simplified, over-generalized descriptions of facts.*

I. *The fallacy of unsubstantiated assertion.* I hope that none of my readers are so destitute of the ability to think critically as not to understand what is wrong with trying to prove something merely by asserting it is so. Any assertion which is at all debatable requires empirical evidence to corroborate it. Without such evidence, the assertion has to be regarded as unproved or uncorroborated.

Considering Rand's emphasis on proving everything by reason, it is surprising to discover how often she fails to provide supporting evidence for her assertions. Her theory of emotions is one very prominent example of this failing. Nowhere in her published writings did Rand see fit to offer a shred of empirical evidence supporting her belief that man's emotions are determined by his thinking. Instead, she simply asserted it is so and left it at that. (1961, 162-163; 1964a; 1964b, 27; 1982, 4) Now while this might have been justified if she were merely asserting something so obvious or so well founded that no reasonable person could possibly object, it is certainly not justified in regards to a theory as highly debatable as her theory of emotions. Rand's theory literally screams for empirical evidence. Yet none is provided.

Many other instances of this fallacy can be found in the Objectivist literature. As evidence, I offer the following examples:

"No injustice or exploitation can succeed for long without the sanction of the victim." (Rand, 1961, 53) An extremely dubious assertion. What about the Black slaves in the Americas? Or the Jews in Nazi Germany? Or the cheks in the Gulag? Rand should have had the courtesy to explain why these counter-examples fail to invalidate her assertion. But she makes no attempt to introduce evidence backing her assertion. She merely asserts it and expects the rest of us to go along with it.

"[A man's] body will always follow the ultimate logic of his deepest convictions." (Rand, 1961, 119) Again we run across a highly questionable assertion that Rand fails to support with valid evidence.

"[An animal's] senses provide it with an automatic code of action." (1961, 148) Same problem as before: no supporting evidence.

"Make no mistake about the character of mystics. To undercut your consciousness has always been their only purpose throughout the ages—and *power*, the power to rule *you* by force, has always been their only lust." (Rand, 1961, 199) While this might be true of *some* mystics, it is probably not true of *all* mystics. To justify such an assertion one would need an immense amount of evidence. Yet no evidence at all is provided!

"A wealth seeker in the Middle Ages had to become a bandit or was burned at the stake." (Peikoff, 1985, 7) I doubt that you could find a single historian of the Middle Ages who would agree with this assertion. In any case, an assertion as contrary to the known facts as this one requires evidence on its behalf. In the absence of such evidence, it must be dismissed as arbitrary patter.

"A free country has never lacked volunteers when attacked by a foreign aggressor." (Rand, 1967, 40) Again, another extremely questionable assertion unbacked with evidence. Take World War II as an example: even though the U.S. was attacked by a foreign aggressor, a compulsory draft was deemed necessary to defend the country. Without an exhaustive examination of the relevant facts, this assertion is absolutely worthless.

To sum up: Any assertion about the factual world that is at all debatable requires supporting evidence. In the absence of such evidence, there is no reason why the assertion should be deemed acceptable.

II. *The fallacy of restating the assertion in different terms.* This is another very common fallacy in the Objectivist literature. Instead of trying to prove some theory through mere assertion, an effort is made to prove it by asserting it over and over in different ways, rewording the assertion each time to provide variety of expression. A prime example of this is the Objectivist argument for abortion. "Never mind the vicious nonsense of claiming that an embryo has a 'right to live'," rages Miss Rand. "A piece of protoplasm has no rights—and no life in the human sense of the term....To equate a *potential* with an *actual*, is vicious; to advocate the sacrifice of the latter to the former, is unspeakable." (Binswanger, 1986, 1) Elsewhere Rand fumes: "If any among you are confused or taken in by the argument that the cells of an embryo are living human cells, remember that so are all the cells of your body, including the cells of your skin, your tonsils, or your ruptured appendix—and that cutting them is murder, according to the notions of that proposed law. Remember also that a potentiality is *not* the equivalent of an actuality—and that a human being's life begins at birth." (Binswanger, 1986, 1-2)

As arguments for abortion go, these are not particularly convincing ones. Especially dubious is Rand's *ex cathedra* declaration equating a fetus with other cells in the body. Anyone who seriously believes that there exist no important differences between a fetus and a ruptured appendix is obviously operating under a full steam of dogmatic sentiment. You can be sure that if certain organs of the body, such as tonsils or the appendix, were known to develop into human organisms, our attitude towards "cutting them" would be vastly different from what it is presently.

Yet the fallacious equation of a fetus to the cells in the body is not what is primarily wrong with these two arguments. The problem with both the arguments is that they fail to prove anything. They merely try to prove the point at issue by restating it in different terms. According to the science of logic, this is called begging the question and is a form of the *Petitio Principii* fallacy.

What *precisely* is Rand trying to prove in these episodes of torrential rhetoric? Merely this: that it is perfectly okay to butcher a woman's fetus because such a creature does not constitute an actual human life. Now whether this thesis is true of false is not a question we have any intention of solving here. What we are concerned with is the quality of Rand's arguments.

What evidence does Rand provide in support of her thesis that a fetus is not a human life? A fetus is not a human life, she argues, because it is a mere "potentiality," by which she means that it is only a *potential* human life. But what can Rand possibly mean by claiming that a fetus is a mere *potential* human life? The term potential here means: something that is not yet actual. A *potential* human life is therefore merely an organism that is not yet a human life. In other words, to say that a fetus is a *potential* human life is the same as saying that a fetus is *not* a human life. The term *potential* adds nothing to the argument. *Potential* is just a synonym for *not yet actual*. By using it in this context Rand is merely restating her thesis in different terms.

In addition to this potentiality argument, Rand tries to prove her case by describing a fetus as "a piece of protoplasm" which fails to constitute a "life in the human sense of the term." The phrase "piece of protoplasm" is a mere shred of useless rhetoric: any human being could be described as mere piece of protoplasm, but this would not make such an individual any less human. As for the wonderful assertion that a fetus is "no life *in the human sense of the term*," the phrase *human sense of the term* is redundant: it adds nothing to the argument. All terms used by human beings are used in the "human sense of the term." What other sense is there? A canine sense? An extra-terrestrial sense? (And if a fetus should in fact constitute a human life in some other sense of the term, would it still be okay to go on butchering them? What if, for instance, a fetus should be a human life in *God's* sense of the term, as most Christians believe? Obviously, the entire phrase *human sense of the term* is merely Rand's way of restating her thesis in different terms. But in doing so she is guilty of assuming the very point at issue—i.e., whether a fetus constitutes a human life.)

Another example of this fallacy can be found in Peikoff's attempted refutation of supernaturalism. Peikoff tries to show that since only nature exists, the supernatural *cannot* exist. "'Supernatural,' etymologically, means that which is above or beyond nature," he asserts. "'Nature,' in turn, denotes existence from a certain perspective. Nature is existence regarded as a system of interconnected entities governed by law; it is the universe of entities acting and interacting in accordance with their identities. What then is 'super-nature'? It would have to be a form of existence beyond existence; a thing beyond entities; a something beyond identity." (1991, 31)

Peikoff could have saved himself a lot of trouble if he had merely contented himself with asserting that the supernatural does not exist because only nature exists, for he says nothing else in this empirically vacuous paragraph. The phrase "viewed from a certain perspective" is a pleonasm: anything viewed must of course be "viewed from a certain perspective." The phrase "system of interconnected entities governed by law" is another piece of empty rhetoric. Since it fails to specify what sort of interconnected entities exist or what kind of law governs them, this proposition is entirely useless. It is simply a vague and empirically indefinite description of existence. The same can be said of the phrase "universe of entities acting in accordance with their identities," which is simply a restatement in different terms of the previous phrase. To think that all this empirically destitute verbiage proves anything is to be sadly deluded. The whole paragraph simply reasserts the propositions "the supernatural does not exist" and "only nature exists" in different terms and in roundabout ways. Nothing else is accomplished. No empirical evidence is brought forth to corroborate these assertions. Indeed, since Peikoff fails to define the terms nature and supernatural all that clearly, we cannot be sure whether Peikoff's claim that only nature exists isn't a mere tautology. What specific empirical event does it rule out? Or would Peikoff simply regard any occurrence in the real world of fact, no matter how strange or contrary to our conception of a nature, to be natural? In that case, there is no need to refute the existence of the supernatural. If you insist on calling everything that exists "natural," then of course the supernatural will no longer exist. But this does not mean that those occurrences which are considered supernatural, such as miracles and the like, will be proved nonexistent. No, not at all. They will have only been redefined as purely natural occurrences.

Whether the supernatural does in fact exist is something that can only be determined by the light of experience. The manipulation of empty rhetorical phrases is of no consequence in such matters. As Santayana wisely observes: "If, abandoning the narrow grounds of experience, the rationalist appeals to reason, and says that miracles are impossible because they would be unintelligible [or, as Peikoff would say, contrary to the law of identity], he falls into a verbal trap, baited to snare the innocent." (1946, 79) That is all that the Objectivist argument against the supernatural really is: a mere verbal trap baited to snare the innocent.

III. *The fallacy of reasoning on the basis of indefinite terms.* This is another widespread fallacy in Objectivism. It often assumes the following form. Rand begins with some extremely vague principle which, because it lacks any sort of definite empirical meaning, can be used to prove anything she pleases. Then she proceeds to infer from it whatever is needed to carry the burden of her argument. Never mind the fact that the diametric opposite could also be proved from the very same principle. So absorbed is she in rationalizing her own convictions that she never realizes the logical and factual destitution of her arguments.

The most prominent example of this fallacy in Objectivism occurs in Rand's metaphysical theories, where she tries to draw all sorts of empirically definite conclusions from axioms completely barren of any *specific* empirical content. Another prominent example occurs in her theory of ethics, where she argues that the standard of moral judgment is "that which is required for man's survival *qua* man." Such a standard (as I will argue in Chapter

5) could be used to justify almost any action, no matter how morally perverse or shocking.

We will run across several other prominent examples of this fallacy in our discussions of politics and aesthetics. So many of Rand's arguments are laced with indefinite or ambiguous terms that fail to carry the empirical burden of her arguments. I have in mind, specifically, such terms as *absolute, consciousness, existence, free will, self, common sense, context, essence, fundamental, rational, reason, teleological measurement, good, evil, happiness, independence, justice, ought, rights, selfish, freedom, tyranny, romanticism, benevolent universe premise*, and *malevolent universe premise*, among others. Some of these terms are indefinite because they apply indiscriminately to nearly all facts of reality and are therefore too "abstract" to convey any significant information about those facts (e.g. such terms as *absolute, existence, identity*). Others derive their inexactness from their failure to convey any sort of precise, objective information. Words like *hot, cold, heavy, light, large, small*, etc. constitute classic examples of this type of empirically indefinite terms. When individuals use such terms no one really knows exactly what they mean. You are told that the water in the pool is cold. But that information only gives you, at best, a vague idea of the water's temperature. The term cold means different things to different people. Individuals with a low tolerance for cold water might think that 75 degrees is cold. On the other hand, someone with a high tolerance for cold water might consider 75 degrees to be warm.

In the list of vague terms provided above, such terms as *context, common sense, fundamental, rational, reason, freedom, happiness, tyranny, benevolent universe premise*, and *malevolent universe premise* are similar to terms like hot, cold, large, small, etc. in the sense that, although all these terms may correspond to something in reality, they do not tell us anything specific about what they correspond to. We all think we know what *common sense* is. But on closer examination it would be found that *common sense* is a far more ambiguous conception than most of us realize. Often *common sense* is nothing more than a misleading synonym for the phrase *seems obvious to me*. So instead of saying "*X* is obviously true to me" we say: "Anyone with any common sense would realize that *X* is true."

Objectivists do not use the term *common sense* in this manner all that often. They usually prefer the term *reason*, because, strangely enough, they regard it as the more precise term. This, of course, is hardly the case. The term *reason*, at least in the sense used by Rand and her leading expositors, is a far less definite term than most Objectivists realize. Although Rand attempted on many occasions to describe what reason is, none of her descriptions are entirely precise or enlightening. The following represents a sample:

(A) "Reason is the faculty that identifies and integrates the material provided by man's senses." (1964b, 20)

(B) "Reason integrates man's perceptions by means of forming abstractions or conceptions….The *method* which reason employs in this process is *logic*." (1982, 62)

(C) "Reason is man's only means of grasping reality and of acquiring knowledge." (1971b, 84)

D) "Reason is a faculty that man has to exercise *by choice*. Thinking is not an automatic function." (1964b, 20)

(E) "Reason is man's tool of knowledge, the faculty that enables him to perceive the facts of reality." (1964a)

F) "*Reason* is the only *objective* means of communication and of understanding among men" (1982, 70)

(G) "This—the supremacy of reason—...is...the essence of Objectivism....Reason in epistemology leads to egoism in ethics, which leads to capitalism in politics." (Binswanger, 1986, 410) (What she is really saying here is that reason leads to Objectivism.)

In these seven selections, Rand describes reason alternately as a "faculty," a "means of grasping knowledge," a "tool of knowledge," and as an "objective means of communication." Reason is furthermore, we are told, an identifying and integrating faculty which can only be exercised by choice and which enables man to perceive the facts of reality. Now while all this may seem, to uncritical persons, to contain substantial information about the nature of reason, as a matter of fact, no one, after reading these selections, will have any very definite idea what reason is. The most specific of these descriptions is selection B, where we are told that reason "integrates man's perceptions by means of forming abstractions or conceptions" and that the method employed by reason is logic. The trouble with this description is that if we examined it critically we will find that it contradicts itself. If reason is merely the process involved in forming abstractions, then logic simply cannot be reason's method, because, as I explained in the previous section, Rand's theory of abstraction depends upon a process of induction—which, from the standpoint of logic, is a completely invalid form of reasoning. And so if logic really were the method of reason, then reason simply could not have anything to do with integrating perceptions into abstractions.

To be sure, Rand's description of reason is not meant to be examined as critically as I have done so here. The point of selection B (as well as all the others) is to provide a mere semblance of precise meaning, so that Rand's followers will not be alerted to the fact that this term does not refer to anything definite.

Further evidence for this supposition can be gathered by an examination of some of Rand's other descriptions of *reason* quoted above. Note the preponderance of vague terms: *faculty, material, grasping, integrate, means of communication, understanding among men.* In ordinary parlance, such terms may have obvious meanings; but for the purposes of determining anything as complex as the nature of human knowledge, they are close to worthless. What, for example, can it possibly mean to say that reason is a "faculty"?—or a "means of grasping knowledge"?—or a "means of communication"? Can reason really be all these things at once? Can a faculty really be a means of communication? Can a means of communication really be the *only* means of grasping reality? I will concede that these terms are not entirely indefinite. They do convey *some* meaning. They express Rand's conviction that reason constitutes the method whereby individuals make sense of experiential reality. But to say that reason is the method— or the means—by which reality is "grasped" does not really convey a whole lot of specific information concerning the nature of reason. In some sense, it merely turns reason into a tautological concept, a word used to reinforce Rand's conviction that her conclusions are always right. Whenever someone questioned the validity of her opinions, Rand could always reply that her opinions were valid because they were founded on reason, and since reason is the only means of grasping reality, then anything founded on reason must *ipso facto* be valid!

Rand is not the only philosopher to misuse the term *reason* in this way. The complexity of the cognitive process makes it difficult to specify exactly what *reason* is. In the absence of such specification, *reason* simply becomes an indefinite term that can be misused in all sorts of appalling ways. Rand tried to circumvent this problem by defining reason as concept-formation and then proceeding to write an entire treatise devoted to this topic. Yet I seriously doubt that anyone, after reading Rand's book, will come away with a definite understanding of what concept-formation, let alone reason, is all about. Rand spends most of the book explaining concept-formation in terms of other concepts that are equally vague and destitute of empirical substance.

The great advantage of indefinite terms is that you can use them to prove anything you like. If I claim that *reason=X*, for my claim to have any sort of empirical validity, X must be something empirically definite. Otherwise it would be as if I had described reason in terms of gibberish.

The situation is further complicated when the claim *reason=X* is used as the first premise of a syllogism. Suppose you want to prove that *reason=B*. Now if you can back up your claim that *reason=B* with scientifically validated evidence, then all you have to do is provide your evidence and the matter is settled once and for all. But what if you don't have any evidence? Then the best way to proceed is to hide the empirical worthlessness of your arguments under a cloak of empty verbiage. This is where X comes in. In order to make our argument seem convincing, all we have to do is make sure *X* does not accord with anything definite. That way, we can use it to mean anything we please. So why not let it mean *B*? This allows us to construct a very neat syllogism, as follows:

Reason=X
X=B
Therefore, Reason=B

As long as X remains indefinite, we can use this syllogism to prove that reason is just about anything we please. Such are the miraculous powers of indefinite terms. Of course, such proofs, from the viewpoint of experiential reality, are entirely worthless. But anyone who would stoop to such verbalist trickery obviously doesn't give a fig for empirical reality.

Rand uses an argument very much like this one to prove that r*eason* is "the only means of grasping reality." She begins with the premise "Reason is the faculty that integrates perceptions into abstractions." This premise is equivalent to *reason=X*. What follows is an enthymeme, or unstated premise corresponding to *X=B*: i.e., "The faculty that integrates perceptions into abstractions is the only means of grasping reality." From here we can easily deduce the conclusion *Reason=B*: i.e., "Reason is the only means of grasping reality."

As verbalist arguments go, this is actually a pretty good one, because X *seems to* be more definite than it really is. The worthlessness of the argument is only made apparent when you try to apply X to a specific empirical situation. For example, suppose two individuals who claim to be using Rand's faculty of reason end up reaching diametrically opposite conclusions. Now at least one of these individuals must be reasoning incorrectly. For if they had both been reasoning correctly, they should have arrived at the same conclusion. The trouble is, you will never be able to determine which of these two individuals is guilty of fallacious reasoning on the basis of X. Although the proposition *The faculty that integrates perceptions into abstractions* might seem definite to those innocent of the ability to think critically, you will never be able to extract a standard from it that will allow you to judge between two different applications of reason. This can be illustrated by imagining a dialogue between two individuals who, though each believed they were following reason, wound up arriving at different conclusions. Suppose the first individual, Paul, concluded that womanizers have low self-esteem, while the second individual, Peter, concluded the opposite. Peter begins by asking Paul how he knows that womanizers have low self-esteem:

Paul: I know because my reason tells me so.

Peter: But my reason tells me it isn't so.

Paul: That's because your reason is wrong. In order to reason correctly, you have to integrate your perceptions into abstractions.

Peter: But that is precisely what I did.

Paul: You must have done it incorrectly, or else you would not have reached a conclusion opposite mine.

Peter: But in what way have I not done it incorrectly?

Paul: Well, obviously you have integrated the abstractions *womanizer* and *self-esteem* incorrectly. Ayn Rand, in her *Introduction to Objectivist Epistemology*, explains precisely how perceptions are integrated into abstractions.

You have to first distinguish the womanizer from other types of men, then you have to find out what is fundamental to all womanizers, that is, the characteristic of womanizers that is most helpful in explaining the rest of a womanizer's characteristics. Then you have to follow the same method in forming the concept *self-esteem*. If you had done all this, you would have seen that it is not possible for a womanizer to have a high self-esteem.

Peter: I did precisely as you advised and reached a completely different conclusion. This leads me to infer that you were the one who has not correctly applied Rand's method of integrating perceptions into abstractions, because if you had, you would agree with my conclusions about womanizers. (Peter and Paul could go on like this for some time without reaching any resolution of their differences. There is no way an argument of this sort can be settled by examining how each of them formed their concepts. Concept-formation is too complex and nebulous a process to provide standards for judging the veracity of an individual's reasoning.)

Nearly all Rand's arguments involving the term *reason* are no better than those used by Peter and Paul. Nor is it very difficult to see why this should be so. For Objectivists, the term *reason* is a sort of mystical entity whose purpose is to assure them that they are right. As Nathaniel Branden, formerly Rand's closest associate, once admitted: "*Reason* was a word we used a great deal. It was a code word, or shorthand, that stood for…the entire Objectivist philosophy." (Branden, N., 1989, 252) *The essence of Objectivism*, Rand tells us, *is reason*. But she might as well have just said "I believe that Objectivism is right," for these two propositions express the exact same idea. Certainly, nothing is added by bringing in the term *reason* and constantly harping on it. No fact can be proven by asserting that it is established by reason. You cannot prove, for example, that womanizers have low self-esteem by asserting that reason tells you it is so. On the contrary, in order to find out whether womanizers have low self-esteem, you must first define, in precise empirical terms that can tested against reality, what is meant by *womanizer* and *self-esteem* (e.g., "a womanizer is any man who sleeps with ten or more women a year"—"low self-esteem involves a rooted feeling of self-worthlessness leading to various neurotic symptoms which can be observed and specified by a practicing psychiatrist"), and then you have to go out into the world and observe a scientifically determined sample of actual womanizers and test them for low self-esteem (if that is even possible!). Of course, this takes a lot of work. It is much easier to pretend you can figure these things out through "reason"—in other words, through the manipulation of empty verbiage.

The indefiniteness of a term is a matter of degrees. Some words, although vague, still manage to correspond to something in reality, although it is difficult to determine in precisely what degree the correspondence occurs. Other terms, however, are so vague that they do not correspond to anything that can be objectively tested at all. Terms like *good, evil, ought, justice,* and *rights* not only suffer from a deplorable vagueness, they also lack any sort of objective, scientific status whatsoever. If two people disagree about whether sodium chloride in solution precipitates silver nitrate, they can go into a laboratory and conduct an experiment to determine who is right. But if they disagree as to whether a person ought to devote his life to God or give all his money to the poor, there is no way in which the argument can be settled by objective, scientific means. The term *ought* is not compatible with the rigors of scientific thought. As Pareto shrewdly points out: "The chemist does not say: 'Sodium chloride in solution *ought* to precipitate silver nitrate.' He says—a very different matter—that sodium chloride in solution *precipitates* silver nitrate." (1916, §1689)

Such terms as *ought, good, just,* etc. are merely symbols describing various subjective states. If Peter's sentiments are favorably aroused by a certain object, that object is deemed good or just or beautiful or whatever term of subjective approbation seems most applicable. If Peter's sentiments are not favorably aroused, then terms like *bad, evil, ugly, unjust* are brought into service. Yet all the while Peter has failed to say anything which can be objectively established in the same sense that a fact of nature can be objectively established.

Many thinkers believe they can avoid the fallacy of reasoning on the basis of indefinite terms by making an effort to define their concepts. Now while this may be, in some respects at least, a worthy goal, it is an error to suppose that all you have to do in order to make your terms exact is to define them. This is hardly the case at all. In many cases, the reliance on definitions to give words definite meanings only serves to make the terms more vague and misleading than they were to start with. The reason for this is that definitions are nothing more than a restatement of one word in terms of other words. Thus the term *puppy* is defined as a "young dog." But does the phrase "young dog" really tell us what a puppy is? No, not quite, because it fails to tell us how young a dog has to be to qualify as a puppy. Many definitions suffer from this same lack of specificity. One vague term is defined on the basis of other vague terms. For this reason, it is quite common to find some of the worst abuses of verbalist reasoning among those very philosophers who are most scrupulous about defining their terms.

Given the verbalistic character of so many of Rand's arguments, it is not surprising to find her emphasizing the importance of definitions in human thought. "The truth or falsehood of all man's conclusions, inferences of thought and knowledge rests on the truth or falsehood of his definitions," she tells us. (1990b, 65) But this, at best, is an exaggeration. A definition can be entirely true yet, at the same time, entirely useless in regards to enabling the individual to understand the meaning of a concept. The definition of a puppy as a "young dog" is perfectly true in its way, but perfectly useless if you are trying to help someone who knows virtually nothing about dogs to distinguish a puppy from a fully-grown dog. For a definition to be of any use, it must be specific and it must describe the unknown in terms of the known. But this is just the problem: most definitions fail on both counts.

The problem stems from the extreme brevity of definitions. As Rand herself admits: "A definition is the *condensation* of a vast body of observations." (1990b, 48) The very fact that a definition condenses information causes it to lose the very specificity necessary to convey any sort of precision of meaning. And without exactness of meaning, no concept can successfully define the unknown in terms of the known. The fact that Rand does not seem to have been aware of this demonstrates the extent of her verbalistic tendencies.

According to Objectivism, a definition is the final step of concept-formation. Definitions are necessary, we are told, to keep our concepts tied to reality. This, however, is hardly the case. The inability to define a concept has little if any bearing on whether that concept is understood by the individual using it. There are many concepts individuals use without knowing how to define them. If you ask any non-intellectual person to define all the terms he uses, chances are he may not be able to define any of them. But does that mean he doesn't know what he is talking about? No, not at all. It is merely an indication of his inability to articulate what he knows. Often it is precisely when a person most thoroughly understands the terms he uses that he is least able to define them. The reason for this is because a person who thoroughly understands a concept derives this understanding from experiential reality itself rather than from mere words. Consequently, he doesn't need to define his terms to know what they mean. A shepherd does not have to be able to define what a sheep is to know what the term means. He knows what sheep are from experience, and he proves he knows what they are from how skillfully he tends his flocks. The best definition is always experience. If you really want to know what a term means, go out into the world and find a concrete example of it and experience it for yourself.

Now this is not to say that definitions are entirely useless. When you are using terms that are either vague or refer to something outside the experience of your readers, then definitions may be of some use. But they are only of use if they help your readers understand what you mean in terms of experiential reality. The trouble with the sort of definitions advocated by verbalistic thinkers like Rand is that they try to explain one vague term by defining it on the basis of another equally vague term. Thus we find Rand attempting to define man as a "rational animal." But the phrase "rational animal" serves no other purpose than to draw the reader's attention away from experiential reality into the world of empty verbiage. Knowledge of man cannot be derived from empty verbiage. Only from experiential reality—i.e., from the observation of the behavior of particular men—can we know what man is.

IV. *The fallacy of reasoning on the basis of oversimplified descriptions of facts.* Most verbalists would prefer to support their doctrines with facts, since arguments based on factual evidence tend to be more convincing than arguments based solely on the clever manipulation of rhetorical constructions. But if the facts do not support the doctrines in question, what is the verbalist to do? Many verbalists try to get out of this dilemma by presenting supporting facts which have been skillfully distorted, usually through over-simplification. This is very common in arguments about historical causation. Those ideologues who hate capitalism, for instance, will assert that this or that crisis in history (e.g., World War I, the Great Depression, the Cold War, the "Me Decade," etc.) was *caused* by capitalism. As a statement of fact, these assertions usually represent gross oversimplifications. Crises in history normally have many causes. They cannot all be caused by capitalism.

Rand and her followers are egregious abusers of this fallacious mode of describing historical facts. Consider the following passage from one of Rand's lectures, a passage which is rife with overly simplified descriptions of historical facts: "Only three brief periods of history were culturally dominated by a philosophy of reason: ancient Greece, the Renaissance, the nineteenth century. These three periods were the source of mankind's greatest progress in all fields of intellectual achievement—and the eras of greatest political freedom....The rest of human history was dominated by mysticism of one kind or another... All the centuries dominated by mysticism were the eras of political tyranny and slavery, of rule by brute force—from the primitive barbarism of the jungle—to the pharaohs of Egypt—to the emperors of Rome—to the feudalism of the Dark and Middle Ages—to the abortive monarchies of Europe—to the modern dictatorships of Soviet Russia, Nazi Germany, and all their lesser carbon copies." (1990a, 89)

What Rand is trying to do in this passage is provide historical evidence for her assertion that "reason" leads to freedom, progress, and cultural achievement, while "mysticism" leads to political tyranny, slavery, and brute force. The evidence she provides is in the form of vague references to historical periods like the Renaissance or the nineteenth century or to various political states like the Roman Empire or Nazi Germany. Ancient Greece, the Renaissance, and the nineteenth century are described as periods of history "culturally dominated by a philosophy of reason." But what on earth can this possibly mean? In what respect was ancient Greece *culturally* dominated by a philosophy of reason? As far as I can tell, the main respect appears to be a diminution of the influence of what Rand calls "mysticism," by which she means superstition, religion, or any views she strongly disagrees with. Yet if we were to examine Ancient Greece, or the Renaissance, or the nineteenth century, we would find, at best, only a very slight diminution of the influence of religious belief and practice. The most dramatic diminution of religious belief took place in Ancient Greece—or, more precisely, in Periclean Athens. The Renaissance, on the other hand, exhibits only a slight decrease in religious belief—far less, in fact, than is commonly supposed. The nineteenth century represents a somewhat more complex scenario. At the beginning of the nineteenth century, religious belief actually intensified, especially in England and America. Later in the century, religious belief began to wane among the intellectual classes. But even so, most people in both England and America remained committed to some sort of religious faith. And so if the cultural dominance of a philosophy of reason is incompatible with widespread religious belief, than Rand's assertion about the nineteenth century must be dismissed as a serious distortion of facts.

Rand goes on to assert that the cultural dominance of a philosophy of reason leads to freedom and intellectual progress. Again, this represents a gross over-simplification of the facts. While it is true that freedom and intellectual progress are incompatible with religious fanaticism, this does not mean they are incompatible with religion as practiced by the majority of believers. Nineteenth century history proves this beyond any doubt. Despite the deep religiosity of the English and American peoples during that century, both nations enjoyed a high degree of political freedom and intellectual progress.

This is not to say, however, that there isn't an element of truth in Rand's assertions. If by reason we mean either logical thinking or the scientific method, than it is quite true that the influence of reason did in fact increase in Ancient Greece (i.e., Periclean Athens), the Renaissance, and the nineteenth century. But this increase does not quite constitute the sort of "cultural dominance" that Rand is alleging. Nor is it quite true that this increase in the influence of "reason" led to greater political freedom. In both Ancient Greece and the Renaissance, the precise opposite occurred. Athens lost its freedom to Sparta, Macedonia, and Rome. The Renaissance occurred hand in hand with the centralization of power in England, France, and Spain and the flourishing of petty tyrants in Italy.

The historical evidence Rand provides in support of her claims regarding the influence of mysticism is not a whit better. We have already seen what is wrong with her view of the Dark and Middle Ages. But it goes beyond just a mere misrepresentation of actual facts. There is a deeper problem here, one that runs to the very heart of Rand's method of collecting evidence to support her contentions. Rand and her followers seem incapable of the intellectual modesty necessary to understand why such blatant judgments of large chapters of human history must be regarded with great suspicion. History will not yield up its secrets to those who treat it with such irresponsibility and disdain. Understanding is rarely furthered by ideological presumption.

The tendency of Rand to rationalize her sentiments by over-simplifying and distorting the facts of reality is itself rationalized in one of her theories of knowledge—specifically, in her theory of essence. According to Peikoff, Rand devised a "whole new form of thought" out of her theory of essence. Instead of consulting the supernatural or trying to judge in a vacuum, Rand, we are told, first made an effort to "abstract the essence of a series of concretes." Then she proceeded to "identify, by an appropriate use of logic, the necessary implications or result of this essence." This allowed her to reach "a fundamental generalization, a *principle*, which subsumes and enables you to deal with an unlimited number of instances—past, present, and future." Peikoff describes this procedure as "thinking in *essentials*, which," he advises us, "was an essential part of Ayn Rand's method of thought." He then goes on to explain that "For Ayn Rand, thinking in essentials…was a method of understanding any complex situation by deliberately setting aside irrelevancies—such as insignificant details, superficial similarities, unimportant differences—and going instead to the heart of the matter, to the aspects which, as we may say, constitute the distinctive core or being of the situation. This is something Ayn Rand herself did brilliantly." (Rand, 1990a, 341-342)

From a superficial point of view, none of this appears all that objectionable. If thinking in essentials simply means avoiding what is irrelevant, how could anyone possibly be against it? Certainly, no reasonable person would advocate thinking in non-essentials! Nonetheless, there are some serious problems with this view of knowledge. According to Peikoff, if you can find the "essence" of a particular group of concretes, then from this essence you can extract a principle that "enables you to deal with an unlimited number of instances." But what makes Peikoff so certain that all groups of concretes actually have this magical essence that makes it so easy to understand complex situations? What if a given group of concretes is so complex that it cannot be reduced to a single essence or principle? What then? And even if these wonderful essences do in fact exist, how *precisely* are we to find them? Peikoff's account of the whole process is rather vague. To say that we reach them through abstraction is simply not specific enough. Suppose two people abstract different essences from the same group of concretes. How are we to determine which of them has abstracted the "correct" essence?

Unfortunately, Rand's own remarks about the nature and function of essence are of little help in this respect. In her book on epistemology, she defines an essence as the "fundamental characteristic" of a concept's units upon "which the greatest number of other characteristics depend, and which distinguishes these units from all other existents within the field of man's knowledge." (1990b, 68) Again, we are confronted with the problem of vagueness. Phrases like "fundamental characteristic" and "upon which the greatest number of other characteristics depend" are intolerably imprecise. What on earth *is* a "fundamental characteristic"? Rand claims that a fundamental characteristic is merely that characteristic "which all the others (or the greatest number of others) depend, i.e., the fundamental characteristic without which all the others would not be possible." (1990b, 45) In other words, the term *fundamental characteristic* is just a synonym for the term *essential characteristic* and the term *essence*. But this means that we are running in circles. What do these phrases mean in terms of empirical reality?

In an attempt to illustrate this principle, Rand turns to the concept *man*. One can observe, she argues, that "man is the only animal who speaks English, wears wristwatches, flies airplanes, manufactures lipstick, studies geometry, reads newspapers, writes poems, darns socks, etc. None of these is an essential characteristic: none of them explains the others; none of them applies to all men; omit any or all of them…and he would still be *man*. But observe that all these activities (and innumerable others)…are expressions and consequences of man's rational faculty, that an organism without that faculty would *not* be a man—and you will know why man's rational faculty is his *essential* [and, *ipso facto*, his fundamental] distinguishing characteristic." (1990b, 45-46)

This example provides a good illustration of what is wrong with Rand's theory of essence. In the first place, characteristics like speaking English, wearing wristwatches, flying airplanes, etc. "depend" on other characteristics besides "rationality." You cannot explain them by rationality alone. Moreover, there are many other characteristics of man that have no connection to rationality at all. All man's basic motivations, for example, are non-rational in nature, as I have already demonstrated; and, as Pareto has shown, many of his actions are non-rational as well. (1916) By insisting that man's essential characteristic is his rationality, Rand is guilty of blinding herself to all those characteristics of man that she does not want to acknowledge.

For the most part, this theory of essence is merely a justification for arbitrarily ignoring any characteristics found in reality that contradicted Rand's theories. Whenever Rand found herself confronted with a characteristic she did not approve of, all she had to do was claim that the characteristic in question was "inessential," and by uttering this one word she conjured the characteristic clean out of existence.

We catch her doing just this in another passage from her book on epistemology, where she says that if a man is in doubt about the validity of some social theory, all he has to do is recall that "man is a rational animal and he will know how to evaluate the theory." (1990b, 86) This strikes me as a very inadequate method of checking social theories. If you want to know whether a theory is true, you have to consult, not some arbitrarily chosen essential characteristic, but the actual facts of reality. If you want to know, for instance, whether Max Weber's theory about the crucial role of the Protestant Ethic in the formation of modern capitalism is true, you have to consult the relevant facts. Certainly, you will never be able to determine the degree of truth or falsity in Weber's theory by recalling that man is a rational animal. To even entertain such a delusion demonstrates a serious flaw in one's thinking. Again, let me repeat what I have said before: matters of fact cannot be determined on the basis of verbal constructions! No significant fact about reality can be discovered by hunting for "essential" characteristics and other such nonsense. If you want to understand the nature of some object in reality, such as man, you have to go out and study that object in order to determine its behavioral propensities. It is from such propensities, carefully observed and documented, rather than from some arbitrary essence, that one learns to understand an object as complex as man. Of course, it will be a lot of work to discover the behavioral propensities of human beings using this method. No doubt it is much easier simply to hunt for the "essential" characteristics of man and draw your principles from that. But make no mistake about it: knowledge of the complexities of reality is not discovered by taking such dubious shortcuts. Rand's theory of essences is not merely a rationalization of her penchant for

over-simplifying the facts of reality; it is also a rationalization of her own intellectual laziness.

*   *   *

(4) One of the more curious aspects of Rand's personality was her absolute insistence that her disciples strictly
adhere not merely to her philosophy, but to her personal
aesthetic tastes as well. "[Rand] had said, and continued to
say, that the validity of one's musical tastes could not be
philosophically demonstrated," Barbara Branden, Rand's
biographer, noted. "Yet if one of her young friends
responded as she did to Rachmaninoff, or especially to her
lighter musical loves, she attached deep significance to
their affinity. On the other hand, if a friend did not
respond as she did, she left no doubt that she considered
that   person   morally   and   psychologically
reprehensible....If she was now demanding adherence
even in areas of subjective preferences, her demands in
realms she deemed rationally demonstrable became obses-
sive." (1986, 268)

Rand's insistence on absolute conformity seems anomalous in someone who made her mark preaching one of
the most extreme individualist creeds ever inflicted upon
the human race. Individualism, Rand insisted, means the
absolute refusal to run anyone's life or have anyone else
run your life. This being so, what business did Rand have
telling her friends and disciples what kind of music they
were supposed to like?

Regardless of how we choose to judge Rand's fanatical
insistence upon complete conformity among her closest
followers in both philosophical conviction and artistic and

musical appreciation, we can hardly describe it as logical behavior. It is the product, not of reason, but of sentiment, passion, and resentment. Rand was obviously traumatized by any expression of disagreement, whether intellectual or emotional in character. Such trauma is not unusual in human nature. The will to conformity is a very powerful motivational complex in many human beings. If any person departs from a uniform standard of judgment or behavior, there will always be those who will be disturbed by this departure and who will seek to prevent it either through persuasion, censure, psychological manipulation or brute force. This desire to demand conformity from other human beings is, according to Pareto, "especially assertive in matters of logic. From the logical standpoint the maximum of absurdity would seem to be reached in condemning a man to the stake because he did not think as others think on some theological question....[While Rand certainly didn't advocate burning anyone at the stake, her insistence that her followers agree with every detail of her philosophy, including her aesthetic judgments, is equally ridiculous from the viewpoint of logic.] But that criticism is valid only for the...logical reason devised to explain what has been done. The act itself is just the manifestation of a sentiment of hostility to a violation, regarded as particularly flagrant, of a uniformity." (1916, §1127)

Rand's insistence on conformity differs in one respect to that of most people: instead of demanding that her friends conform to standards prevalent in society at large, she merely expected them to conform to her *own* standards. Another important difference is that Rand had no intention of using force against those who violated her standards. She might censure them, bully them, denounce them, but she would not initiate violence against them. Part of the reason for this might have been that she did not have the power to use force. But even more important in this respect was her principled opposition to the initiation of force against dissenters. It must be said on Rand's behalf that no matter how badly she might have treated her disciples, she never advocated the use of force against those who disagreed with her. Not that this alone would have prevented her from actually using force if she had enjoyed the power to do so. Many the occasions in history when individuals have said one thing when they were powerless and done the opposite when the levers of power were in their hands.

In any case, there can be little doubt of the virulence of Rand's passion to make sure that those within the inner circle of the Objectivist movement thought and felt exactly as she did. Nor can there be much doubt as to the influence this passion had on her philosophy. Her fanatical determination to subject nearly every aspect of human existence to the dominion of "reason" testifies to the strength and tenacity of this passion. Since "reason" is supposedly objective, its application will always lead to the same conclusion. Now if everyone applied "reason" to every aspect of their lives, they would all reach the same conclusions and conformity would be the rule of the day. Objectivism, if it were one hundred percent successful, would lead to absolute conformity among human beings. This consideration should make those who regard Rand as a great champion of freedom and individualism rethink their views on the matter.

It is not only in her idolatry of "reason" that one finds evidence of Rand's passion for conformity. One also finds it in her belief in the certainty of man's knowledge. Those who insist that other people should think and feel like themselves will of course regard their own thoughts and feelings as correct beyond any doubt. For if there were any doubt, how could they justify insisting upon conformity? You can hardly expect people to conform to a principle that might prove mistaken. Dogmatism is then a necessary adjunct to conformism. Where dogmatism is lacking, there is no reason to insist upon absolute conformity to prevailing standards.

From a purely scientific point of view, the question whether human knowledge can be certain hardly arises. Such a question only arises for those dogmatic thinkers who do not have the courage to admit that they might be wrong. The man of science is much humbler. He knows from experience that many individuals who were sure they were right later discovered they had been mistaken. Man is not omniscient. All his knowledge about the factual world comes from experience. But his experience can never be exhaustive. He cannot experience every manifestation of a given law of nature.

For example, as far as we know, water freezes at 32° F. No evidence has ever surfaced suggesting that water does not freeze at 32° F. However, this does not mean that we can be *certain* that water always has and always will freeze at 32° F. Our experience of water freezing is limited to a finite number of instances in the past. From a strictly logical point of view, we must remain open to the possibility that water might have frozen at different temperatures in the distant past or that it may freeze at different temperatures in the future. Since we have no experience of either the distant past or the future, we cannot know for certain at what temperature water froze in those periods. The evidence would *suggest* that the freezing temperature of water has always been 32° F. But in the absence of direct corroborative experience, we can never be absolutely certain. The belief that water has and always will freeze at 32° F is a mere conjecture. As conjectures go, it is a very well-corroborated one—so well corroborated, in fact, that it can be treated from a purely practical point of view as approximating certainty. But from a strictly logical point of view, it cannot be regarded as certain. From a logical point of view, no theory that is based only on partial evidence can be regarded as certain. Before anyone has any logical justification to conclude that "All X is Y," he must experience every manifestation of X. Otherwise, how can he be sure that all X is in fact Y? Perhaps the one X which he has not yet experienced will prove not to be Y. In that case, his theory that "All X is Y" would have been *falsified*.

One of Rand's most dubious assumptions regarding the nature of human knowledge is her conviction that, without certainty, knowledge would be impossible: "The pronouncement [that nobody can be certain of anything] means that no knowledge of any kind is possible to man, i.e., that man is not conscious," Rand once insisted. This is a rather strong statement, to say the least. Rand would appear to be trying to scare her readers into agreeing with her. In the absence of certainty, she goes on to argue, all claims to knowledge would have the same worth: "[I]f nobody can be certain of anything, then everybody can be certain of everything he pleases—since it cannot be refuted, and he can claim he is not certain he is certain (which is the purpose of that notion)." (1982, 14) Rand is here guilty of assuming that the only alternative to absolute certainty is absolute skepticism. Either you are certain or you are completely ignorant—*that* is the unstated premise at the base of her assertions about certainty. But there is no reason to believe that this is the case. As the philosopher Karl Popper has demonstrated, it is entirely possible to have knowledge without certainty.

Popper's rejection of certainty stems from his attack on the validity of induction. "Now it is far from obvious, from a logical point of view, that we are justified in inferring universal statements from singular ones, no matter how numerous," explains Popper; "for any conclusion drawn in this way may always turn out to be false: no matter how many instances of whites swans we might have observed, this does not justify the conclusion that *all* swans are white." (1934, 27)

But if induction is invalid, how can any sort of *general* knowledge about reality ever be justified? To give just one example: Most people take it for granted that the sun always has and always will continue to rise in the East and set in the West. Now this assumption constitutes a generalization about the nature of the sun in relation to the earth. But the evidence upon which this generalization is based is only partial—i.e., it is based on the experience of mankind, which is only a few million years old and covers only a tiny fraction of the earth's existence. How, then, can our belief that the sun will *always* rise in the East and set in the West possibly be justified?

Popper's approach to this problem is bold and ingenious. Human rationality can be saved, he argues, merely by giving up the effort to justify our theories by induction. Instead of trying to justify our theories by collecting evidence that *confirms* them, we should rather seek evidence that refutes them. This may seem a rather paradoxical way of going about the whole business of validating human knowledge, but on closer examination the rationality of Popper's approach will be manifest. Popper's theory of knowledge is based on the idea that the only time we can be certain about a theory is when we have discovered evidence refuting it. The theory *All swans are white* can be used to illustrate the truth of this. As we have seen, no amount of empirical evidence can ever establish the validity of this theory beyond all doubt, since we can never be certain that one of the swans we have failed to observe might be yellow or blue or purple. But if we ever did come across such a gaudily colored swan, that by itself would be enough to invalidate the theory *All swans are white* beyond any reasonable doubt.

Since no amount of evidence, no matter how well gathered and documented, can ever prove the validity of a theory, it follows that such evidence is close to worthless. Only the evidence that refutes a theory is of any value, because only that evidence actually tells us something definite—namely, that a theory has been disproved beyond a reasonable doubt. It follows then that, when examining a given theory, instead of trying to prove it by finding confirmations of it, we should rather seek to disprove it by finding evidence that goes against it. If, after an exhaustive effort, we are unable to find any such evidence, we can at that time begin to entertain the suspicion that maybe the theory is true.

But if theoretical knowledge is only certain when it has been falsified and never when it is confirmed, how are men supposed to know which theories to follow in practice? Popper answers this challenge as follows: "There is no need to be shocked by the discovery that we cannot justify or even support by arguments or reasons the claim that our theories are true. For critical reasoning still has a most important function with respect to the evaluation of theories: we can criticize and discriminate among our theories as a result of our critical discussion. Although in such discussion we cannot as a rule distinguish (with certainty, or near certainty) between a true theory and a false theory, we can sometimes distinguish between a false theory and one which *may* be true. And we can often say of a particular theory that, in the light of the present state of critical discussion, it appears to be much better than any other theory submitted; better, that is, from the point of view of our interest in truth; or better in the sense of getting nearer to the truth." (1983, 26-27)

The advantages of this approach to the problem of theoretical knowledge are readily apparent. In the first place, Popper's method encourages a far more critical outlook than does the inductivist method advocated by dogmatic philosophers like Rand. Inductivists seek to prove a theory by finding evidence that supports it. The trouble with this approach is that it inclines people to look only for evidence which affirms or "verifies" their theories, blinding them, in effect, to evidence which might falsify them. He who searches for evidence to justify a pet theory almost always finds exactly what he is looking for. That is why it is much better to test a theory by looking for negative evidence. If such negative evidence exists, the sooner one

finds it, the better. If it doesn't exist, the best way to corroborate its non-existence is by one's failure to find it,
despite having looked as hard as one could. The best that
can be said on behalf of a theory is that it has survived
every attempt to refute it.

This approach has the additional advantage of keeping
the path to inquiry open. Those who, like Rand, regard
themselves as certain are far more prone to that sort of
dogmatism that refuses to consider any evidence that
might prove embarrassing to their convictions. Nathaniel
Branden, who, before his break with Rand in 1969, had
been her leading disciple for nearly two decades, writes of
his mentor's dogmatism in the following terms: "I was
astonished at how closed she typically was to any new
knowledge....When I tried to tell her of some new
research that suggested that certain kinds of depression
have a biological basis, she answered angrily, '*I* can tell you
what causes depression; I can tell you about rational
depression and I can tell you about irrational depression—
the second is mostly self-pity—and in neither case does
biology enter into it.' I asked her how she could make a
scientific statement with such certainty, since she had
never studied the field; she shrugged bitterly and snapped,
'Because I know how to think.'" (1989, 347)

The question whether depression does or does not
have a biological basis can only be determined, if it can be
determined at all, by scientific inquiry. Those who are
unfamiliar with the relevant scientific evidence have no
business making *ex cathedra* declarations about it in the
manner of Ayn Rand. Whether the individual knows how
to think has absolutely no relevance in the matter.
Empirical evidence must always be given the first priority

in the determination of any fact of reality. But in order for empiricism to be given the first priority, the path to inquiry must always be left open. By insisting that she could be certain concerning matters of fact which can only be determined by a critical examination of all the relevant empirical data, Rand is guilty of closing the path of inquiry and shutting up her mind to reality.

Rand devised an elaborate rationalization to justify her faith in certainty. It is presented by her protégé, Leonard Peikoff, as follows. Man's knowledge, we are told, is limited. Omniscience is therefore impossible. Even so, this does not mean that we cannot be certain of what we do in fact know. The reason for this has to do with what Rand called the *contextual* nature of human knowledge. It is only within the specified context of a man's knowledge that he can ever be certain.

But what precisely is this *context* of knowledge? Consider the following explanation provided by Peikoff in one of his lectures on Objectivism: "By 'context' we mean the sum of cognitive elements conditioning the acquisition, validity, or application of any item of knowledge. Knowledge is an organization or integration of interconnected elements, each relevant to the others....In regard to any concept, idea, proposal, theory, or item of knowledge, never forget or ignore the context on which it depends and which conditions its validity and use." (Binswanger, 1986, 104)

With the concept of *context* well in hand, Peikoff proceeds to insist that all the absolutes he believes in, from absolute certainty to the moral absolutes of the Objectivist Ethics, are *contextual* absolutes. What this means is that they are conditioned by circumstances—in other words, that they are not really absolutes at all.

I regard Rand's use of the term *context* as a conceptual escape hatch. Rand wanted to believe that absolute certainty is possible. The trouble is that all the relevant evidence suggests that absolute certainty, at least in regards to theoretical knowledge, is not in fact possible, since many theories which were at one time considered certain were later soundly refuted by new discoveries. For this reason, Rand had to be careful about insisting upon the absolute certainty of any given theory, because if at some future date evidence were discovered refuting the absolute validity of the theory in question, Rand's belief in certainty would have been shown to be unwarranted. So Rand devised an escape hatch that would enable her to weasel out of any such embarrassment. If some principle which she had declared as absolutely certain were later refuted, she (or one of her followers) could merely point out that, since all absolutes are contextual, her claim to *contextual* certainty had not been invalidated in the least. Within the specific context in which she accepted the theory, it remains *certainly* valid. It is only within the *new* context that the theory no longer remains certain.

If this seems like a cheap verbal trick, well, that is precisely what it is. Rand wanted to convince herself that she could be certain, but since there is a great deal of evidence suggesting that certainty is not humanly feasible, she invented the notion of "contextual" certainty. The trouble is that this notion of contextual certainty is entirely worthless. The reason why individuals want to be certain is because in practical matters, mistakes in judgment can be very serious. Thus the skydiver wants to be certain his parachute will open, because if it doesn't open, he will die. The skydiver would derive little comfort from being told that he can be "contextually" certain that his parachute will open. "But I don't give a fig for your contextual certainty!" he would protest. "What I want to know is whether I can be certain that the parachute will open." If we tried to apply Rand's theory of certainty to this specific problem, we would be forced to conclude that it does not guarantee that the parachute will open. Rand's contextual certainty is only valid within the specific context of an individual's knowledge. But if the skydiver happens to be ignorant of a defect in his parachute, that ignorance obviously lies outside the context of his knowledge, and as such would not prevent him from feeling "contextually" certain that his parachute would open once he has made his jump. From the logic of Rand's theory we are confronted with a paradoxical conclusion: namely, that it is possible to be contextually certain that something is true and yet be wrong about it. "But then what's the use of contextual certainty?" To this query Rand never provided a coherent answer.

If Rand's theory of contextual certainty is so useless, why did Rand go to the trouble of devising it? I have suggested she devised it as a kind of trick. This is not to imply that she did so with the purpose to deceive. Most likely she was not altogether aware of the mendacious nature of her theory. Because of the dogmatism of her personality, Rand was eager to believe that men could be certain in the commonly accepted sense of the word. But when she attempted to rationalize this kind of certainty, she unwittingly wound up devising a theory which, in a subtle, technical sense, denied the very type of certainty that she had originally set out to justify. Only, because of the verbalistic character of her reasoning, she failed to realize this. And so these two conceptions of certainty—the commonly accepted one and Rand's contextual variety—became confused in her mind and, I fear, in the minds of her followers as well.

To sum up. Rand's theory of certainty was a byproduct of her hunger to preserve various uniformities of thought and feeling among her closest friends and disciples. Since this hunger did not square with her belief in individualism nor with her rejection of aggression, she sought to justify it by devising a theory which would allow her to get away with claiming that her beliefs and emotional reactions were absolutely true and certain. This rationalization granted her the right to bully and manipulate her disciples into behaving precisely as she saw fit. In so doing, she ended up depriving them of the very individuality that her philosophy purportedly sought to uphold.

As usual with rationalizations of this sort, the arguments advanced to defend it were inept and confused. Certainty, she claimed, was possible because it was contextual. But Rand's contextual certainty turned out to be something entirely different from what most people mean when they claim they are certain. What most people mean by certainty is that they cannot be wrong. Contextual certainty, however, in no way guarantees that an individual cannot be wrong. The skydiver can be as contextually certain that his parachute will open as he pleases; yet it still might not open. What, then, is the use of the concept?

CHAPTER 4:

▼

THEORY OF METAPHYSICS

"Metaphysics is the finding of bad reasons for what we believe upon instinct."

—F.H. Bradley

In the previous chapter, I subjected Rand and her followers to heavy criticism for supporting many of their doctrines with proofs largely made up of logical and moral constructions—that is, with words instead of facts. I promised that we would see more examples of such verbalistic argumentation in later chapters. In this chapter, I will begin to make good on this promise.

Before going into the weaknesses of Rand's metaphysical theories, perhaps I should briefly describe what Rand means by the term *metaphysics*. "I use the word 'metaphysical' to mean: that which pertains to reality, to the nature of things, to existence," she explained. (1964b, 2)

Peikoff defines metaphysics as "the branch of philosophy that studies the nature of the universe as a whole." I realize these are rather vague descriptions. The best way to understand what Rand and her Objectivist cohorts mean by the term *metaphysics* is to examine what sort of doctrines they consider metaphysical. In this chapter, we will be examining the Objectivist critique of several "metaphysical" doctrines, including philosophical idealism and monotheistic creationism. We will also examine the Objectivist view of causality and the Objectivist contention that reality is logical.

One thing else before we get started. Rand is known to have entertained a personal aversion towards certain words, some of which she went so far as to describe as "anti-concepts." (Included among her anti-concepts are "duty," "consumerism," "meritocracy," and "simplistic.") (Binswanger, 1986, 24) I, too, entertain a personal aversion to certain words (though I would not go so far as to call them anti-concepts); and there is no word in any language that I detest more than the term *metaphysics*. The reason why I detest this word is because I have come to regard it as the symbol of everything I most deplore about philosophy. The metaphysician is that philosopher who, in the words of Santayana, "attempt[s] to determine matters of fact by means of logical or moral or rhetorical constructions." Metaphysics, Santayana tells us, "is neither physical speculation nor pure logic nor honest literature, but (as in the treatise of Aristotle first called by that name) a hybrid of the three, materializing ideal entities, turning harmonies into forces, and dissolving natural things into terms of discourse." (1923, vii) Since I do not believe facts can be discovered in this way, I deplore just about everything that parades under the metaphysical head.

The greatest metaphysician of all time is undoubtedly Professor G.W. Hegel, the German "philosopher," as he is described in textbooks. Hegel appears to have entertained an extremely high opinion regarding his own intellectual powers, for he believed he could explain matters of fact without the aid of empirical observation. The results of the professor's ripest cerebrations literally drip with unintelligible sapience. Consider, as evidence for this assertion, Hegel's demonstration of Kepler's third law: "As root, time is only empirical magnitude. As quality, it is nothing but abstract unity. As an aspect of a developed totality, it is in addition, a determined unity, a reflected totality. It produces itself, and in producing itself it does not transcend itself. But as it has no dimensions, in producing itself it attains only to formal identity with itself, to the *square*; and space, on the contrary, which constitutes the positive principle of external continuity, attains the dimensions of the concept, to the *cube*....That is Kepler's third law concerning the ratio of the cube of the distance to the square of time." (Pareto, 1916, §503)

There is no use asking what all this vast assemblage of idiotic verbiage means; that is not the point. It is not supposed to be comprehensible; otherwise it would not be metaphysical. It is because of passages like this that Hegel's philosophic rival, the acidic Mr. Schopenhauer, could hardly contain himself at the thought of Hegel's reputation as Germany's greatest philosopher. "The Germans are accustomed to accept words instead of ideas," griped Schopenhauer. "Are they not trained by us for this purpose from early youth? Just look at Hegelry: what is it but empty, hollow, even nauseous verbiage? And yet how brilliant was the career of this philosophical creature of the ministry! It needed only a few mercenary fellows to sing the praises of the bad, and their voices found in echo in the hollow emptiness of a thousand numskulls, an echo resounding and spreading even at the present time. See how soon a great philosopher was made from a common head, indeed from a common charlatan!...I refer to the fact that in Germany men proclaim as a great mind and profound thinker a dull, ignorant philosophaster, a scribbler of nonsense, who, by his ineffably hollow verbiage, thoroughly and permanently disorganizes their brains; I refer to our dearly beloved Hegel." (1847, 60-61)

Schopenhauer's malicious sarcasms did little to efface Hegel's posthumous reputation. Nowadays there are still reputable scholars who regard Schopenhauer as a vindictive beast for describing Hegel with such delectable accuracy. When Karl Popper, in his book *The Open Society and Its Enemies*, denounced Hegel's philosophy for exemplifying "a terrible decline in intellectual sincerity and intellectual honesty," (1945, II, 393) many scholars around the world, including the eminent Walter Kaufmann, raised their hands in holy horror. It seems to me, however, that any philosopher who writes of matters of which he is ignorant in a language so destitute of empirical content that it becomes impossible to determine what it means deserves even worse than what Hegel received at the hands of Messrs. Schopenhauer and Popper.

I mention this so there will be no doubt as to my sentiments concerning metaphysical studies. Not only do I have absolutely no use for most of what passes for metaphysics, but I have serious doubts whether anything legitimate can be found in a branch of philosophy that, since that old pedant Aristotle first systematized it, has been subject to some of the most intellectually perverse and stupefying speculations on record. As far as I am concerned, knowledge of the nature of reality must be gathered, not from verbalistic speculation, but from a detailed observation of the facts of reality. According to my philosophy, facts come first. No principle, whether we choose to call it metaphysical or not, can take precedence over a fact. Metaphysicians always want to enslave facts to some arbitrary principle founded upon "reason." I, however, believe that this bondage should be the other way around: facts should be the masters of principles, not principles the master's of facts. If a fact contradicts a principle, it is the principle that must be rejected, not the fact.

It is from this perspective that I will judge Rand's theory of metaphysics. I will focus especially on the question whether Rand regards principles as prior to facts, or facts as prior to principles. On this question, I fear we will find Rand's position closer to Hegel's than to mine.

    *   *   *

(1) I find it most interesting that Rand scholar Chris Sciabarra, in his book *Ayn Rand: The Russian Radical*, should accuse Rand of being a "dialectical" thinker in the Hegelian sense of the term. Rand was engaged, he tells us, in a "dialectical revolt against dualism," which means she sought, among other things, to preserve "the analytical integrity of the whole" and to examine "the dynamic tensions within a system." (1995, 17-18) Those of my readers who cannot make heads or tails of what such phrases as

"dialectical revolt" and "analytical integrity" and "dynamic tensions" mean are urged to read Mr. Sciabarra's book, where all such mysteries receive illumination. What I find most interesting about Sciabarra's accusation, or rather thesis, against Rand is his linkage of Rand with Hegel. Although I agree with very little of what Sciabarra says about "dualism" and Hegel's "dialectical method" (such terms are too vague for my overly matter-of-fact mind), I do believe his suggestion that Hegel and Rand shared the same basic method of thought comes pretty close to hitting the nail on the head. If instead of using the questionable term "dialectical method" we substituted "verbalistic method" or "metaphysical method," we would come even closer to the truth.

The verbalistic character of Rand's Objectivist philosophy is apparent almost from the start. "Objectivism begins by naming and validating its premises," Peikoff tells us. "Ayn Rand does not select questions at random; she...begins deliberately at the beginning—at what she can prove is the beginning, and the root of all the rest." (1991, 4) And what, may we ask, constitutes this precious "root of all the rest" which Rand "can prove is the beginning"? Why, it is nothing less than the three "basic axioms" of Objectivism: the axioms of *existence, consciousness*, and *identity*. The *axiom of existence* is responsible for informing us that "existence exists." The *axiom of consciousness* explains that we "exist possessing consciousness, consciousness being the faculty of perceiving that which exists." And finally, the *axiom of identity* makes it clear that "to be is to be something, to have a nature, to possess *identity*." (1991, 4-6) Or, as Rand liked to put it, "A is A." (1961, 12) According to Peikoff, these three axioms are "inescapable primaries: no conceptual knowledge can be gained apart from these principles." (1991, 12)

At first blush, Peikoff's assertion might seem obviously untrue. I can't speak for anyone else, but as for myself, I don't recall ever finding these axioms "indispensable" to the formation of my conceptual knowledge. In fact, until I ran across them in Rand's writings, I had never even heard of them. Does this mean that all my knowledge acquired before I first came into contact with Rand's axioms must be regarded as non-conceptual? After all, if no conceptual knowledge can be gained apart from these axioms, then wouldn't that mean that all of us poor souls who have never been exposed to them would be incapable of gaining conceptual knowledge? But no, luckily for the human race, this is not the case at all. These axioms, Peikoff assures us, are grasped even by those who have never heard of them. Even primitive savages, we are told, have an implicit knowledge of them!

No doubt this is all very wonderful. These axioms, although explicitly grasped by the few, are nevertheless implicitly grasped by the many (how very democratic of them!), so that no one need feel left out. However, there is one little problem concerning these axioms that needs to be addressed. Rand and her followers seem to believe that, by merely uttering these axioms, they have asserted something definite and palpable. But in this belief they are sadly deluded. The problem with the Objectivist axioms is that they are destitute of empirical content. They tell us little, if anything, about reality. In regarding them as something substantial and informative, Rand and her followers have once more allowed themselves to be seduced by verbalist mumbo-jumbo.

What, actually, do these axioms tell us? Not very much. At bottom, they are merely pretentious reformulations of several irrelevant truisms. "Existence exists" and "A is A" are mere tautologies. They tell us neither *what* exists nor *what* is A. The second axiom asserting the existence of consciousness is simply a vague way of describing the indisputable fact that people are conscious of *something*. But it fails to specify not only what that something is, but what consciousness is as well.

It is these three cognitively empty truisms which, according to Peikoff, form the starting point and basis of the entire Objectivist philosophy. But is this possible? Can anything be constructed from principles that are so destitute of specific empirical content? I don't believe so. The problem with indefinite principles like the Objectivist axioms is that nearly anything, no matter how contrary to the facts of reality, can be inferred from them. By including everything, they end up saying *nothing*. As cognitive principles used to interpret the data of reality, they are absolutely worthless.

*   *   *

(2) Let us begin with an examination of the first axiom, "Existence exists." As Rand herself acknowledged, this axiom fails to specify precisely *what* exists. (1990b, 247) Yet this consideration does not prevent her from saying in another place that the phrase *existence exists* "means that an objective reality exists independent of any perceiver's emotions, feelings, wishes, hopes or fears." (1964a) But is this really what the phrase *existence exists* means? No, I don't think so. To reason from *existence exists* to

"what exists is an objective reality" is to commit a palpable *non sequitur*. The very fact that this axiom fails to specify precisely what exists means that no statement concerning the specific nature of existence can be derived from it.

From *existence exists* we proceed to the second Objectivist axiom: "you exist possessing consciousness, consciousness being the faculty of perceiving that which exists." This axiom is not as empirically destitute as the first one: but it is rather amorphous in regards to its empirical significance. The term *consciousness* is often used by Rand and her followers in several different senses, none of which are entirely compatible with the others. What is worse, Rand never specifies which sense of the term she is using. The confusion that results enables Rand and her followers to devise sophistical constructs for refuting philosophical idealism and monotheistic creationism. The most important of these constructs is the principle of the "primacy of existence." "Existence, this principle declares, comes first," explains Peikoff. "Things are what they are independent of consciousness—of anyone's perceptions, images, ideas, feelings. Consciousness, by contrast, is a dependent. Its function is not to create or control existence, but to be a spectator: to look out, to perceive, to grasp that which is." (1991, 18)

This principle is next contrasted to its diametric opposite, the principle of "the primacy of consciousness." "This is the principle that consciousness is the primary metaphysical factor," Peikoff informs us. "In this view, the function of consciousness is not perception, but creation of that which is. Existence, accordingly, is a dependent; the world is regarded as in some way derivative of consciousness." (1991, 18)

According to Objectivism, the validity of the primacy of existence is implicit in the axiom of consciousness. Also implicit in this axiom is the *invalidity* of the primacy of consciousness view. Since consciousness is the faculty which perceives that which exists, existence must *ipso facto* take precedence over consciousness.

So far, I have no argument with the Objectivist elaboration of these principles. Existence is undoubtedly prior to and independent of consciousness; and consciousness is undoubtedly dependent upon existence: that much I can agree with. Where I find a problem with these principles is *how* Rand and her followers choose to use them. They draw conclusions from them that have no warrant in either logic or fact.

It must be kept in mind that Rand's assertion of the primacy of existence over consciousness still fails to enlighten us concerning the precise nature of this "primary" existence. For this reason, nothing of any relevance can be drawn from it. Rand, however, in her eagerness to refute certain views of existence that she disliked, blinded herself to this fact. Two views in particular she wished to invalidate: (1) philosophical idealism; and (2) monotheistic creationism. Both of these doctrines, according to Rand, violate the principle of the primacy of existence. Let us examine her argument first in regards to philosophical idealism, then in regards to theological creationism.

Philosophical idealism. Peikoff defines an idealist as someone who regards "reality as a spiritual dimension transcending and controlling the world of nature, which…is regarded as deficient, ephemeral, imperfect—in any event, as only partly real." (1991, 30) This view of reality is invalid, Peikoff argues, because it asserts the primacy of a spiritual dimension, which is tantamount to asserting the primacy of consciousness. The assumption here is that the terms *spiritual dimension* and *consciousness* are synonymous. Peikoff's entire argument rests on the identity of these two terms.

In this attempted refutation of idealism we find all the trademarks of the classic verbalist argument. First you have a vague premise made up of words which are either indefinite in meaning (e.g., the term *consciousness*) or lacking in empirical content (i.e., the term *existence*). You add to this a vague definition of *idealism* and a questionable definition of *spiritual*, and you have yourself a neat little refutation of the idealist creed. Unfortunately, it is entirely invalid.

To begin with: Where did Peikoff get the idea that the term *spiritual* is synonymous with consciousness? That may be how Peikoff himself chooses to define *spiritual*, but it is not necessarily how idealists themselves choose to define it. If they choose to define spiritual as being separate from consciousness, then Peikoff's argument collapses from its own verbalistic ineptitude.

The only way to determine whether philosophical idealists are guilty of believing in the primacy of consciousness is to investigate their actual beliefs. Such an investigation will show that very few idealists, if any, believe in the primacy of consciousness. On the contrary, nearly all of them believe, like Rand, in the primacy of existence. Where they differ from Rand is in regards to the question, *What, specifically, exists?* Some idealists (but not all) deny the existence of an external material world. This does not mean, however, that they believe consciousness creates existence. Berkeley, for example, regarded the mind of God as the primary existent. Schopenhauer, on the other hand, blamed existence on what he chose to call "the Will." Both of these "idealist" philosophers centered existence in something *outside* human consciousness.

Even solipsists believe in the primacy of existence. You ask a solipsist: "Do you believe that existence exists?" he will answer: "Of course I do. I believe that *I* exist." If you proceed to ask him whether he believes he exists possessing consciousness, consciousness being the faculty that perceives existence, he would answer: "Well of course I exist possessing consciousness. How else would I know that I exist?" And then finally, if you asked him whether he believes in the primacy of existence, he would answer: "Of course existence is primary! All that exists is myself, and since there is no other existence, this existence must be primary. All else is delusion."

To sum up. The Objectivist refutation of idealism is based on a confusion between the terms consciousness and spiritual. Since both terms are scandalously vague, it is easy to assert that they are one and the same. But this is not necessarily the case.

Monotheistic creationism. This doctrine asserts that the universe is the handiwork of a supernatural deity. Objectivism once more trots out its principle of the primacy of existence in order to refute it. Peikoff begins by asserting the identity of the term *God* with the term *consciousness*: "According to Christianity (and Judaism), God is an infinite consciousness who created existence." (1991, 21) From this point, it is easy to prove that creationism denies the primacy of existence. If God is regarded as mere consciousness, then obviously the assertion that God created existence is tantamount to a denial of the primacy of existence. For if a supernatural consciousness did in fact create existence, then *that* consciousness must be regarded as primary to existence. Therefore, concludes Peikoff, monotheistic creationism denies the primacy of existence. Q.E.D.

There are several glaring falsehoods in this argument. In the first place, where did Peikoff ever get the idea that Christianity regards God as "an infinite consciousness who created existence"? I know of not a single Christian who holds such a belief. If there are such Christians, I wish Mr. Peikoff had provided their names. In the absence of evidence for this assertion, I am inclined to suspect that Mr. Peikoff is merely playing a verbal trick on his readers. Since most Christians regard God as a spiritual being who created the universe, Peikoff merely substitutes the term *spiritual being* for the term *consciousness* and the term *universe* for the term *existence*. Yet it is an open question whether these terms are in fact meant to be equivalent by the theology of Christianity (or Judaism). After all, no Christian would say: "I believe that God's *consciousness* created the universe." No, what the Christian believes is that *God*, not his consciousness, is responsible for the universe. This is important consideration to keep in mind. The terms God and God's consciousness are not equivalent. God's consciousness is simply the medium through which God experiences his omniscience. It is something deeper in God—either His mind or His spirit or His will—that, according to Christian doctrine, is responsible for the creation of the universe.

The same goes for the terms *universe* and *existence*. No Christian theologian who is not terribly confused would ever accept the statement "God created existence."

According to the basic premises of Christian theology, this would be impossible. Nearly all Christians believe that God has always existed. Since God did not create Himself, this means that God could not have created existence. What He created is the universe. As it says in *Genesis*: "In the beginning God created the heaven and the earth." Note that it says nothing about God creating existence.

Even if, however, we drop these objections and agree with Peikoff that theistic creationism denies the primacy of existence, this still would not mean that monotheism violates the Objectivist axiom of consciousness. This axiom is supposed to be "self-evident." Now although I consider the term *self-evident* to be scandalously vague, let us waive this objection and pretend for a moment that the axiom of consciousness is in fact "self-evident." But it should be plain that Rand's axiom of consciousness can only be self-evident in regards to the nature of *human* consciousness, because that is the only type of consciousness we have any experience of. The concept of self-evidence, if it has any meaning at all, must refer only to those things which the self has first-hand experience of. Now the consciousness of God is something we have had no experience of; consequently, we can have no "self-evident" knowledge about it. For this reason, the Objectivist claim that monotheistic creationism violates the principle of the primacy of existence is irrelevant. Even if monotheistic creationism did violate Rand's principle of the primacy of existence, this would not constitute a refutation of creationism. The principle of the primacy of existence is self-evident only in regard to the individual's own consciousness. Whether this primacy is valid in regards to other types of consciousness, that we can never know.

Only from experience could we ever make such a determination. But on this question, experience has nothing to say.

A is A. The last of the Objectivist axioms, the so-called "axiom of identity," or "A is A," would appear to have been Rand's personal favorite, for she refers to it more than any other and deduced some of her most important metaphysical principles from it. This axiom, as the reader will recall, insists that everything that exists must have a specific nature. "A leaf cannot be a stone at the same time, it cannot be all red and all green at the same time, it cannot freeze and burn at the same time," explains Rand. (1961, 152) "The point is that to be *is* to be something," adds Peikoff. "If something *exists*, then *something* exists; and if there is a *something*, then there *is* a something." (1991, 7)

Having cleared that up, we can now proceed to critique the relevance of this axiom. Like the axiom of existence, Rand's identity axiom suffers from a severe paucity of empirical content. All the axiom declares is that things have specific identities. But it fails to enlighten us what these specific identities might be. They could be *anything*—provided, of course, that they are "something."

Why did Rand formulate so useless an axiom? She formulated it so that she could advance certain notions about empirical reality that she wished to validate without going to the trouble of collecting empirical evidence. The first of these notions is the idea of cause and effect, which, according to Objectivism, "is a universal law of reality" whose validation rests on the fact that every entity has a specific identity that causes it to act in a uniform, non-contradictory fashion. (Peikoff, 1991, 14)

The second of the two notions that Rand tries to smuggle in under the cover of her axiom of identity is the view that reality is essentially logical. "The principle which logic provides to guide man's mental steps *is* the fundamental law of reality," declares Peikoff. (Rand, 1990b, 121) How does he know this? Because "A is A"—which means: *contradictions cannot exist in reality.* (Rand, 1961, 154) Unfortunately, neither Peikoff nor his mentor Rand ever bothered to provide any empirical evidence for this proposition. Both of them believe that the logical nature of existence is self-evident. As we shall see, this is hardly the case.

Causality. Let us begin with Rand's attempted validation of causality. According to Rand's philosophy, causality is a "corollary" of the axiom of identity. This means that causality is regarded by Objectivism as a logical implication of the fact that things have identity. Since everything in the universe must have a specific identity, each thing must act in a specific way. Otherwise, the entity in question would be acting apart or against its fundamental identity. "A thing cannot act against its nature, i.e., in contradiction to its identity, because A is A and contradictions are impossible. In any given set of circumstances, therefore, there is only one action expressive of its identity. This is the action it will take, the action that is *caused* and necessitated by its nature." (Peikoff, 1991, 14)

People destitute of the ability to think critically are often impressed with such arguments. Little do they realize the vacuity of such reasonings; nor can they imagine how easily it would be to defend the precise opposite conclusion from the same premises. Since the axiom of identity is a mere tautology devoid of empirical content, you can use it to defend any claim about objective reality you wish to advance, no matter how absurd. Suppose I wished to deny the existence of cause and effect. Could I do so without contradicting Rand's axiom of identity? Of course I could. All that Rand's axiom of identity asserts is that everything has a specific nature. But it fails to assert what sort of nature everything actually has. And so if I were to assert that the nature of everything is to interact on the grounds of pure chance instead of on those of cause and effect, neither Rand nor any of her followers could refute me on the basis of their axiom of identity.

Whether objects in the real world of fact are subject to cause and effect can only be determined by scientific observation and experiment. Arguments on the basis of empty tautologies are entirely useless for determining the specific nature of factual reality. Matters of fact simply cannot be discovered through the manipulation of verbal or logical constructions. If you want to know whether causality is valid, study the empirical world of facts. Only by observing the facts can you know what they are.

Reality as logical. This vague phrase expresses almost the same thing as the law of causality. I only separate them for the sake of analytical convenience.

One of the cardinal doctrines of Objectivism is the view that contradictions cannot exist in reality. At first blush, this doctrine would appear to be easily refuted. As proof, I submit the Congressional Record: I am sure you will find scores of contradictions within its pages. But those are not the sort of contradictions whose existence Objectivism would deny. Rand and her followers have something else in mind altogether. They are eager to prove that the universe is governed by natural law and that miracles are impossible. When an Objectivist claims that contradictions cannot exist in reality, what he is really saying is that events which violate natural law cannot exist. "[T]he laws of nature are inherent in the identities of the entities that exist," Peikoff tells us. "A violation of the laws of nature would require that an entity act in contradiction to its identity; i.e., it would require the existence of a contradiction. To project such a violation is to endorse the 'miraculous' view of the universe." (Rand, 1990b, 115)

This argument shows the same flaws as the argument for causality. Since it fails to specify precisely what the laws of nature are, it leaves the door open to anyone who is clever enough to suggest that maybe it is a law of nature for miracles to occur. Once again, the Objectivist finds himself checkmated.

It is not only religious miracles which Objectivism wishes to invalidate; Rand's philosophy also seeks to refute those skeptics who have the malice to suggest that the laws of nature might change in the future. The skeptic argues that, since all our knowledge comes from experience, we can never be sure whether the laws of nature will change in the future. After all, no one has ever experienced the future, so no one really can say for certain what the future will be like.

Objectivism tries to get around this argument by insisting that the laws of nature have to remain the same because otherwise there would be a contradiction, and contradictions cannot exist in reality. But what if it is in the nature of things to observe different laws of nature at different periods of time? Then there would be no contradiction in supposing the laws of nature might change over time, because this fact itself would be a law of nature.

To a certain extent, the Objectivist doctrine asserting the logical nature of reality can be viewed merely as a way of justifying Rand's penchant for determining matters of fact on the basis of logical constructions. As I have already noted, Rand was a lazy philosopher who eschewed the difficulties involved in empirical research. She preferred to discover the facts of reality through metaphysical introspection. But, as Pareto wisely remarks, "mankind has never discovered the puniest uniformity in the facts of nature in that fashion." (1916, §111)

In order to demonstrate the futility of determining matters of fact *solely* on the basis of logical principles, I thought I would mention a little experiment conducted by the philosopher Karl Popper. In order to determine whether a proposition validated solely by logic must be universally valid in regards to the physical world, Popper decided to test the proposition "2+2=4" as if it were a physical, rather than a logical, theory. As a physical theory, Popper argues, "we cannot be sure it remains universally valid. As a matter of fact, it does not....If you put 2+2 rabbits in a basket, you may soon find 7 or 8 in it. Nor is it applicable to such things as drops. If you put 2+2 drops in a dry flask, you will never get four out of it....If you answer that these examples are not fair because something has happened to the rabbits and the drops, and because the equation '2+2=4' only applies to objects in which nothing happens, then my answer is that, if you interpret it in this way, then it does not hold for 'reality' (for in 'reality' something happens all the time), but only for an abstract world of distinct objects in which nothing happens." (1963, 211-212)

If a proposition that is logically true (like "2+2=4") can be shown to be, in at least some instances, factually *un*true, then we must reject any theory that asserts the absolute logicality of the natural world. Reality is neither logical nor illogical; it just *is*. Logic is a quality that applies only to the realm of thought. It is our ideas, our deductions, our conclusions that can be either logical or illogical. Facts are what they are, irrespective of logic.

Those who, like Rand, assume that reality is logical, are guilty of the fallacy of confusing our ideas about reality with reality itself. What is true of the realm of ideas is not necessarily true of the realm of facts. Thoughts are one thing, facts are something else altogether. This is true even when the ideas in question constitute a more or less "accurate" representation of reality. Just as a painting is not identical with its object, so a man's thoughts are not identical with *their* object. My idea of reality and reality itself are not one and the same thing. The representation is not identical with the object represented.

Where, then, does logic come in? Logic is a quality applicable only to thought. If our thinking is to be efficacious, it must observe the laws of logic. Otherwise, we will lapse into confusion and our thoughts will be riddled with errors and misconceptions concerning the external world of fact. Our thoughts about reality must be logical if they are to correctly represent reality. That is why logic is important. But note: the importance of logic does not depend on whether reality itself is logical. Superficial philosophers like Rand assume that, in order for logic to be valid in the realm of thought, it must also be valid in the realm of fact. But this is not in the least true. Our mental representations about reality do not need to be precisely symmetrical to reality in order for them to be veracious. No two languages are entirely the same, yet this does not mean that one language cannot be translated into another. Any language can be translated into another, regardless of how asymmetrical the terms or the grammars. The same holds true of our thinking about reality. Although reality is continuous, irreducible, and in flux, this does not mean reality cannot be translated into terms of thought that share none of these qualities. Our ideas can never perfectly represent the objects that they symbolize. If they could, they wouldn't be symbols. But this does not mean that our ideas cannot be close enough to the facts for the practical purposes of everyday life. The fact that we have been able to construct a highly advanced technological civilization based on scientific discoveries demonstrates that, regardless of whatever incidental inadequacies may occur in our efforts to represent one medium (i.e., reality) in terms of another (i.e., thought), such inadequacies can be considered largely irrelevant. As long as we never forget that the facts *of* reality must always take precedence over our thoughts *about* reality and that no principle found solely on the basis of the laws of thought can be assumed, in the absence of empirical corroboration, to be applicable *to* reality, then we need not be excessively concerned with the asymmetrical character of the relationship between our mental representations and factual reality.

* * *

(3) Rand considered herself to be an objective realist, but if her method of determining the facts of reality is any

indication, then it would appear that she also had a trace of subjective idealism in her makeup. Subjective idealism can be defined as an inclination of thought that gives primacy to ideas, concepts, and principles. In any conflict between an idea on the one side and a fact on the other, the subjective idealist tends to side with the idea.

During the course of this book we have on a number of occasions found Rand giving ideas precedence over facts. In her theory of human nature, Rand declared that man's character is the mere product of his ideas. In her theory of history, Rand declared that ideas *cause* history. And in her metaphysical theory, Rand placed a handful of vague and empirically empty ideas—she called them "axioms"—at the very center of her philosophical system, giving these axioms precedence over objective reality and using them to determine matters of fact.

If Rand really understood what it means to believe in the objectivity of the material world, she would have made an effort to comprehend the world on *its* terms, rather than on hers. Existing realities always take precedence over our conception of them. That is why any universally applicable assertion about reality can only be conjectural in nature. To claim that an idea concerning the nature of reality is "certain" is tantamount to giving that idea precedence over reality.

This *fallacy of idealism*, as I choose to denote it, is committed by every philosopher who, like Rand, believes in "axiomatic knowledge." According to Rand, axiomatic knowledge consists of those concepts that identify "a primary fact of reality. [Axiomatic knowledge]," Rand goes on to say, "is implicit in all facts and in all knowledge. It is fundamentally given and directly perceived or experienced, which requires no proof or explanation, but on which all proofs and explanations rest." (1990b, 55)

Knowledge "fundamentally given and directly perceived" would not really be knowledge at all—it would be a contradiction in terms. Nothing is fundamentally given or directly perceived except images and feelings— and images and feelings do not constitute knowledge of the real world. (Santayana, 1923) The real world is something substantial and permanent: it exists whether a mind perceives it or not. This is not, however, the case with images and feelings—or, indeed, with any of the phenomena of consciousness. Such phenomena are produced by the mind and exist only in the consciousness that perceives them. They are neither substantial nor objective when considered in and of themselves. They are here one moment, gone the next. By themselves, such phenomena, though fundamentally given and directly perceived, cannot be considered as forms of knowledge, because they do not exist as material realities. At best, the images and ideas present to consciousness are mere symbols of knowledge; they are not knowledge itself. When I turn and look at the tree outside my window, what is fundamentally given and directly perceived by the mind is not the tree existing in time and space, but only an image of the tree which my mind, in its poetic fancy, has painted across the canvas of my consciousness. The image, by itself, tells me nothing of the tree. The tree exists independent of my mind, yet the image of the tree disappears as soon as I close my eyes or turn my head. For this reason, my knowledge of the tree's existence cannot be predicated merely on my perceiving an image of it in my mind. In order for me to posit the independent existence of the tree, I must first make a conjectural leap from the image in my mind to the tree existing in time and space. No axiomatic knowledge can make that leap for me, because there is nothing about that leap which is "self-evident." On the contrary, it involves what Santayana called an act of "animal faith"—a leap from the given to the not-given.

The only kind of knowledge that is "self-evident" is tautological knowledge, which is merely knowledge of some sort of ideal system of relations (such as geometry or mathematics) that may or may not have any applicability to the real world of fact. The question of whether a given tautological system of ideal relations is applicable to reality can only be answered by testing it against factual experience. It would be erroneous, for example, to assume the applicability of any set of mathematical equations to the real world were these equations not corroborated by experiment and observation. The validity of the proposition "$E=MC^2$" rests, not on any mathematical axioms, but on the scientific evidence corroborating its validity. In the absence of such evidence, "$E=MC^2$" would have to be regarded as pure speculation, with no empirical value whatsoever; its "validity," such as it is, rests entirely on observation and experiment, not on any axioms.

When Objectivists assume the empirical validity of axiomatic concepts, they unwittingly adopt the idealist assumption that reality must conform to their ideas. Now if Rand herself had been an idealist and Objectivism an idealistic philosophy, we could understand her adoption of idealist assumptions. But, as we know, Rand did not consider herself an idealist. On the contrary, she was an emphatic opponent of idealism who repeatedly insisted upon the primacy of objective reality. Unfortunately, her insistence that certain principles of logic are valid, not merely ideally, according to the laws of thought, but also existentially, according to the laws of matter, contradicts the very principles of objective realism which her axioms are meant to uphold and validate. Her error in this regard should serve as a lesson to all those who believe that man's knowledge of the real world can ever be self-evident and axiomatic. As Santayana judiciously observed: "All the axioms of philosophers declaring the world to be necessarily infinite or everlasting or rational or conscious must be received as applying only to their respective systems: the world meantime is just as it is, has been what it has been, and will be what it will be." (1942, 277-278)

*   *   *

(4) As we discovered in the previous chapter, one of Rand's favorite modes of verbalistic argumentation is to try to prove her thesis by restating it in different terms. Nowhere does one find more evidence of this than in her metaphysical theories. It often seems as if the Objectivist axioms of existence, consciousness, and identity serve no other purpose than to allow Rand and her followers to express their differences of opinion with other philosophers in entirely new and exciting ways. Instead of trying to explain precisely why a philosophical viewpoint she disagrees with is wrong, Rand prefers to merely accuse it of denying one of her metaphysical axioms. Thus we are told that what is wrong with Locke, Berkeley, and Hume is that they did "not really have a concept of existence as a metaphysical fact." (1990b, 250) But this is just another

way of saying that Locke, Berkeley, and Hume are wrong. The phrase "concept of existence as a metaphysical fact" adds nothing to the discussion, because it is utterly lacking in empirical meaning.

Rand's favorite method of expressing disagreement is to accuse her ideological opponents of denying that A is A. An example of this can be found in her novel *Atlas Shrugged*, where the hero of the story, John Galt, chastises the entire country in a nationally broadcast radio speech: "Are you seeking to know what is wrong with the world? All the disasters that have wrecked your world, came from your leader's attempt to evade the fact that A is A. All the secret evil you dread to face within you and all the pain you have ever endured, came from your own attempt to evade the fact that A is A. The purpose of those who taught you to evade it, was to make you forget that man is man." (1961, 153)

Rand's hero could have saved himself the trouble of uttering so many words if he had just come out and said: "All the disasters that have wrecked your world and all the evil you dread and pain you have endured have come about because you and your leaders refused to follow my philosophy." But expressing it in this way would have made the empirical vacuity of the passage apparent even to those uncritical persons who are most taken in by such piffle. That is why Rand choose to express it in the terms of her vacuous axiom of identity.

The truth of the matter is that the problems of the world are *not* caused by people evading the fact that A is A. No, that is absurd. Everyone more or less agrees that A is A. Where they disagree is concerning the nature of A. Now the only way to determine the precise nature of A is by consulting the facts of reality. This, however, can be a time-consuming process involving years of research and hard work. Hence Rand's preference for using empty philosophical axioms in place of empirical evidence. Her opponents, she claims, are wrong, not because their views are contrary to the facts, but because they deny that A is A. Her own views, on the other hand, are right precisely because of her wholehearted support of this trivial little tautology. Can anyone imagine a more wonderful way of determining who is right on a given issue? And yet there are people who continue to insist that Rand is a great philosopher and an impeccable logician!

CHAPTER 5:

▼

THEORY OF MORALITY

"Civilized people naively imagine that they follow in practice the principles of a certain theoretical ethics. In point of fact, they act very differently indeed and then resort to subtle interpretations and ingenious casuistries to reconcile theory and practice that are ever and anon discordant."

—Vilfredo Pareto

The central problem of morality is that there exists no objective method of determining whether one moral value can always be regarded as "better" or "loftier" or more "right" than another. In this sense, morality differs from science. If two individuals are in disagreement about some testable fact of empirical reality—say, about the density of a certain metal or the radius of the sun—there are scientific tests designed to determine who is right and thus settle the disagreement. If, however, two individuals differ as to the goodness of a given moral end, there exists no objective method for settling their disagreement. Let us suppose that Peter believes that the highest moral end is to serve others. Paul, on the other hand, regards his own personal happiness as the highest end. How is anyone ever going to determine which of these two is right?

This problem in morality was first identified by David Hume. It is sometimes referred to as the naturalistic fallacy, or Hume's Law. It asserts that statements about what ought to be cannot be deduced from purely factual statements about what is. Hume, in a famous passage, expressed the difficulty in the following terms: "In every system of morality, which I have hitherto met with, I have always remarked, that the author proceeds for some time in the ordinary way of reasoning, and establishes the being of a God, or makes observations concerning human affairs; when of a sudden I am surpriz'd to find, that instead of the usual propositions, *is*, and *is not*, I meet with no proposition that is not connected with an *ought*, or an *ought not*. This change is imperceptible; but is, however, of the last consequence. For as this *ought*, or *ought not*, expresses some new relation or affirmation, 'tis necessary that it shou'd be observ'd and explain'd; and at the same time that a reason should be given, for what seems altogether inconceivable, how this new relation can be a deduction from others, which are entirely different from it." (1739-40, 521)

To date, no philosopher has been able to answer Hume's challenge. There have been attempts to refute Hume, but none have been successful. The problem of deducing a rational morality from the facts of reality remains unsolved.

Rand, however, believed she had found a way to get around Hume's Law and construct a morality based on "reason." By beginning her argument with the question, *Why does man need a morality?* she thought she could avoid the pitfalls of Hume's infamous gap between *is* and *ought*. Man, she argued, needs a moral code in order to survive. Since survival is a factual problem that can only be solved by reason, Rand concluded that it is possible—and, indeed, even necessary—to construct a reason-based morality.

As I hope to demonstrate over the course of this chapter, Rand's theory of a rational morality is a complete failure. From start to finish, it is laced with *non sequiturs*, dubious premises, blatant appeals to sentiment, and other sundry logical irrelevancies. As usual with Rand, she has seen fit to try to establish her various moral principles on the basis of verbal and rhetorical manipulations, which she attempts to reinforce by intimidating her readers with all sorts of *ad hominem* slurs against those who refuse to accept her ethical cerebrations *en toto*. Given the absence of anything even remotely approaching logical rigor in Rand's theorizing, it is difficult not to suspect that she is once more engaged in blatant rationalization of preconceived notions. And since those who are seeking reasons to justify what they already believe on the basis of instinct and sentiment never fail to find precisely what they are looking for, Rand had little difficulty constructing arguments that purportedly demonstrate what she had believed all along. "Him who seeks shall always find"— such is the maxim of inveterate verbalists everywhere.

What is most curious, however, about Rand's theory of morality is not the bad logic and dubious premises that went into it, but the banal and empty conclusions that came out of it. After all, it was not as if Rand was logically obligated to deduce conclusions destitute of practical import. Given her verbalistic method, she could have deduced any damn thing she pleased. The sky was literally the limit. Yet she chose to deduce principles which, as practical moral principles, are so abstract and so removed from the concerns of everyday life as to be close to worthless. How can we explain such a glaring anomaly?

The most obvious explanation is that it never occurred to Rand that her conclusions were empty because they were the product, not of reason, but of her personal sentiments. Those operating under the influence of sentiment often don't realize the extent to which their intellectual judgment has been warped by their emotions. They sincerely believe that what has been founded on the basis of their own emotional prejudices is in fact founded on reason. Hence their own sentimentality blinds them to the emptiness of their conclusions.

I believe something of this sort happened in Rand's case. All along, as she formulated her moral theory, she believed herself to be following the counsels of reason. But these counsels were actually sentiments dressed up in rational guise. Hence Rand's blithe acceptance of principles so vacuous and banal. Since such principles satisfied her sentiments, it never occurred to her that they were not in accord with either logic or the facts of reality.

In this chapter, I will set out to demonstrate why I regard Rand's attempt to formulate an objective standard of value applicable to all human beings as a complete failure. Both the logic of the arguments and the factual validity of her premises will be subjected to rigorous scrutiny. I will also examine the practicality of her view of good and evil and the degree to which her theory of human sexuality accords with known facts.

*　　　　　　*　　　　　　*

(1) Rand defines morality as "a code of values to guide man's choices and actions—the choices and actions that determine the purpose and the course of his life." (1964b, 13) The principle aim of Rand's theory of morality is to show how such a code of values can be objectively validated on the basis of reason and observation. She begins by asking: "What are *values*? Why does one need them?" A value, we are told, "is that which one acts to gain and/or keep." (1964b, 15) But why would anyone act to gain and/or keep something? What could possibly be the motivation of valuing?

It is at this point that Rand commits her first palpable error. Values, she declares, presuppose "an entity capable of acting to achieve a goal in the face of an alternative. Where no alternatives exist, no goals and no values are possible." (1964b, 15) Here Rand is guilty of confusing the *act* of valuing with the *pursuit* of values. It is only the *pursuit* of values that presupposes an alternative, since no one could pursue a value if there were no alternatives and they had to accept the values destined to them by fate. But even if human beings were incapable of choosing among alternatives, this would not necessarily mean they were incapable of having values. A prisoner whose entire life was regulated by the prison warden could still value certain meals or clothes or books that were given to him, even though he did not have any alternative but to accept them.

From this point Rand goes on to argue that, since life is the *fundamental* alternative, then life must be the *standard* of value. The argument upon which she bases this conclusion, it must be admitted, is not terribly coherent. It is built on a series of banal trivialities dressed up to look like profound truisms. She begins by noting that only living beings face the alternative of life and death. Since values, according to Rand, can only be pursued in the face of the "fundamental" alternative of life and death, she concludes that only living beings can have or pursue values. Following this momentous discovery, she proceeds to note that "An organism's life depends on two factors: the material or fuel which it needs from the outside, from its physical background, and the action of its own body, the action of using that food *properly*. What standard determines what is *proper* in this context? The standard is the organism's life, or: that which is required for the organism's survival." (1964b, 16)

This passage illustrates to perfection Rand's method of demonstration. She begins with an appalling banality: life depends on "the material or fuel which it needs" and on the "action of its own body." This vacuous assertion is used to introduce the next appalling banality. Rand asks: "What standard determines what is proper in this context" (i.e., in the context of the requirements for man's life)? Rand answers: "The standard is the organism's life." In other words, the standard proper for determining the requirements of man's life is man's life! Imagine the profundity of the woman who could come up with such an insight!

Luckily for us, this is not the least of Rand's wisdom. She has even more pearls of sapience to bestow upon our ignorance. Did you know, gentle reader, that you have no choice regarding the method required for your survival? Only a certain specific course of action will sustain your life! A few paragraphs later she goes on to assert: "Metaphysically, *life* is the only phenomenon that is an end in itself: a value gained and kept by a constant process of action. Epistemologically, the concept of 'value' is genetically dependent upon and derived from the antecedent concept of 'life.' To speak of 'value' as apart from 'life' is worse than a contradiction in terms. 'It is only the concept of "life" that makes the concept of "value" possible.'" (1964b, 17)

Here Rand commits a palpable *petitio*. Her thesis is that life is the ultimate value. She tries to prove this by arguing that the concept *value* is "genetically dependent" on the concept *life*. But what on earth can this mean? Does Rand believe that concepts copulate with one another and engender offspring? If so, then Rand is guilty of committing one of the cardinal fallacies of philosophical ratiocination: she has reified her concepts into sexual entities. But actually, she has something else in mind in this passage. She is trying to convince us that the concept value makes no sense or has no valid meaning apart from the concept life. The problem is, she makes no effort to explain why this should be so. As far as the impartial critic can determine, the only reason why the concept value is genetically dependent on the concept life is because life is the standard of value. Rand seems to be arguing in a circle. Either that, or she is not arguing at all.

Leonard Peikoff, in his treatise on Objectivism, at least presents Rand's argument with less incoherence of exposition and greater clarity of style. Nonetheless, problems remain with the argument itself. The terms in which the argument is presented are rather vague and nebulous in content. Words like *value, life, man, metaphysically given, fundamental,* and *ultimate* are tossed around as if they referred to something definite. The truism that life is the only alternative to death is again reasserted in several different guises, until we finally get to main conclusion—namely, that the "alternative of existence or non-existence is the precondition of values." (1991, 208) "Once we remove the alternative of life or death," argues Peikoff, "we remove the possibility of need satisfaction or need frustration, at least on the physical level, since 'need' in this context denotes that which is required for survival. We thereby remove also the sensory incentives, the pleasure and pain sensations, which accompany need satisfaction or frustration in conscious creatures." (1991, 210)

Peikoff's entire argument here is based on a verbal trick. According to Peikoff, if human beings did not face the alternative of life and death, they would be incapable of having any needs. How does Peikoff know this? Because, he tells us, "'need' in this context denotes that which is required for survival." Let us ignore the phrase *in this context,* which is simply another way of saying "in the context of the argument's assumptions." (But it is precisely these assumptions that are the point at issue!) This leaves us with an assertion defining the term *need* as: *the requirements of survival.* Now while Peikoff is at liberty to define his terms any way he pleases, we must keep in mind that there exist certain desires in men which most people would regard as needs *yet which are not required for survival.* People are said to need recreation, more money, sexual gratification, television, etc. yet none of these needs have any bearing on the question of survival. They do have a very definite bearing on the question of pleasure and pain. This being the case, how can Peikoff justify his assertion that, without the alternative of life and death, there can be no "sensory incentives," no "pleasure and pain"?

Peikoff, of course, cannot justify the assertion. Nor does he really try. He simply repeats it over and over, giving it a different wording or emphasis each time he reasserts it. An indestructible entity, he insists, would be incapable of having any values because nothing would make any difference to it. (1991, 209-210) But how can Peikoff possibly know whether an indestructible entity would be incapable of having values? Since we have no first hand experience of what an indestructible entity is really like, how can we know anything of such an entity beyond the fact that it is indestructible?

Peikoff's argument, when reduced to its barest essentials, amounts to the assertion that no sentient creature would be capable of experiencing needs, interests, and motives if it were not faced with the possibility of destruction, because if its existence were assured, nothing would make any difference to it. But is this really true? If God were to make us immortal, would we immediately cease to care about anything?

To answer this question, it is best to inquire why human beings care about anything in the first place. Do they care because they are faced with the alternative of life or death? Or do they care for some other reason?

Given the fact that there are things people care about which have no relation to the alternative of life and death, I believe we can safely dismiss the Objectivist view of the matter. A mother cares very much about her children. Yet the welfare of her children often has no bearing on her own personal survival. Indeed, if anything, a mother's concern for her children may turn out to be inimical to her survival. It may lead her to put her life at risk to safeguard the well-being of her offspring. If the alternative of life and death is what makes caring possible, how can we explain this?

There is an enormous amount of evidence to suggest that the alternative of life and death has little, if anything, to do with providing sentient beings with the motive to care about what happens to them. This motive is the product of desire, sentiment, emotional preference—call it what you will. In the absence of such a purely emotional motivation, the alternative of life and death would have no significance whatsoever. A man who is incapable of experiencing any kind of desire or pain would be incapable of caring about whether he lived or died. As J. Charles King, one of Rand's most penetrating critics, has aptly noted, life is only valuable as a means rather than an end in itself. (1984, 111) No one would care to survive for survival's sake. "Survival is something impossible," wrote Santayana, "but it is possible to have lived well and died well."

To a certain extent, Rand would not have necessarily disagreed with Santayana's apothegm. Although she pretended to regard survival as the ultimate goal of human existence and life as the standard of value, she nevertheless rejected the notion of "survival at any price." This, of course, is a contradiction. If life is the ultimate standard of value, then survival at any price must be accepted as the logical consequence. But Rand had no intention of advocating a morality exclusively concerned with mere survival. Her aim was to rationalize her own moral

sentiments, none of which entirely squared with a morality exclusively devoted to staying alive. The only reason
why she chose life as her ultimate standard of value is
because she needed a standard that could be applied
equally to all men, despite congenital differences of character. Had she chosen some other standard—say, for
instance, happiness or the avoidance of pain—she could
not have justified her claim that her system of ethics was
completely objective, since people differ in what gives
them happiness or relieves them of pain. The standard of
life, on the other hand, seemed to avoid this kind of sub-
jectivity. There are some forms of behavior which can be
shown to imperil *all* human life, despite intrinsic differences of character. For instance, all human beings, regardless of their specific character, will put their lives in serious
danger if they drink cyanide, jump off bridges, publish
anti-Islamic literature in Islamic countries, uncover evidence of mob-related corruption in the U.S. government,
or play Russian roulette. These are all activities which,
when judged by a moral system which makes the preservation of life the ultimate standard of value, must be
regarded as bad or evil irrespective of the sentiments or
inclinations of the individuals who may wish to engage in
them. And since it is this sort of absolute objectivity which
Rand was aiming at when she first put together her theory
of morality, this is why we find it occupying so prominent
a place in her Objectivist Ethics.

The main problem with Rand's standard of value is
that it is far too narrow. There exist many human actions
that cannot be judged by such a standard. Many human
activities have little if any relation to the question of survival. Take adultery, for instance. Most conventional

moralities regard adultery as immoral. But since the question of adultery rarely has any bearing on the issue of the preservation of life, a morality based on life as the standard of value would be incapable of formulating any judgment about it.

This is true of many other forms of behavior considered immoral by conventional moralities. Take fraud as one example. If the preservation of life is our ultimate concern, why should an individual shrink from engaging in fraudulent transactions? After all, even if he is caught, the worse that will happen is that he will go to prison. Since his life is not at stake one way or the other, Rand's morality of survival is useless in determining whether an individual should engage in fraud.

If morality really is, as Rand defines it, "a code of values to guide man's choices and actions," it is difficult to see how a morality based on life as the ultimate standard of value could be practicable. Since not all our choices and actions have any bearing on the issue of survival, a morality based on Rand's standard of value would often prove utterly worthless as a guide to conduct.

None of this troubled Rand in the least. Since her primary concern was to discover a standard of value that merely *seemed* objective, once she had found it, she was satisfied. What she next had to do was find some way of showing how this standard of value led to those very moral prejudices that she hoped to rationalize in her theory of morality. Since there was no logical or factual connection between Rand's theory of value and her own personal values, she had no alternative but to once again resort to verbal chicanery. By playing fast and loose with vague terms, she could argue that it is not life per se which is the standard of value, but *man's life qua man*. What she meant by this enigmatic phrase is difficult to say. In the next section, we will attempt to unveil this mystery.

                    *   *   *

(2) Once Rand had established to her own satisfaction the principle that life is the ultimate standard of value, she turned her attention to the question of what this standard means in the context of practical living. If life is the ultimate standard of value, what sort of values should men choose to follow? Obviously, argued Rand, they should follow those values that will enable men to survive. Man, she points out, cannot survive by just any code of values. On the contrary, since man has "a specific nature that requires specific actions to sustain his life," only those values which enable him to meet the challenges of existence will be appropriate to his life. But in order to know what those values are, man has to use his reason, his rational faculty. Only through reason can man discover the values he needs to properly guide his life and insure his survival. From this premise, Rand concludes that "reason is man's basic means of survival." (1964b, 22-23)

It is at this point that Rand brings in her phrase *man's life qua man*. What Rand is trying to communicate by this peculiar combination of words is that man has to aim not just at survival per se, but at a specific type of survival—a survival appropriate to his nature. There is, however, a serious logical problem with introducing a distinction of this sort. As soon as you admit that only a special type of survival is the ultimate standard of value, you have introduced into your morality an element that has nothing to do with the alternative of life and death. Once you make survival conditional upon some other principle, then survival ceases to be your ultimate standard.

Rand tries to get around this problem by asserting that the only type of survival that has value for man is the type of survival proper to a rational being. This view of the matter supposedly follows from her conclusion that reason is man's basic means of survival. According to Rand, human beings can only survive as rational beings. To attempt to survive as anything else would be self-destructive. "Man cannot survive as anything but man," Rand sententiously observes. (1964b, 24) And since the nature of man is such that he can only survive through the use of his reason, Rand concludes that the only survival proper to man is his survival as a rational being. However, if we accept Rand's premise that man must use his reason in order to survive, then it would seem redundant to insist that the only type of survival proper to man is his survival as a rational being. If reason is man's basic means of survival, then of course man must be a rational being in order to survive. Yet there is more to Rand's argument then the affirmation of this hollow tautology. There is something else she is up to which has nothing to do with the logic of her position. Rand wants to trick herself and her readers into believing that her own personal moral prejudices are in accord with her theory of value. In order to achieve this end, she engages in what can only be described as verbal sleight of hand. The phrase *man's life qua man*, which is simply a restatement using different words of the phrase *survival proper to a rational being*, is invested with two logically incompatible senses. According to the first sense, the phrase basically means what I have explained it to mean—that is, it means that man must use reason in order to survive. In the second sense, Rand interprets the phrase to mean that the only type of survival worth having is a "rational" survival. In the first sense, reason is seen as a *means* to an end (i.e., survival). In the second sense, reason is regarded *as an end in itself* (i.e., the only survival worth striving for is man's survival as a rational being).

Now what Rand seeks to accomplish in her theory of morality is to derive the second meaning from the first. In other words, she argues that, since reason is man's basic *means* to survival, then it follows that the *end* of human existence is man's survival as a rational being. But this inference is entirely without justification in logic. Means are one thing, ends are something else. Simply because a particular means is necessary to secure a given end does not prove that the means in question can be substituted for the end. Yet this is precisely what Rand, in effect, is arguing.

The reason so many of her followers have fallen for this verbal trick is that most of them take it for granted that the term *survival* and the phrase *survival as a rational being* are equivalent. They are not equivalent. The phrase *survival as a rational being* clearly implies a conditioned type of survival, i.e., the individual's life only has value if he survives as a rational being and not in any other way. By placing this condition on survival, Rand is guilty of surreptitiously substituting *reason* for *survival* as her ultimate moral end and standard of value.

Once reason is substituted for survival as the ultimate moral end of human existence, Rand can proceed to justify her rejection of the maxim "survival at any price": since reason is the ultimate standard of value, anything which is contrary to reason, even if it proves necessary to survival, must be rejected out of hand. And so the maxim "survival at any price" is replaced by the maxim "*reason* at any price."

Rand's cute little phrase *man's life qua man* is her way of expressing the maxim "reason at any price." Since man's essential characteristic, according to Rand, is his reason, it follows that what he is *qua* man is a rational being. Now if it is man's life as a *rational* being, rather than just as a *human* being, which is his ultimate standard of value, then it follows that his first priority is to remain rational at all costs. This is precisely Rand's view of the matter—although, to be sure, she expresses it in different terms than I have here. "Man's basic virtue," she contends, is his "rationality," which she describes as "the recognition and acceptance of reason as one's only source of knowledge, one's only judge of values and one's only guide to action." (1964b, 25)

If man's ultimate standard of value and his fundamental goal of existence is to survive as a rational being, what does this mean in terms of everyday life? What does it mean to accept reason as "one's only judge of values and one's only guide to action"?

It is at this point that Rand's theory of morality becomes totally arbitrary and subjective. By making man's life as a rational being her ultimate end and rationality his basic virtue, Rand unwittingly adopted a standard of morality which could be used to defend just about anything, no matter how shocking or conventionally immoral. The reason for this has to do with the nature of human rationality. Human beings, as I pointed out in Chapter 1, sec. III, are motivated exclusively by desire,

sentiment, passion. It is impossible for men to be motivated by reason because reason cannot determine by its
own devices the moral ends of human action. At best, reason can only determine (a) whether the end in question
can be achieved and (b) the means appropriate to achiev-
ing the end in view. Reason cannot determine whether a
given end is desirable because desire is a psychological
given: either you desire something or you don't. No
rational argument will ever persuade you to desire something which you cannot help finding undesirable.

Since reason cannot determine the ends of human
action, any attempt to formulate a moral code based on
rationality as the ultimate standard of value will necessarily
fail from a logical point of view. No values can be derived
logically from such a standard, because there is no such
thing as a "rational end." Ends are like facts: either they
exist (i.e., are pursued by human beings) or they don't. To
describe an end as "rational" or "irrational" is merely to
express a personal opinion. Such terms have no logical status when applied to ends. Generally speaking, any moral
end which accords with our personal sentiments and
desires we will tend to regard as "rational"; any moral end
which does not accord with our personal sentiments and
desires we will tend to regard as "irrational."

Although Rand's attempt to make reason and human
rationality her ultimate standard of value must be regarded
as a failure from the logical point of view, the very fact that
it is a failure allows Rand to infer anything she wants from
it. That is the great advantage of adopting principles
which, logically speaking, are destitute of content: you can
make them mean anything you like. The principle *man's
life qua man* is like a verbal rubber band: it can be

stretched to fit any occasion. Any sort of conduct, no matter how outlandish or bizarre, can be justified on the basis of this logically vacuous standard. And since Rand's standard is incapable of logically specifying the precise ends that human beings should pursue, it leaves moral values at the mercy of whim and casuistry.

In the next four sections, we will supplement the logical objections that have been advanced against Rand's moral theory with empirical criticism of some of the factual assertions she made on behalf of her theory. As we should expect from a philosopher who tries to formulate a moral system on the basis of verbalist sophistry, we will find Rand advancing statements of fact that contradict empirical reality.

*   *   *

(3) *Reason as man's basic means of survival.* Any empirical critique of the Objectivist Ethics must begin with an examination of Rand's claim that reason is man's basic means of survival. Rand took the empirical truth of this claim for granted, never having once troubled herself with trying to provide scientific evidence for it. Although she was willing to admit the existence of men who did not live by reason, she argued that such men could only survive by depending on those men who *did* live by reason: "If some men choose not to think [i.e., use their reason], but survive by imitating and repeating, like trained animals, the routine of sounds and motions they learned from others, never making an effort to understand their own work, it still remains true that their survival is made possible only

by those who did choose to think and discover the motions they are repeating." (1964b, 23)

The only way to determine whether this view of the matter accords with the facts is to check the facts themselves. Is it really true, as Rand claims, that human survival depends on reason?

Before we can answer this question, we must have a precise notion of what is meant by the term *reason*. Rand defines reason as a faculty which "integrates man's perceptions by means of forming abstractions or conceptions....The *method* which reason employs in this process is *logic*." (1982, 62) This definition is clearly inadequate, since there is some question whether a process of abstraction can in fact be logical, and, in any case, it would be very hard to judge whether the conduct necessary to maintain human life does or does not proceed from an integration of man's percepts into abstractions. If we are going to test Rand's claim regarding the necessity of reason for human survival, we will need a more precise standard of judging what to accept as a product of reason than what Rand herself provided.

I propose that instead of setting up a criterion to distinguish the rational from the irrational, we should be less ambitious and merely seek to set up a definite but by no means exclusive criterion which will help us distinguish those forms of human conduct which *must* proceed from a non-rational basis from those which *might* proceed from a rational basis. This criterion will be based upon the notion that all conduct that does not use logically appropriate means to attain a given end *must* be considered non-rational. And so if a quack doctor tries to cure an appendectomy by dousing his patient with herbal medicines, or if a would-be globetrotter tries to get from New York to London by taking the subway, both individuals will unquestionably be regarded as guilty of non-rational conduct. I say "unquestionably" because I do not believe there can be any argument about it one way or the other. If an action uses means logically inappropriate to the ends in view, I do not see how anyone, even Rand, could consider such an action rational. No matter what kind of standard you want to adopt to judge the rationality of human conduct, you have to agree that no act can be rational unless the means are logically appropriate to the end in view.

This is not to say, mind you, that *only* those actions that use logically inappropriate means can be considered non-rational. This may or may not be the case. Rand believed, for instance, that reason was capable of distinguishing between ends which are rational and ends which are not rational. Now if Rand's position were correct, this would mean that even conduct that uses logically appropriate means for the ends in view could be non-rational. It would all depend on whether the ends pursued were themselves rational. If the ends were not rational, no conduct proceeding from them, even if that conduct used logically appropriate means, could be considered rational.

Now if I can prove that human beings can survive largely on the basis of conduct that fails to use logically appropriate means to the ends in view, then I will have, *ipso facto*, disproved Rand's contention that reason is man's basic means of survival. If entire social groups can survive largely on the basis of conduct which in no way can be described as rational, then Rand's view of the matter will have to be rejected as contrary to the facts.

For an act to use means logically appropriate to the ends in view, several basic qualifications have to be met. In the first place, the individual engaging in the conduct in question must have knowledge of both the ends which he has in view and the means appropriate to that end. If he is ignorant of either the ends or the means—or, more plausibly, if the ends or the means are not clearly understood—then the resulting conducting cannot be considered rational. For this reason, any behavior which proceeds from habit or instinct cannot be considered rational, even if it leads to results that appear rational to an enlightened spectator. Furthermore, no action can be considered rational if the individual fails to understand why the means he chooses are appropriate to the ends in view. A witchdoctor who randomly combines some herbs into a potion and then uses the potion to cure a sick child is not acting rationally in the sense defined above, because he doesn't understand why the means he chose to cure the sick child turned out to be appropriate. His success is simply an accident that has nothing at all to do with reason.

Now if we apply the principles formulated above for judging human conduct we will find that many actions crucial to human survival proceed from conduct which in no way can be described as rational. Language, etiquette, social mores, political and economic institutions, and common law are all *largely* the product of non-rational conduct. This may come as a shock to admirers of Rand's view of human rationality, yet it is true nonetheless. Human beings did not one day get together and decide to formulate language, etiquette, morals, institutions, laws, etc. To even think such a thing would be to entertain a palpable absurdity. None of these social phenomena could have been developed *prior* to their existence, because prior to their existence no one had any notion of them. This is most clearly true in the case of language. Those who believe that, in order for human conduct to be effective, it must proceed from reason, have a great deal of trouble explaining the origin of language. Obviously, human beings could not have gotten together one day to discuss the formation of language, because prior to the emergence of language, human beings were incapable of speaking with each other. Language, like so many other necessities of human civilization, developed as the unintended consequence of non-rational (probably instinctive) conduct. It is only in very recent human history, comparatively speaking, that an attempt has been made to influence language according to standards developed by rational thought. I have in mind, specifically, such books as *Modern English Usage* by H.W. Fowler and other books of that sort which attempt to demonstrate why certain uniformities of language are rationally superior to others. Outside the proselytizing efforts of grammarians like Fowler, human language has been (and will continue to be) pretty much at the mercy of the non-rational.

The importance of non-rational conduct is further corroborated by what I wrote in Chapter 3 concerning the role of intuition in human thought. Since what proceeds from intuition is not a consequence of rational deliberation, conduct based on intuition can in no way be regarded as rational in the sense defined above. Intuition is non-rational in nature. It develops independently of conscious reason and operates on the basis of principles that often defy conceptual articulation.

When we stop to think how important intuition-based conduct is to human survival, we must begin to doubt Rand's claim that reason is man's basic means of survival. In chapter 3, I gave, as examples of conduct based on intuition, linguistic, moral, judicial, and aesthetic conduct. There are of course other types of conduct as well. A man's ability to either manipulate other human beings for his own advantage or defend himself against the manipulations of others will almost certainly depend in large part on an intuitive component. The so-called "man of the world" is often nothing more than an individual who has developed a remarkably perceptive intuition of other people that allows him to distinguish, with a high degree of accuracy, wolf from sheep, while the perennial sucker who is constantly being fleeced is usually someone sadly lacking in this skill. What separates the successful speculator and the man who ruins himself on the Stock Market is often nothing more than the speculator's greater intuitive knack for playing the market. In many many instances, it is intuition, rather than just mere reason, which contributes most to the prosperity, and sometimes even to the survival, of individual men. Indeed, it is difficult to imagine how human beings could possibly survive without intuition. There are too many skills necessary to human prosperity and survival that simply cannot be accounted for on the basis of reason, from the skill of walking to the skill of operating agricultural equipment.

Again I must remind the reader that my emphasis on the importance of intuition and non-rational conduct should in no way be interpreted as an attempt to denigrate reason or logic or to imply that intuition is somehow "superior" to rational thinking. I am simply attempting to

describe the way things are in empirical reality. Both intuition *and* reason play an important role in the survival of
human beings living in modern civilization. This is a fact
that can be corroborated many times over. Reason—by
which we mean rational scientific thought—has enjoyed
conspicuous success in the arts and crafts, in the technical
and theoretical sciences, in agriculture, industry, and commerce, and in military strategy and tactics. It has been less
successful, however, in morals and religion, in politics and
the organization of society, and in literature and the arts.
Since reason is incapable of discovering objectively
absolute values, human beings have no choice but to allow
their values to be shaped by intuition and sentiment.
Moreover, many of the skills necessary for human prosperity require a subtlety of judgment so refined and a dexter-
ity of motor coordination so intricate and complex that no
conscious mind governed by reason alone could ever direct
them. Imagine a medical student without any experience
in an operating room trying to perform brain surgery by
the guidance of reason alone! In the absence of an intuitive
capacity developed by decades of study, practice, and experience, the surgery would, without question, be a failure.
At the same time, we must not forget that, without the
capacity of rational thought, no one would have ever considered attempting to apply man's extraordinary intuitive
skills to the problem of curing brain ailments through surgery. That is why it would be just as great an error to denigrate reason in favor of intuition as it would be to
denigrate intuition in favor of reason. The existence and
prosperity of modern civilization depend on both.

While the existence of modern civilization almost certainly depends, at least in part, on reason, there is some

question whether the existence of primitive man has anything at all to do with rational thinking. Indeed, if the testimony of anthropologists can be trusted, primitive man's habitual mode of thinking is incompatible with the logic and reason of civilized man. According to the French anthropologist Lucien Levy-Bruhl, the mental representations of primitives do not have the logical character of civilized man's ideas and concepts. "If I were to express in one word the general peculiarity of the...representations which play so important a part in the mental activity of undeveloped peoples," wrote Levy-Bruhl, "I should say that this mental activity was a *mystic* one." (1931, 774) To say that primitive man's mental activity is "a *mystic* one" is tantamount to saying that primitive man's mental activity is not the product of reason, for mysticism and reason are hardly compatible, as Rand herself would have acknowledged. But as soon as we admit that primitive peoples do not, as a rule, think rationally, Rand's theory of morality is confronted with a very serious problem. Rand would have us believe that man depends on his reason for his survival. But if primitive men are not even capable of using reason, how then can we explain *their* survival? If human beings really are dependent on reason, as Rand alleges, then we simply cannot explain how the human race survived during its first several million years of existence, before men learned how to reason in the fashion of civilized human beings. The very fact that the human race did survive during those first several million years demonstrates that reason is *not* man's basic means of survival, that he can and has survived by other means.

Rand appears to have sensed the threat that the survival of primitive man posed to her theory, for we find her meeting this threat with the full weight of her rhetorical fury. The savage's life, she argues, is so horrible that it cannot count as a legitimate type of survival. "To a savage, the world is a place of unintelligible miracles where anything is possible to inanimate matter and nothing is possible to *him*," asserts Rand. "His world is not the unknown, but that irrational horror: the unknowable....He believes that nature is ruled by demons who possess an omnipotent power and that reality is their fluid plaything, where they can turn his bowl of meal into a snake and his wife into a beetle at any moment, where the A he has never discovered can be any non-A they choose, where the only knowledge he possesses is that he must not attempt to know. He can count on nothing, he can only *wish*, and he...wishes, begs and crawls, and dies, leaving you, as a record of his view of existence, the distorted monstrosities of his idols, part-man, part-animal, part-spider, the embodiments of the world of non-A." (1961, 195)

Once more we find Rand discoursing upon a subject she knows nothing about. I would seriously doubt whether you could find a single anthropologist with extensive experience in the field who would regard Rand's description of primitive man as veracious. While it is true that primitive man's view of reality is not based on reason, it does not therefore follow, as Rand would have us believe, that his life is an unmitigated exercise in helplessness, misery, and horror. As far as we know, savages appear quite content with their existence. Some primitive peoples (e.g., the Bushman of the Kalahari desert) are known for their gentleness of temper and their accepting, stoical, thoroughly peaceable attitude towards life. Nor is it true that primitive man regards reality as a fluid plaything: the fact that primitives do not reason as we do does not mean that they do not recognize certain uniformities in nature. Again, it is a case of having a different view of what constitutes *A*, rather than of rejecting *A* out of hand or believing in non-*A*. And while it is true that the savage's view of reality can hardly be described as rational, this still does not prevent the savage from living out his life, and this, according to the premise of Rand's theory of morality, is all that should count.

The vehemence of Rand's contempt for primitive man is easily explained: she cannot forgive the savage because his non-rational method of survival disproves one of the basic premises of her theory of morality. In order to circumvent the embarrassment occasioned by the survival of primitive man, she tries to disparage this survival by describing it as horrible and irrational. However, even if we accepted Rand's view of the primitive man's survival as true, this alone would not extricate Rand from her difficulties. If survival and survival alone is the ultimate end, why should it matter whether one's survival is horrible? To condemn a horrible survival as not proper to a rational being is tantamount to admitting that survival is not your ultimate value after all.

Rand, as I have already tried to explain, attempted to get around this problem by arguing that survival as a rational being is the only acceptable type of survival because reason is man's basic means of survival. But the survival of primitive man falsifies this contention and leaves us once more wondering why survival as a rational being is preferable to survival as a non-rational being.

There exists one final argument in the Objectivist arsenal that might prove useful in extricating Rand out of her difficulties. It could be argued that survival as a rational being is preferable because, generally speaking, rational beings live longer than non-rational beings. This would be a much better argument than any of the others we have so far refuted, because it can be supported with at least a modicum of evidence. Civilized man, who survives to some extent on the basis of reason, tends to live longer than primitive man, who survives almost exclusively on the basis of non-rational conduct. But this difference is only a tendency, and it is not clear how well it would be borne out by a comparison between individuals from equivalent levels of civilization. In any case, the empirical data for making such a comparison is woefully lacking. Any theory, therefore, which uses this line of reasoning must be regarded, at best, as a mere hypothesis.

$$*\qquad\qquad *\qquad\qquad *$$

(4) *Egoism versus altruism.* Rand's most controversial ethical doctrine is her condemnation of altruism, which she once described as a "doctrine of moral cannibalism" and "a morality for the immoral." (1961, 174) Altruism, for Rand, is the greatest of all evils. "Since nature does not provide man with an automatic code of survival," she wrote, "since he has to support his life by his own effort, the doctrine that concern with one's own interests is evil means that man's desire to live is evil—that man's life, as such, is evil. No doctrine can be more evil than that. Yet this is the meaning of altruism." (1964b, xi)

It is unlikely that anyone who regards altruism in a favorable light would accept this characterization of altruism as valid. And for good reason: for it is clear that Rand is guilty of redefining altruism to mean something different from what it means to most people in everyday life. She makes a straw man out of it so that it can more easily be set afire.

Rand's denunciation of altruism goes hand in hand with another one of her most shocking moral theories: to wit, her unmitigated advocacy of selfishness. While it is true that, to a certain extent, Rand's praise of selfishness stems from her love of ruffling the fur of her adversaries, it must nevertheless be admitted that there is more to her theory than just the desire to shock conventional moralists.

Many of Rand's detractors assume that anyone who would dare to make a virtue of selfishness can be dismissed out of hand. But *philosophical* criticism must take nothing for granted. No matter how appalled some of us might be at Rand's advocacy of selfishness and condemnation of altruism, we have no business assuming that Rand is wrong until we can bring forth evidence to *demonstrate* that she is wrong. And feelings of shock and outrage do not constitute evidence.

Let us begin by trying to determine exactly what it is that Rand meant by her incendiary phrase "the virtue of selfishness." The sense in which she uses the term *selfishness* does not in all respects accord with how the rest of us tend to use it. Most people use the term selfish to mean someone who pursues his own interest without giving any consideration to the interests of others. Rand uses it to mean simply a concern for one's own interest. According to Rand, being concerned for one's own interest does not mean having no consideration for others, because it is sometimes in one's own interest to have consideration for others. It is important to note this alteration in Rand's usage of the term *selfish*. When she describes selfishness as a virtue, she is not advocating exploiting other people for one's own benefit. She is opposed to any kind of exploitation whatsoever, regardless of who benefits. Her moral ideal is best expressed by an oath propagated by one of the heroes of her novel *Atlas Shrugged*: "I swear—by my life and my love of it—that I will never live for the sake of another man, nor ask another man to live for mine."

Many will no doubt find the moral ideal embalmed in this motto repugnant. Nor am I in any way trying to defend it. I am merely trying to explain it, so that it will not be misunderstood. When Rand says that she does not believe that anyone should live for the sake of another, this does not mean that she is opposed to doing things for others or buying them presents or giving up something to benefit them. Rand believes you should only do things for others if there is something in it for you. In other words, she believes in the principle of reciprocity. You cannot expect people to just give, give, give without getting anything in return. Nor is it fair for someone merely to take, take, take without ever giving something back. Hence Rand's contention that the "principle of *trade* is the only rational ethical principle for all human relationships." (1967, 38)

One of the reasons why many people find Rand's praise of selfishness so unpalatable is because of their narrow conception of what constitutes a person's self-interest. To such people, the concept of self-interest includes only the least respectable values in human nature—e.g., money, sex, pleasure, entertainment, etc. Spiritual values, on the other hand, are often excluded from a person's self-interest, especially when they involve the welfare of another person. For example, most people would regard a mother's devotion to her son as evidence of the mother's willingness to sacrifice her personal self-interest for the benefit of her son. But this is not the only way of looking at it. One could easily interpret a mother's devotion to her son as being part of her self-interest. Nor would this simply be a matter of semantics. As anyone who has ever observed motherly devotion should know, there are few things more selfish than a mother's devotion to her son. Her very happiness depends on the son's welfare. She seeks *his* happiness in order to attain happiness for herself, and what can be more self-interested than that!

What is true of motherly devotion is true of the devotion between friends and lovers as well. It is simply not true, as so many people appear to assume, that acts of devotion, caring, tenderness, and "sacrifice" are contrary to an individual's self-interest. As Rand herself points out, "Concern for the welfare of those one loves is a rational part of one's selfish interests. If a man who is passionately in love with his wife spends a fortune to cure her of a dangerous illness, it would be absurd to claim...that it makes no difference to *him*, personally and selfishly, whether she lives or dies." (1964b, 44)

Given the fact that Rand included, in her concept of selfishness, behavior that most people would regard as unselfish and altruistic, it may be wondered to what extent Rand's view of morality differs from the common view. Is it simply a matter of different terminology? Or is there a real, material difference between Rand's moral values and those of the rest of us?

In some respects—though not in all—it is just a matter of terminology. Rand, we must remember, had an agenda which she wanted to rationalize into a system of philosophy. Part of this agenda involved finding a way to explain why most people are opposed to laissez-faire capitalism. She needed a scapegoat to blame for capitalism's failure to win the allegiance of society. She believed she had found this scapegoat in the morality of altruism. According to Rand, altruism is a theory of morality that preaches "that man has no right to exist for his own sake, that service to others is the only justification of his existence, and that self-sacrifice is his highest moral duty, virtue and value." (1982, 61) Such a code of morality, Rand contended, is incompatible with capitalism, because capitalism depends on the profit-motive, which is fundamentally selfish and non-altruistic in nature. Since altruism has been the dominant code of morality during the last 2,000 years of human civilization, capitalism has never had much of a chance. But if you could only convince people that altruism is evil and selfishness and the profit motive is good, then you could get them to support an economic system based on the principles of complete and unmitigated *laissez-faire*.

This theory of Rand is, as I explained in chapter 2, entirely without foundation in fact. The morality of altruism had little, if anything, to do with the demise of the so-called "unrestricted" capitalism of the nineteenth century. Changes in social institutions are not brought about by moral theories. Such changes proceed from the innovations of certain ambitious members of the ruling elite eager to find new ways of enhancing their interests. Moral theories are only used to justify these innovations. They do not cause them.

To assume that the morality of altruism *caused* any major social development is to demonstrate an astonishing obtuseness and naiveté regarding human nature. What, after all, *is* the morality of altruism? Mere wisps of over-heated rhetoric, that is all. Many human beings get pleasure out of hearing such rhetoric, just as they get pleasure from listening to music or poetry. The same principle applies in both instances. The primary effect of altruistic rhetoric is aesthetic in nature; its moral effect, when it even has any, is usually secondary and minimal.

This is not to say that there is no such thing as altruistic behavior. People do in fact "sacrifice" themselves for others. Soldiers die to save their country. Firemen put their lives at risk to save complete strangers from burning buildings. A mother starves so that her child may have something to eat. Conduct of this sort can be considered altruistic in the sense that these individuals are putting themselves in harm's way in order to benefit other people. The point in question is whether such conduct is motivated by altruistic rhetoric or whether something else is the cause of it. My contention is that altruistic behavior is primarily caused, not by some moral theory draped in a shroud of rhetoric, but by sentiments pure and simple. The soldier who willingly throws himself on an exploding grenade to save five of his comrades is acting to satisfy a powerful sentiment throbbing in his breast. If he had lacked this sentiment, no amount of altruistic rhetoric would have persuaded him to do anything as detrimental to his well-being as throwing his unprotected body on a live grenade. What I said earlier in the first chapter about every act requiring a motive applies in this case as well. No motive, no act. And since motivation requires some sentiment or desire to bring it into active existence, it follows that every act, even an act detrimental to one's well-being, must be the product, not of slogans or ideas or anything of a merely intellectual nature, but of some sentiment throbbing in the human breast.

But even if Rand is wrong about the origin of altruism, this does not necessarily mean that she is wrong in her condemnation of altruism. Is Rand right about altruism? Is altruism the greatest of all evils?

In order to answer this question, we have to know what *evil* means. Rand defines evil as that which negates, opposes, or destroys man's life as a rational being. (1964a, 23) This definition, however, is far too vague to be of any use. What on earth does Rand mean by the term *man's life*? Who *specifically* is she referring to? The term *man's life*, as far as we can tell, refers indiscriminately to *all* men. But when a man sacrifices his life to save the lives of other men, we are confronted with not just one man's life, but with several. Which man's life is the concept *man's life* supposed to refer to? If it refers to all the men involved in the sacrificial act, then it would be impossible to say whether the sacrifice was good or evil. It was good for the men saved and evil for the man not saved, which is tantamount to saying that the act was both good and evil at the same time.

One thing should be clear from the start. If an individual benefits from an altruistic sacrifice, it would seem rather churlish of him to adopt Rand's view and condemn the sacrifice as evil. Mere common decency would obligate the individual to feel grateful towards those who sacrificed

themselves for his benefit. In any case, it is a fact easily testified by everyday experience that most people feel gratitude towards those that have sacrificed themselves for
others. We see this very clearly in the gratitude shown to
soldiers who sacrificed their lives to prevent their country
from being conquered by a foreign power. War memorials,
posthumous decorations, holidays to commemorate veter-
ans, etc. are a product of the gratitude which all decent
people feel towards those who have put their lives at risk to
safeguard their fellow countryman from the rape, pillage,
and slaughter of an invading army.

Rand tended to regard any praise of altruism with deep
suspicion, as if it were something horribly sinister. But this
is mere paranoia on her part. While the praise of altruism
may not be as morally pure as naive people habitually
assume, this does not mean that it is a sinister or evil thing
at bottom. True enough, there are somewhat mixed
motives behind the whole business. People sometimes
praise altruism because they feel guilty about having benefited from the altruistic service of others. They feel a need
of making some kind of sacrifice in return, in order to
show their appreciation and to, as it were, pull their moral
weight. But altruistic sacrifices are not easy to make. Men
are predisposed against making them. And so a division is
created within the psyche between the guilt-driven need to
make a sacrifice and the selfish instincts opposed to any
sort of sacrificial behavior. In such circumstances, human
beings often prefer to substitute rhetoric for deeds. Instead
of boldly stepping forth and sacrificing themselves for
someone, they merely talk about making sacrifices,
indulging in a veritable gush of self-righteous rhetoric
about the moral necessity of altruistic conduct and going

out of their way to exhort others to do what they themselves shrink from doing.

In addition to this, let us not forget the aesthetic effect of altruistic conduct. The altruistic sentiments of human beings are favorably stirred by any spectacle of one man sacrificing himself for the sake of others. Many human beings can hardly imagine anything so noble as a man giving his life for his family, his country, and his God. Never mind the fact that only a few human beings would voluntarily make such a sacrifice if they had the opportunity.

This is a point that seems lost on Rand. She hears all this rhetoric praising altruistic conduct to the skies and exhorting everyone to sacrifice themselves and makes the mistake of taking it seriously, as if everyone were suddenly going to engage in an orgy of self-sacrifice. But since very few people can be talked into sacrificing themselves, it does not appear that altruistic rhetoric, no matter how extreme and unbalanced, constitutes any very serious threat to human welfare.

Does this mean that Rand is entirely wrong about altruism? No, not necessarily. I believe there is an *element* of truth in Rand's condemnation of altruism. Most people are uncomfortable acknowledging this element of truth, because it violates deeply held sentiments regarding the nobility of those who gave their lives to their country or who made great sacrifices for the benefit of others. To admit that altruism is not always good strikes many as a slur against those who have engaged in altruistic conduct from which others have benefited. But it is important in matters such as these not to let ourselves be carried away by sentiment. Indeed, that is just the problem with altruism. Since it is a sentiment, it is subject to all the vagaries and hazards of passion. People under the influence of strong passion are capable of doing many very stupid things. This is no where more true than when they are under the spell of altruistic passion.

Generally speaking, altruistic conduct is largely the product of what could be called, following the example of Pareto, the "sentiment of asceticism." Asceticism involves an impulse of renunciation. Most human beings feel this impulse to at least *some* degree, although in only a very few does it exist to an *appreciable* degree. Regardless of how strong its force, it is nevertheless a vital sentiment in human nature. Without it, society would probably be impossible. At least some human beings have to be willing to curtail their inordinate desires so that cooperation and give-and-take can have a chance in social relationships. Mere rational self-interest alone cannot provide the motive for such cooperation, because human motivation is not rational. Motivation comes from sentiment and desire. Where such sentiments or desires fail, no motive occurs.

Now even though the ascetic impulse is necessary in order to preserve the social order, this does not mean that asceticism is always beneficial. It all depends on the degree of its manifestation. If it exists in little or no degree, the result is a society torn by conflict. If it exists in an inordinate degree, the result is ascetical fanaticism such as we find in the mendicant friars and the stylites of the Middle Ages or the pacifists and extreme environmentalists of more recent times. Only when ascetic sentiments are moderate can they be regarded as beneficial.

There is, alas, one important exception to this rule. Even moderate ascetic sentiments can be dangerous when they are mixed with certain deleterious traits of character. The most dangerous mixture involves the trait of cowardice. Men who are congenital cowards often try to conceal their pusillanimity under a mask of virtuous self-renunciation. Thus the unwillingness of the timid man to stand up and fight for his interests is ascribed to his "hatred of violence" or his "indifference to mere things." These rationalizations of pusillanimity, when mixed with asceticism, form the basis of the creed of humanitarianism, the ideology of cowardly asceticism *par excellence*. According to the theory of humanitarianism, the aim of society should be to reduce the sufferings of human beings as much as possible. As usual in such matters, practice somewhat diverges from theory. In practice, humanitarians tend to be preoccupied with alleviating the sufferings only of those individuals who constitute, in at least some degree, a threat to the social order. Humanitarians tend to be far more sympathetic to the sufferings of criminals, the dysfunctional poor, sexual deviants, revolutionary troublemakers, traitors, and aggressively hostile foreign nations intent on world domination than they are to the sufferings of normal people who pay their taxes and don't make a fuss about being oppressed by the system. There is a very good reason for this. The sufferings of normal people are of only marginal concern to the typical humanitarian, *because such people will never have to be controlled through the use of violence.*

This is not the case with those social elements that constitute a legitimate threat to society. At some time in the future there may come a day when the humanitarians in the ruling elite find themselves confronted by the necessity of using force to keep some socially dysfunctional element of society in line. In order to prevent such a confrontation, the humanitarian goes out of his way to appease the socially dysfunctional. Such appeasement is rationalized as "social justice" or some equivalent thereof. The claim is put forth that society is to blame for able-bodied individuals who refuse to work and for the dysfunctional behavior of criminals. People who refuse to work should be supported at the public expense because it is society's fault that they cannot find employment. Criminals should not be punished because that would be equivalent to "blaming the victim."

The attitude that leads to appeasement of this sort is most prominent among those individuals who regard themselves as "liberals." It is also prominent among the radical Left. If such people continue to exercise their deleterious influence within the ruling elite, they will almost certainly bring this country to ruin. In saying this, I am not attempting to make a moral statement, I am merely stating a fact that can be verified by scientific analysis. From the viewpoint of morality, the liberal humanitarians may very well be right. Perhaps the sufferings of the socially dysfunctional are more important, from a moral point of view, than the preservation of the social order. It all depends on what sort of ethical standard you adopt. But regardless of your moral standard, it is a fact testified by history that you cannot evade the necessity of using force to preserve the integrity of the social order by appeasing the socially dysfunctional with favors and bribes. The Roman Empire attempted to use such a method to keep the barbarians in check. Eventually, this policy led to the collapse of the Empire and nearly a thousand years of economic and intellectual destitution for most of Western Europe. Louis XVI of France attempted a similar method with the dissatisfied elements in French society, a policy that led straight to the guillotine. A similar disaster awaits America if the cowardice of humanitarian liberalism continues to have its way in the conduct of foreign and domestic policy.

To the extent that Rand's condemnation of altruism applies to the pusillanimous humanitarianism described above, to that extent does her theory have at least some merit. It has less merit when it is directed solely at the rhetoric of altruism, because such rhetoric has very little influence on the behavior of most human beings. It has no merit at all when directed at that moderate form of asceticism that encourages individuals to be less exclusively concerned with the satisfaction of their own personal desires than otherwise would be the case. If this moderate asceticism did not exist in most human beings, social cooperation would be very difficult, if not impossible.

Because of her failure to make these distinctions, Rand's adverse comments on altruism can hardly be regarded as the final word on the subject. She was correct in assuming that altruism is not totally beneficial; but she is wrong in condemning it altogether.

What about Rand's view of selfishness? Is there an element of truth here, as well? And if so, how much of an element of truth is there?

The best part of Rand's view of selfishness is her conviction that relations between human beings should follow the "trader principle." According to this principle, all social relations should be conducted so that each member of the relationship profits, spiritually and/or materially, from the association. If we ignore the ethical aspect of this principle and treat it instead as a description of facts, we get a theory that accords very closely to reality. Voluntary human relationships tend to cohere and flourish to the extent that they adhere to the trader principle advocated by Rand. Relationships that do not observe this principle quickly become unstable and deteriorate. Two human beings simply cannot get along for any length of time if one of them is benefiting from the relationship while the other is not. This view of the matter is corroborated many times over by common experience. Healthy relationships are those in which both individuals benefit from their association. Unhealthy relationships occur when one or both of the parties in the relationship fail to get anything out of it (or are harmed by it).

Where Rand goes seriously amiss in her advocacy of selfishness is in her assumption that most human beings are capable of pursuing their self-interest rationally. Anyone who views human beings as they are rather than as one might *wish* them to be cannot fail to recognize that most human beings simply are not intelligent enough to figure out what is in their rational self-interest. This is why non-rational conduct is not necessarily a bad thing. Human beings are often better off following the guidance of sentiment, intuition and tradition than they would be if they tried to direct their efforts on the basis of reason alone. The inordinate complexities of life are just too great for most people. It is for this reason that traditional methods of doing things often are better than newer methods determined by "reason." A method established by tradition at least enjoys the advantage of having stood the test of time. This cannot be said of those methods based merely on speculative reason. Experience, not reason, is always the better test of the effectiveness of a given mode of conduct. Thinkers who, like Rand, regard "reason" as the answer to all man's problems make the error of disregarding this fact.

*   *   *

(5) *Happiness as the purpose of man's life.* Despite Rand's conviction that man's life is the ultimate value and goal of his existence, she nevertheless maintained at the same time that happiness was man's "highest moral purpose." This, however, would appear to be a contradiction. If the ultimate value and goal of existence is man's life, how is it that happiness can be man's highest moral purpose? Aren't such terms as *ultimate goal and value* and *highest moral purpose* merely synonyms signifying the same thing? And if so, how can both life *and* happiness be man's ultimate value *and* highest moral purpose?

Rand seems to have recognized that there might be a problem with this none too logical formulation, for we find her making an effort to explain it away in her essay on the Objectivist ethics. "The maintenance of life and the pursuit of happiness are not two separate issues," she argued. "To hold one's own life as one's ultimate value and one's own happiness as one's highest purpose are two aspects of the same achievement. Existentially, the activity of pursuing rational goals is the activity of maintaining one's life; psychologically, its result, reward and concomitant is an emotional state of happiness. It is by experiencing happiness that one lives one's life, in any hour, year or whole of it. And when one experiences the kind of pure happiness that is an end in itself—the kind that makes one think: '*This* is worth living for'—what one is greeting and affirming in emotional terms is the metaphysical fact that *life* is an end in itself." (1964b, 29)

Again we find ourselves confronted with another of Rand's incoherent, verbalistic arguments. What are we to think of such a declaration as "It is by experiencing happiness that one lives one's life"? Does this mean that one cannot live one's life if one does not experience happiness? And how can Rand say that the kind of "pure happiness" that makes one think "*This* is worth living for" constitutes an emotional affirmation of the "metaphysical fact" that life is an end in itself? If pure happiness is what causes a person to think "*This* is worth living for," doesn't this prove that "pure happiness," and not life, is the "end in itself"? And if only pure happiness is what makes life worth living, why didn't Rand choose this type of happiness as her standard of value?

The reason Rand did not choose happiness as the ultimate value of her moral system is because (as I explained earlier) she feared that this would lead to moral subjectivism. Happiness is an emotion and emotions are subjective. If you make happiness your ultimate value, then you are in effect letting your emotions decide what you should value. But this, argued Rand, is tantamount to letting oneself "be guided by nothing but emotional whims." (1964b, 29)

Rand here makes the mistake of confusing means and ends. It is perfectly conceivable that one can pursue an emotional end like happiness yet still be "guided" by reason. It all depends on how you determine the method by which you will attain your emotional end. If it is happiness you are pursuing, you can make an effort to use your reason to figure out the best way of making yourself happy. In such a case, happiness is your ultimate value and goal of your action and reason the method by which happiness is pursued.

Rand, however, could not accept the idea that reason could only be applied to the *means* of human action and not to the *ends* as well. She was after the Holy Grail of rationalists everywhere—the "rational end." But reason is helpless when it comes to the task of trying to distinguish between rival ends. Only by resorting to our sentiments and desires can we determine whether an end is really worth pursuing.

Rand's unwillingness to accept this fact is one of the reasons why her moral theory is so incoherent and so lacking in logical rigor. She wanted two things that are fundamentally incompatible: first, an objective, absolute standard of value which could be verified by reason and, second, a moral theory which advocated happiness as the highest moral purpose. She believed she had found her absolute standard of value in her doctrine that man's life is his ultimate standard of value. The problem she faced was how to reconcile this standard with her conviction that happiness is man's highest moral purpose.

She tried to reconcile these two contradictory principles as follows. Happiness, she argued, can only be attained by choosing man's life as one's ultimate goal. "It is only by accepting 'man's life' as one's primary goal and by pursuing the rational values it requires that one can achieve happiness," Rand tells us. (1964b, 29) "Just as man cannot achieve self-preservation arbitrarily, but only by the method of reason," argues Rand's protégé, Leonard Peikoff, "so he cannot achieve happiness arbitrarily, but only by the same method. The method is the same because self-preservation and happiness are not separate issues." (1991, 339)

There are two problems with this argument, one logical and the other empirical. The logical problem has to do with the sudden transformation of an ultimate value into a means. By arguing that man has to regard his life as his ultimate value in order to attain happiness, she has made the act of holding life as the ultimate value a *means* to a greater end, i.e., to personal happiness. But logically speaking, there can be no greater end than an *ultimate* value. Rand has pulled a fast one on us. She has substituted *happiness* for *man's life* as her ultimate goal and value without ever admitting it in plain terms.

The empirical problem with her theory is somewhat more serious. Attentive readers of Rand's ethical writings will have noted that she no where makes an effort to corroborate her theory of happiness with empirical data. As usual with Rand, she simply assumes that her theory has to be true because it accords with her personal sentiments.

It is just as well that Rand did not try to substantiate her theory with factual data. Her theory is too incoherent and uses too many vague terms to ever be successfully tested against reality. That is essentially the problem with all theories declaring that happiness can only result from following a specific moral code or principle. How is such a claim to be tested against reality? How are we supposed to distinguish individuals who follow a specific moral code from those who do not? Are we supposed to take their word that they follow the code in question? Or are we supposed to follow them around and make certain that they are following it? And once we have determined with any degree of accuracy who has followed the code and who hasn't, how on earth are we to determine which of them is happy? It is not as if the happiness of an individual can be measured with scientific instruments. But without such measurements, how can we ever know whether a given code of morality did or did not lead to happiness?

Most people try to answer such questions on the basis of their own personal experience. If they believe that adherence to a certain code of morality has made them happy, they will conclude that the moral system in question will make anyone else who follows it happy. But this does not necessarily follow. In the first place, we can never be certain whether an individual's happiness is in fact caused by the moral code he believes he is following. It may have another cause that has little, if anything, to do with his morals. Moreover, there is some question whether individuals do in fact follow abstract codes of morality. They may *believe* that they are following such codes, but this belief may be an illusion. Since most moral codes are scandalously vague, they can be used to justify almost anything. I have already noted in an earlier chapter how Rand's adultery with Nathaniel Branden can be justified on the basis of her own moral system. Adultery could no doubt be justified on the basis of many other moral systems as well, including the moral system of Immanuel Kant. (Santayana, 1940, 62-63) The moral principles of philosophers are simply too general and too lacking in specific normative content to be of any use in precisely determining how the individual should act in every circumstance confronting him in life. Moral codes tend to be very simple; but life is inordinately complex. Hence the normative emptiness of nearly all philosophical systems of morality.

Since most moral codes do not specify the behavior that is supposed to follow from them, claims that such codes lead to happiness are completely worthless. If your moral principles are so vague that they can be used to justify just about any sort of conduct you please, it should be obvious that no specific act can arise on the basis of those principles. Rand's principle *man's life qua man* and Kant's categorical imperative are two examples of moral principles from which you can logically deduce nearly anything you damn please. And since these principles exclude nothing, to say that such principles lead to happiness is tantamount to saying that all conduct leads to happiness, which is absurd.

Another reason why it is impossible to determine whether a given moral code leads to happiness arises from the fact that no two individuals will necessarily find happiness in precisely the same way. What makes Paul happy will not necessarily make Peter happy. For this reason, no individual can conclude from his own personal experience that just because his own personal code of morality has made *him* happy, that it will therefore make everyone else who follows it happy as well. It all depends on what kind of individuals they are. Some people are made happy only by living strictly within their means and taking no financial risks. Does this therefore mean that only those who follow a moral code that condemns risk-taking can attain happiness? Of course not! There are some people who love the excitement that comes with taking risks and who would be bored stiff if they spent their entire existence obsessed with preserving their financial security. People can only find happiness by pursuing those values that are in accord with their unique individuality. And since not everyone has the same character, it follows that no method for attaining happiness can be valid for all human beings.

One other consideration needs to be mentioned about the attempt to link morality and happiness. Those who believe that men can become happy by following this or that moral code are guilty of forgetting the role of fortune and bad luck in human affairs. Machiavelli claimed in *The Prince* that fortune plays the role of arbiter in half our actions. Whether fortune enjoys *that* great a role in human affairs would be difficult to say; but certainly it has at least *some* role, even if not a very large one, and this has to be taken into account when discussing the relation of morality and happiness. There are certain individuals who, through no fault of their own, endure terrible misfortunes. Some are born in extremely averse circumstances; others are born with severe physical ailments or an ill-constituted psyche. One can hardly blame the misery and unhappiness of such individuals entirely on their conduct. To suggest that they would have been happy if only they had followed some particular code of morality is not only absurd, it is also cruel and slanderous, for it implies that their misfortunes are a consequence, not of circumstances beyond their control, but of their own immorality.

The fact of the matter is that there does not appear to be any tried and true method of determining whether this or that principle leads to, let alone guarantees, personal happiness. Each individual must discover for himself what, if anything, makes him happy. Moral principles are useless in such matters because there exists no way of proving that they do in fact lead to happiness. All we can go by is anecdotal evidence. But anecdotal evidence is personal, unscientific, ambivalent, and inconclusive. Consequently, it is entirely futile to try to use such evidence to prove that virtue leads to happiness.

          *   *   *

(6) *The problem of evil.* Although there is no way of knowing the precise relation between morality and happiness, it is a matter of common observation that people who are considered "virtuous" and "good" sometimes come to bad ends, while people who are considered "vicious" and "evil" sometimes prosper. Whether virtue insures happiness and vice sorrow we have no way of knowing; but we do know that virtue does not always lead to material prosperity or to physical well-being and that vice does not always lead to financial ruin and physical misery. One need only mention events like the holocaust, the Ukrainian Peasant Famine, or the killing fields of Cambodia to realize the power of evil to cause misery and devastation to more or less innocent individuals.

That evil should sometimes prosper at the expense of virtue is a fact which many people find deeply disturbing. It is felt that unless those who do evil are in some way made to "pay" for their crimes, there is no hope for man and life becomes a cruel farce in which the virtuous are persecuted *because* they are virtuous and the wicked prosper *because* they are evil. Since most people do not want to live in a congenitally unjust world, they are eager to believe in any doctrine which assures them that, ultimately, justice will win out in the end. Religions like Christianity satisfy this need by assuring the faithful that those who do evil in this world will be punished in the next. Not everyone, however, is capable of taking the leap of faith necessary to accept the religious solution. But the need for a secular equivalent remains. The most common secular solution to the problem of evil involves the claim that only the virtuous are capable of "true" happiness. This is essentially the solution adopted by Rand, but she adds a twist to it that is uniquely her own. She argues that evil is not only incapable of bringing about true happiness, but that it is "impotent" as well. (1961, 167) It has no power but that which it extorts from its victims.

Given the immense amount of material devastation and physical misery inflicted upon the world by individuals generally regarded as evil, it is difficult to understand how anyone could ever regard evil as impotent. And indeed, although Rand claims to believe this, on closer examination we find her adding a very important condition to her contention. According to Rand, evil is only impotent to attain the good. It does, however, have the power, admits Rand, to destroy the good. (Peikoff, 1991, 329-331)

At the heart of this doctrine of the impotence of evil is the conviction that it is impossible to attain a good end through an evil means. Objectivists believe that only those who are virtuous and refrain from dishonesty, parasitism, injustice, and irrationality can be successful. But since we find many examples in the real world of men prospering because, rather than in spite of, their wicked deeds, Objectivists have felt obliged to offer some kind of explanation for this. According to Leonard Peikoff: "The success of evil, to the extent that such phenomenon exists, flows not from any inherent efficacy on the part of evil, but from the errors or flaws of men who are essentially (or in some issue) good. Above all, such success flows not from any individual's compromise or weakness, but from the fact that throughout history, the good has failed to recognize itself or to assert its rightful claims." (1991, 333)

From this we can easily deduce a solution to the problem of evil. If evil can only be successful as long as the good fails to recognize itself and assert its rightful claims, then in order to keep evil in check, all we have to do is somehow get the good to recognize itself and demand its rightful share. But what does it mean to say that the good should "assert" its rightful claims? Does this mean that the good should merely verbalize its claims? Or does this mean that the good should use physical force to assert them? If the former meaning is what Rand was driving at, then it is obviously false. If an armed robber comes into your house to plunder your valuables, you cannot stop him by merely asserting your rightful claim not to be robbed. The robber will simply laugh at such futile and silly rhetoric. If, on the other hand, you assert your rightful claims by resorting to violence, then you might actually have a chance of accomplishing something. But then again, if the robber is better at using force than you are, he will probably succeed despite your resistance.

What is true of the armed robber is true of evil in general. When evil has physical force on its side, it can only be defeated by a greater force. But there exists absolutely no guarantee that this will always be the case. As long as evil enjoys a military advantage over the good, evil will continue to be successful, Rand's theory of evil's impotence notwithstanding.

Rand and her followers attempt to get around this fact by insisting that, since evil is impotent, it is incapable, by its own devices alone, of securing for itself a military advantage. Military advantage depends on the quality and effectiveness of one's weapons and the strategic and tactical skills of one's generals. But both of these factors depend on man's reason, which Rand defines as man's primary good. From this Rand concludes that evil must depend on the good for its military advantage. If the good would merely stop supporting evil, evil would no longer have the overwhelming force it requires to succeed in the world.

This view of the matter, I fear, grossly over-simplifies the basic realities of the situation. Rand would have us believe that there exists some kind of dichotomy between the initiation of physical force and human intelligence, so that anyone who would try to prosper in the world by the initiation of force must be, by definition as it were, too stupid and irrational to succeed without the help of a rational person who, by virtue of his rationality, would be opposed to the initiation of physical force. But this view of the matter assumes that all evil people are irrational in all things. This is not how things are in the real world of fact. History is full of examples of individuals who would be regarded by most people as evil but yet who were fully capable of pursuing their "evil" ends by rational means. Just think of the great conquerors in human history— Tamerlane the Great, Ghengis Kahn, and Stalin. While these men might not have been paragons of reason in the Objectivist sense, they still had enough cunning to establish powerful empires capable of devastating entire countries.

What about Rand's view that goodness entails rationality? Is she correct in assuming that every good person must be rational and that no rational person can be evil? Since reason cannot, by its own devices, distinguish between a "good" end and an "evil" end, it would be logically absurd to claim that rationality assures goodness. At best, rationality can only distinguish between achievable ends and non-achievable ends. And unless we assume that all achievable ends are good because they are achievable (which is a very dubious assumption), then we have no choice but to conclude that it is entirely possible for a rational man to pursue evil ends. To believe otherwise is to surrender oneself to the irrational influences of wishful thinking.

*   *   *

(7) *Honesty as the best policy.* No where is the verbalistic character of the Objectivist ethics more in evidence than in Leonard Peikoff's defense of honesty. Peikoff is eager to convince us that honesty is necessary for man's survival and that dishonesty undermines man's life because it is incompatible with his reason. "Since man lives in reality, he must conform to reality—such is the argument for honesty," declares Peikoff. "Any other course is incompatible with the requirements for survival." (1991, 269)

It is difficult to know precisely what Peikoff is trying to say here. He seems to be saying that dishonesty is incompatible with survival. But given the fact that there have been many dishonest individuals who have lived long and prosperous lives, Peikoff's assertion would appear to be contradicted by the facts of reality. A more subtle error lies in Peikoff's assertion that, since man must conform to reality, he has no choice but to be honest. If we take this assertion to mean that man must be honest because, in reality, honesty is the best policy, then we have to conclude that Peikoff has merely restated his thesis in different terms. But there is another argument embedded in this assertion that is more in keeping with Peikoff's subsequent remarks about the virtue of honesty. Peikoff apparently believes that dishonesty involves an evasion of the facts of reality. The dishonest man, Peikoff avers, "wages war against reality" and is therefore "guilty of defying all the rules of a proper epistemology. Like the man who evades [reality] in private, without social purpose, he thus subverts at the root the cognitive power of his consciousness. The con man, however, usually makes no pretense of counting on cognition in order to prosper; he counts on his ability to manipulate others. *People* become to him more real than the fragments of reality he still recognizes." (1991, 271)

Peikoff is here guilty of confusing two entirely different issues. He makes the mistake of assuming that *telling* the truth and *knowing* the facts of reality are one and the same thing, so that if someone lies, he cannot possibly know the truth. Obviously, this is absurd. There is no relation between telling the truth and knowing it. Many a dishonest person has a better grasp of the facts of reality than the honest fool whom he cheats and bamboozles. Indeed, this is why dishonesty sometimes pays. If the dishonest person were incapable of recognizing anything more than a few fragments of reality, as Peikoff supposes, then he would be incapable of deceiving others with his lies, because such lies would not conceal any factual realities from which he could benefit. We must remember that the primary motivation of dishonesty is, to prevent others from recognizing the relevant facts of the situation at hand. The con man fleeces his victims by tricking them into investing their money in worthless speculations, like swampland in Florida or shares to a gold mine that doesn't exist. In order for the con man to be successful, he must know that the swampland is worthless and the gold mine nonexistent. Otherwise, he too is likely to lose his shirt. In any successful scam, it is the dishonest trickster, rather than his honest victims, who has the better grasp of the relevant facts and who therefore exhibits the greater conformity to reality.

After Peikoff's ill-advised attempt to link dishonesty with evasion, we next find him advancing the argument that dishonesty is bad because it doesn't work in practice. The first reason why dishonesty doesn't work, Peikoff argues, is because lies breed further lies. In order to cover one lie, the con man is forced to make a second lie, and in order to cover this new lie, he is forced to make a third, and so on and so forth. (1990a, 340) However, since each lie contradicts one or more facts of reality, the more lies he tells, the greater the chances are that someone will catch him in one of his lies and end up exposing his entire scam. And so, even if the con man is fortunate enough to escape detection in his first scam, his success will merely serve to encourage him to embark on further adventures of deceit. Eventually, the law of averages will catch up with him and he will be caught. He "may win the battle," Peikoff acknowledges, but "if such are the battles he is fighting, he has to lose the war." (1991, 271)

While Peikoff is perfectly correct in assuming that dishonesty entails a risk of detection, it does not therefore follow that every dishonest man "has to lose the war," i.e., that he will eventually be caught. Numerous are the politicians and businessmen who have used dishonest means to become wealthy and powerful men without ever being caught. Nor is Peikoff fully justified in assuming that lies will always breed further lies. Lies only lead to further lies when a dishonest person is put under intense cross examination and has to invent lies in order to prevent his interrogator from catching him in a contradiction. But astute con men sedulously avoid those who would put them under such intense scrutiny, preferring instead to confine their scams to the credulous, the foolish, and the gullible.

In a dim sort of way, Peikoff seems to recognize this, for we next find him advancing the argument that dishonesty is bad because it turns the dishonest person into a "parasite...on people who are deludable." "What such people believe and expect—what they expect falsely, thanks to him—this is the power he must deal with and pander to," insists Peikoff. (1991, 271) This argument, it should be clear, is based almost entirely on sentiment. Its logical value is precisely zero. If self-interest is all that counts, there exists absolutely no reason why an individual adept at bamboozling the gullible should not exercise his unique talent. If in doing so he makes himself dependent on the gullible, so what? We are all of us to some degree dependent on other people. The honest businessman who makes his living selling romance fiction depends on the vulgar tastes of his customers. Were his customers to develop better tastes in literature, he would be ruined. Examples such as this can be multiplied *ad infinitum*. It is not the dishonest man alone who depends on the flaws and weaknesses of others. Many an honest man is every bit as dependent on the foolishness of others as is the con man.

As Peikoff proceeds, his argument against dishonesty becomes increasingly mawkish and puerile. At one point, we find him declaring that the dishonest man "betrays every moral requirement of human life and thereby systematically courts failure, pain, destruction. This is true by the nature of dishonesty, by the nature of the principle it involves—even if, like Gyges in Plato's myth, the liar is never found out and amasses a fortune. It is true because the fundamental avenger of his life of lies is not the victims or the police, but that which one cannot escape: reality itself." (1991, 272)

If anyone has any doubt of the influence of sentiment on moral argumentation, one need only examine this passage with a critical eye. Peikoff is basically saying that even if a liar gets away with lying, he will be punished for his lies. And who will be the agent of his punishment? Not his victims, not the police, but "reality itself"? Now let us think about this argument in purely logical terms. How on earth is "reality itself" going to punish a liar who, in reality, has gotten away with being dishonest? If the liar is never found out and ends his days in the lap of luxury and universal esteem, doesn't this mean that reality has in fact failed to avenge his life of lies? And if so, how can Peikoff declare that reality is an avenger from which no liar can escape? Peikoff is here guilty of contradicting himself. Sentiment, rather than logic, has been his guide in the matter.

To cap it all off, we find Peikoff, at the conclusion of his attack against dishonesty, suddenly declaring that, even though lying is "absolutely wrong," its absolute wrongness is "contextual." We have run across this misused term in our chapter on the Objectivist theory knowledge. As the reader will recall, the concept of *contextuality* was used by Rand and her followers as a kind of verbal sleight of hand to explain why people can be absolutely certain and yet still turn out to be wrong. It is used in a similar manner in her theory of morality. "The principle of honesty, in the Objectivist view, is not a divine commandment or a categorical imperative," explains Peikoff. "It does not state that lying is wrong 'in itself' and thus under all circumstances, even when a kidnapper asks where one's child is sleeping (the Kantians do interpret honesty in this way). But one may not infer that honesty is therefore 'situational,' and that every lie must be judged 'on its own merits,' without reference to principle. This kind of alternative, which we hear everywhere, is false." (1991, 275)

Despite all of Mr. Peikoff's palaver about "reference to principle," it is not altogether clear how we are expected to distinguish between those conditions in which lying is "absolutely wrong" and those in which it isn't. Peikoff suggests that dishonesty is bad when it is used to "obtain" a value, but justified when it is used to "protect" one's values from criminals. The trouble with this suggestion is that the terms *obtain* and *protect* are too indefinite. One can use them to justify almost any dishonest act imaginable. Suppose, for example, that an individual uses dishonest means to obtain a burglar alarm system for his home. Why would dishonesty in this situation necessarily be wrong?

After all, the individual is merely protecting his values (i.e., his home) from criminals.

The belief that moral principles are "contextual" and therefore valid only under certain vaguely defined conditions serves no other purpose than to make casuistry the order of the day. And this, in the final analysis, is precisely what the Objectivist ethics amounts to in the end—casuistry, pure and simple. Once you admit that your moral principles do not apply "under all circumstances," then you have, in effect, given yourself the right to break your moral principles any time you choose. If someone should reproach you for not living by your principles, you can merely remind them that these principles, though absolute, are nonetheless contextual and may be broken with complete impunity if the circumstances call for it. And since it is impossible, given the vagueness of the principles involved, to distinguish between circumstances in which breaking one's moral principles is justified and circumstances in which it is not justified, those who are adept at devising verbalistic arguments based on the indefiniteness of words can justify nearly anything they please.

To sum up: Any attempt to defend honesty on the basis of self-interest is bound to fail because plenty of individuals down through history have thrived on dishonesty. Honesty is only the best policy for those who are not good judges of human character and are incapable of distinguishing the gullible from the shrewd. It is not necessarily the best policy for those adept at identifying and swindling the credulous. Nor is it clear that honesty would be the best policy under the kind of market-based capitalist system advocated by Rand. As I will argue in the next chapter, there is some evidence to suggest that deceit is a very important factor in the capitalist system and that without it, capitalism would not have been as successful, economically, as it has been historically.

                    *   *   *

(9) *Sex as metaphysical.* Rand's views on sex are interesting for the light they throw on the influence her gender exercised on her philosophical principles. Had Rand's gender been male, her theory of sex would, in all likelihood, have been different in several important respects. The influence of her feminine gender is clearly seen in her rejection of sexual promiscuity and her belief that individuals who pursue sex for its own sake and not as an expression of their highest values are indulging in a futile attempt to use sex as a method of gaining self-esteem. "The man who despises himself tries to gain self-esteem from sexual adventures," declares Rand. But this cannot be done, she insists, "because sex is not the cause, but an effect and an expression of a man's sense of his own value." (1961, 118)

The point Rand is trying to make here is rather difficult to take seriously if you do not share her sentiments on the matter. Rand had an extremely idealistic view of human sexuality. Sex, she believed, was not just a physical act accompanied by pleasurable sensations, it was also "a celebration of [one]self and of existence" and a rapturous expression of "two interconnected achievements: self-esteem and the benevolent universe premise." (Peikoff, 1991, 344) A man's sex life, insisted Rand, is shaped by his fundamental convictions. "Tell me what a man finds sexually attractive and I will tell you his entire philosophy life,"

Rand once boasted. "Show me the woman he sleeps with and I will tell you his valuation of himself." (1961, 118) These are the kind of views held by a woman who regards sex as some kind of sacred epiphany and who is shocked by the fact that some men regard sex as mere recreation. "Sex is one of the most important aspects of man's life," Rand told Alvin Toffler in an interview for *Playboy*. "Sex must not be anything other than a response to values. And that is why I consider promiscuity immoral. Not because sex is evil, but because sex is too good and too important..." (1964a)

A womanizer could just as easily draw from Rand's premises the precise opposite conclusion. Since sex is so important, the womanizer could argue, one should try to have as much of it as possible. If that means sleeping with 300 women a year, well, what's so bad about that? If sex is so important, then why should it matter how many partners one sleeps with? To say that promiscuity is immoral because sex is too good and too important is to utter a blatant *non sequitur*. If something is good, why not have as much of it as you can?

Such a view of sex would have appalled Rand's feminine sentiments. Women are not given to thinking this way about sex. They want to believe that every sexual act ought to be motivated by the highest values of romantic love. The fact that some men have a more purely hedonistic view of sexuality fills them with horror and moral indignation. They would like to believe that there is something deeply wrong with such men—that they are somehow emotionally and psychologically stunted creatures who do not get as much out of sex as those men who have a more feminine view of romantic love. Rand expresses this view of the matter in her doctrine that all womanizers are men of low self-esteem. The sentimental origin of the doctrine should be obvious from the fact that Rand does not provide so much as a single shred of empirical evidence in support of it. She believes it despite the evidence—which is to say, she believes it, not because it accords with the facts, but because it accords with her own wishful thinking.

In reading over the remarks about sex scattered through the Objectivist literature, I cannot help thinking that philosophy and sex do not mix well. Most philosophers, as soon as they begin hatching abstruse theories about sex, wind up spouting some of the most ridiculous nonsense on record. Consider the following gem from Peikoff's treatise on Objectivism: "Proper human sex...requires men and women of stature, in regard to both moral character and metaphysical outlook. [What, may I be so bold as to ask, would constitute *stature in metaphysical outlook*? And how are we supposed to distinguish a metaphysical outlook of *high* stature from one of *low* stature? It should be obvious that the term *stature* is, in this context, a purely subjective concept. A person of high stature in moral character and metaphysical outlook is merely someone who lives in accordance with Objectivist principles. Peikoff could have expressed what he wanted to say much more clearly by merely insisting that in order to have proper sex, you must be an Objectivist.] It is to such individuals that Ayn Rand is referring when she writes, in summation, that man's spirit 'gives meaning to insentient matter by molding it to serve one's chosen goal.' [What on earth is *that* suppose to mean? What sort of insentient matter is Rand referring to? Is she referring to the human sexual organs? If so, she is in error to consider them 'insentient.' If they were insentient, there wouldn't be so much fuss about sex.] This kind of course, she continues, leads one 'to the moment when, in answer to the highest of one's values,…one's spirit makes one's body become the tribute, recasting it…into a single sensation of such intensity of joy that no other sanction of one's existence is necessary.'" (1991, 348)

It should be clear to anyone whose mind is not clouded by a steamy fog of erotic sentiment that Rand's description of human sexuality contains about as much scientific value as the screeching of a cat in heat. There are many people who regard the ecstasies induced by such activities as recreational drug use, gormandizing, heavy drinking, jogging, and even computer games in the same light; but if they were to speak of their favorite pastime in the same hyperbolic and effusive manner in which Rand gushes about hers, they would be laughed at, and with good reason. Pleasure is all fine and good as far as it goes; but to think that there is something more in pleasure than pleasure itself is to step outside of reality and enter the realm of rhetorical exaggeration.

In saying that pleasure is all fine and good as far as it goes, I am not implying that there can never be anything wrong with pleasure or that human beings should do whatever gives them pleasure irrespective of the consequences. I would be the first to acknowledge that there is a darker side to pleasure which the effusive rhetoric favored by writers of Rand's romantic temperament tends to ignore. What is pleasant in the short-run may not always prove pleasant in the long-run. Some pleasures carry with them, as after effects, serious long-term consequences.

Sexual pleasure is no exception to this. It can lead to unwanted pregnancies, uncared for children, unfit parents, guilt-inducing abortions, venereal diseases, infidelity, heartache, loss, and many other ills that flesh is heir to. Men and women of "metaphysical stature" are no more immune from these ills than anyone else. Just look at the sexual troubles Rand herself experienced later in life with her protégé, Nathaniel Branden. If even Rand had trouble with sex, what are the chances for the rest of us?

If you compared all the pleasures of sex with the pains it sometimes brings in its wake, would the pleasures really outweigh the pains by all that much? Just think of all the personal tragedy that has been brought about by unrequited sexual longings and ill-advised sexual relations down through the ages. Rand would have us believe that all this misery has been brought about because men and women have not been "rational" about their sexuality. Perhaps there is some truth in this view. Perhaps if individuals were "rational" about their sexuality, they wouldn't have made such a mess of things. But what makes Rand think that human beings can in fact be "rational" about their sexuality? If they have not been rational in the past, on what grounds can we assume that they will be rational in the future? And what does it mean to be "rational" about sex? Does it mean that you have to agree with Rand's empirically unsubstantiated and in some cases palpably absurd views on the matter? And if rationality is expected to be the cure-all for sexual suffering, what about those unhappy individuals who cannot have felicitous sexual relations because they are too ugly to attract appetizing partners? Will rationality cure them of their ugliness? If

Quasimodo had been rational, would he have been able to enjoy the tender embraces of Esmeralda?

If Rand had been seriously interested in discovering the actual facts of human sexuality, she would have attempted to give precise, empirically substantiated answers to these questions. But, as usual with her, she had absolutely no interest in discovering the facts of the matter; she merely wished to indulge her own private sentiments.

*   *   *

(10) *Conclusion.* Before concluding, I simply wanted to mention some of the other virtues that Rand draws from that ever fecund principle, *man's life qua man.* She draws from it seven specific virtues, out of which arises a kind of Objectivist septalogue. Two of the virtues, *rationality* and *honesty*, we have already examined. The other five are: *independence, integrity, justice, productiveness* and *pride.* (1961, 156-161) The problem with these virtues is that they are all rather empty and vague: they fail to specify the precise conduct that is expected to result from following them. This enables the adept casuist to use them to justify just about anything under the sun. And indeed, this would appear to be precisely how Rand proceeded in her own personal life. She arbitrarily decided what her moral system meant in practical terms and then expected all the members of her inner circle to act accordingly.

Since her death in 1982, Objectivism has lost the moral anchor she provided for it. Her followers can now infer pretty much what they please from the Objectivist septalogue. This has given Objectivism greater flexibility in meeting the needs of its partisans. No longer do Objectivists feel obliged to conform to the procrustean example of Rand's personal life. Instead, they may interpret the Objectivist morality in light of their own unique moral sentiments.

In some ways, this is undoubtedly a positive development. During the heyday of the Objectivist movement, when Rand could intimidate her followers into conforming to her very exact notions of moral and even aesthetic behavior, complaints arose of the psychological harm done to Objectivists who simply could not live up to Rand's expectations. Human nature is not entirely homogeneous. What is right for one individual may be wrong for someone else. Not everyone is capable of finding happiness by following Rand's personal life to the letter. The emotional repression experienced by many former Objectivists during the sixties probably had its source in this unrealistic conformism. Now that Rand is dead and can no longer intimidate her followers into trying to be something they are not, the hazardous effects manifested by Objectivism are not so conspicuous. Since individuals are free to make of Objectivism what they please, any negative effects that they experience are the result, not of Objectivism, but of their interpretation of Objectivism. Of course, this applies to any positive effects that they might experience as well: they are also the result, not of Objectivism, but of an interpretation of Objectivism. This is the inevitable consequence of promulgating vague principles.

CHAPTER 6:

▼

THEORY OF POLITICS

"Historical evolution mocks all the prophylactic measures that have been adopted for the prevention of oligarchy. If laws are passed to control the dominion of the leaders, it is the laws which gradually weaken, and not the leaders."

—Robert Michels

"Politics, like ethics, is a normative branch of philosophy." No where is the basic problem of the Objectivist theory of politics more aptly expressed than in this statement by Leonard Peikoff. Peikoff is expressing the Objectivist view that political philosophy is primarily concerned, not with the basic *facts* of political conduct in the real world, but with how politics *ought* to be conducted. "Politics defines the principles of a proper social system, including the proper functions of government," Peikoff blithely insists.

"Politics is the application of ethics to social questions."
(Peikoff, 1991, 351)

It is precisely this ethical taint in the Objectivist politics that prevents Rand and her followers from being able to distinguish between political facts and their own wishful thinking. By turning politics into a "normative" branch of philosophy, they have merely subjected it to the whims and vagaries of their own private prejudices. Instead of seeking to connect fact with fact and trying to discover scientifically corroborated uniformities in political phenomenon, Objectivists seek to find rationalizations for their political ideals.

This mania for turning the study of politics into a mere rationalization of one's subjective preferences is not confined to Rand and her Objectivist cohorts. Outside of a handful of practical men who gain their understanding of political reality from first hand experience, knowledge of politics is almost everywhere distorted by an obsession with what *ought* to be at the expense of what actually *is*. Most of the books, articles, and editorials written on politics today are hardly worth the paper they are printed on. Over and over again we find contemporary experts on politics making assertions that are directly contradicted by the empirical facts. Too many commentators on politics assume the existence in the social and political order of simple causation in which the effect is completely dependent on a single cause when as a matter of fact what we find when we study politics scientifically is numerous factors existing in a relation of causal interdependence.

Another widespread error committed by our political pundits involves their unquestioned faith in the power of the ballot. How touching it is to hear them warble their conviction that, in a democracy, power resides in the people! Although this might be the way things are in some theoretical dreamland envisioned by philosophers suffering from a pathological inability to distinguish wishes from facts, in the real world things stand otherwise. "We find everywhere…that the power of the elected leaders over the electing masses is almost unlimited," wrote the political scientist Robert Michels. "That which *is* oppresses *that which ought to be*." (1915, 401) So it always has been and so, in all likelihood, will it continue to be.

As a result of the overwhelming influence of sentiment on political thinking, debates over politics tend to quickly degenerate into futile wrangling over contrary sentiments. This is no where more true than it is of the controversies surrounding Rand's political views. Most of Rand's detractors are motivated by nothing more than the desire to substitute their own moral prejudices for those of Rand. Nothing of any scientific value can be learned by such means. If criticism of Rand's philosophy is going to make us a jot wiser, it must deal, not with mere prejudices decked out in gaudy rhetoric, but with actual facts that can be corroborated by scientific observation. Any other approach would simply be a waste of time.

This being the case, I have endeavored in this chapter to avoid any concern with what *ought* to be, preoccupying myself entirely with the problem of what *is*. In fact, so determined am I to avoid any discussion of the "normative" side of politics, that I will begin my critique of Rand's theory of politics by conceding to her every normative claim about social, economic, and political relations. When Rand's philosophy declares that society *ought* to be subordinated to moral law; or that everyone *ought* to have the right to life, liberty, property, and the pursuit of happiness; or that individualism *ought* to prevail over collectivism; or that government *ought* to protect individual rights; or that laws *ought* to be objective; or that laissez-faire capitalism constitutes an "unknown ideal" that *ought* to prevail in every society: when Objectivism declares any of these things (or their equivalent thereof), I will not utter a single syllable of protest. I am willing to grant that all these things *ought* to be. What I want to do is find out whether any of these *oughts* are factually possible in a world governed, not by abstract concepts masquerading as material powers, but by flesh and blood men governed by passion, ambition, cunning and force. Would it be possible to construct a social order on the basis of Rand's principles? And if it were possible, what is the likelihood that such a society could preserve its structural integrity for any length of time?

I do not believe it would in fact be possible to construct a social order based on Rand's political ideals. They may very well be the finest political ideals ever promulgated in the history of mankind, but they remain unrealistic and impracticable for all that. It is plainly obvious that Rand knew close to nothing about the nature of practical politics. Most of her political knowledge was purely speculative and sentimental. She suffered from the delusion that political problems could be solved by manipulating conceptual constructions. Using such a method, it was very easy for her to attain whatever solution her heart desired. Unfortunately, such verbal solutions are worthless. They fail to tell us anything about actual realities existing in the world of fact. They reflect nothing but the state of mind of their authors.

In the first section of this chapter, I will briefly sketch Rand's theory of politics, suggesting here and there points of difficulty but otherwise refraining from rigorous criticism. Then I will proceed with an examination of the practical viability of her doctrine of individual rights, with special emphasis on the problem of how these rights are supposed to be enforced and protected. A critical scrutiny of Rand's advocacy of laissez-faire capitalism will follow, with the emphasis this time on the question of the *political* viability of that particular economic system. I will conclude by discussing the extent to which Rand's political ideals can in fact be realized and some of the obstacles that stand in their way.

*   *   *

(1) *The Objectivist Politics.* As I indicated at the start of this chapter, Objectivists believe that political theory is a mere logical extension of ethical theory. "The answers given by ethics determine how men should treat other men," declared Rand, "and this determines the fourth branch of philosophy: *politics*, which defines the principles of a proper social system." (1982, 4) The Objectivist politics, then, is merely an application of the Objectivist ethics to political and social problems. But here, at the very outset, we run into a serious difficulty. As we discovered in the previous chapter, the basic principles of Rand's theory of morality are so vague that you can deduce nearly anything you please from them. How, may we ask, can a theory of politics be extracted from principles so lacking in exactitude? Fortunately for Rand, she did not need to deduce a political theory from her principles of morality, because

she had already developed one on the basis of her sentiments. This theory can be described as one of the more
extreme variants of political individualism. Rand contended that men should be free to do whatever they
pleased provided they did not interfere with anyone else's
right to do likewise. According to Rand, the only way anyone's right to do as one pleases can be interfered with is
through physical coercion. "A right cannot be violated
except by physical force," Rand declared. "One man cannot deprive another of his life nor enslave him, nor forbid
him to pursue his happiness [i.e., to do as he pleases],
except by using force against him. Whenever a man is
made to act without his own free, personal, individual,
voluntary consent—his right has been violated.

"Therefore, we can draw a clear-cut division between
the rights of one man and those of another. It is an *objective* division—not subject to differences of opinion, nor to
majority decision, nor to arbitrary decree of society. *No
man has the right to initiate the use of physical force against
another man.*" (Binswanger, 1986, 214)

Whether Rand's principle really is as clear-cut and
objective as she here supposes we will examine later in this
section. Suffice it for now to say that there exists absolutely
no evidence to support Rand's contention that her principle is "not subject to differences of opinion." It most certainly is subject to differences of opinion—differences,
moreover, which are nearly always settled in favor of those
with greater strength, shrewdness, and persistence.

Rand's conviction that no one has the right to initiate
force against others led her to develop her doctrine of
individual rights. The source of these rights, she declared,
"is not divine law nor congressional law, but the law of

identity. A is A—and Man is Man. *Rights* are conditions of existence required by man's nature for his proper survival. If man is to live on earth, it is *right* for him to use his mind, it is *right* to act on his own free judgment, it is *right* to work for his values and to keep the product of his work. If life on earth is his purpose, he has a *right* to live as a rational being: nature forbids him the irrational. Any group, any gang, any nation that attempts to negate man's rights, is *wrong*, which means: is evil, which means: is anti-life." (1961, 229)

This argument contains all of Rand's usual verbal tricks, including the use of that oft-repeated mantra of hers, "A is A," which is simply her way of asserting that what she says is true. If we ignore this empty rhetoric, her argument simply comes down to the claim that, in order for men to be rational, they have to be left free from physical coercion; otherwise, they will not be able to use their minds as they see fit and this will cause them to be irrational, which, as we know from Rand's theory of morality, is supposed to be evil and anti-life.

It is through this linkage of freedom with rationality that Rand harmonizes her ethical and her political principles. As we know, Rand considered politics to be an application of morality to questions of social relations. Politics, she believed, ought to be subordinated to moral law. But what exactly does it mean to subordinate politics to moral law? Some might interpret it as meaning that the state should be used to *enforce* moral law. Such an interpretation, though perfectly logical, would have deeply offended Rand, who believed very sincerely in freedom, even if it meant the freedom to be immoral. And so despite her conviction that politics should be subordinated to moral law, she refused to advocate forcing anyone to be virtuous. To justify this position, she assumed that force was incompatible with man's highest virtue, his rationality. "A rational mind does not work under compulsion," she argued. (1967,164) "To interpose the threat of physical destruction between a man and his perception of reality, is to negate and paralyze his means of survival [i.e., his rationality]; to force him to act against his own judgment, is like forcing him to act against his own sight.... To force a man to drop his own mind and to accept your will as a substitute, with terror in place of proof and death as the final argument—is to attempt to exist in defiance of reality." (1961, 164)

Once Rand had established, to her own satisfaction, the necessity of barring physical force from human relationships, she could turn her attention to the "proper" role of government. "If physical force is to be barred from social relationships, men need an institution charged with the task of protecting their rights under an *objective* code of rules," she averred. "*This* is the task of government—of a *proper* government—its basic task; its only moral justification and the reason why men do need a government." (1964b, 109)

According to Objectivism, the only economic system compatible with such a government is *laissez-faire capitalism*, which Rand defines as "a social system based on the recognition of individual rights, including property rights, in which all property is privately owned." (1967, 19) In practical terms, this means a "full, pure, uncontrolled, unregulated" free market, unencumbered by any sort of state intervention whatsoever. When Rand says that the government's only proper role is to bar physical force from

human relationships, she means it. Entrepreneurs, speculators, businessmen, and lawyers should be left free to pursue their various economic objectives in any manner they
see fit, *provided they refrain from initiating physical force
against other people.* No matter how rude they treat others;
no matter how stingy or cold-hearted they become; no
matter how many people are starving while they bask
amidst piles of lucre: as long as they do not use physical
force against anybody, they may do as they please.

An obvious objection to this scheme of things is that it
would apparently leave unscrupulous persons free to
engage in blatant fraud. Not so, insisted Rand. Fraud, she
claimed, is merely "an indirect use of force." (1964b, 111)
And since Rand's system of political economy does not
tolerate the use of force, direct or otherwise, it would not
allow for fraud, either.

A more serious objection to this system of political
economy involves a problem I have already mentioned on
a number of occasions—namely, the problem of
vagueness. The entire notion of barring physical force
from human relationships is not terribly definite. It is not
always clear how such a principle is to be translated in
every concrete instance in which it would apply. What
would it mean, for example, in relation to corporate law?
Is the principle of limited liability compatible with laissez-
faire? Equally amorphous is the notion of fraud. How are
we expected to define the parameters of fraud? Is insider-
trading fraudulent? What about those unscrupulous but
immensely cunning speculators who use various ingenious
tricks to manipulate the market and create immense
profits for themselves at the expense of other stockholders?
Are we to regard such "underhand" manipulations as

fraudulent? What about the bank manager who loses the bank's assets in unwise speculations? Should the state step in and prosecute him for his negligence? Or should the matter be settled, if at all, in the civil courts?

Questions like these—and there are literally hundreds, if not thousands, of them—cannot be definitely answered on the basis of Rand's principle of barring force from human relationships. The complexity of human relationships does not allow for such reductivism. Nor has Rand helped matters much by her arbitrary introduction of the notion of indirect force, which is even more vague and impractical as a standard of political economy. If fraud can qualify as indirect force, what else might not qualify as well? What about the factory owner who uses his superior economic knowledge to trick ignorant workers into accepting wages below the market value? Isn't he guilty of using indirect force? Certainly, he is guilty of taking advantage of his workers' ignorance. Why, then, should manipulations such as this, which are much more common than is supposed by advocates of unregulated capitalism, not be considered as a form of indirect force?

Perhaps the most noteworthy aspect of Rand's advocacy of laissez-faire capitalism is her insistence that capitalism is the only moral system. (1967, 20ff.) It is for moral reasons, she insisted, not for economic ones, that capitalism must be defended. "No social system (and no human activity of any kind) can survive without a moral base," she claimed. The moral base of capitalism, Rand declared, is her own morality of rational self-interest. Capitalism can succeed on no other moral base. Especially antithetic to capitalism is the morality of altruism. "On the basis of the altruistic morality," wrote Rand, "capitalism had to be—and was—damned from the start." (1967, 30)

Although I am conceding to Rand, for argument's sake, every moral claim she has made on behalf of capitalism, I feel obliged to reiterate what I have said before about her conviction that political and economic institutions are a product of theoretical ethics. There is very little, if any, evidence to suggest that ethical theory plays a significant role in the formation of political and economic institutions. Since such institutions are rarely the product of deliberate rational foresight and design, they can hardly be regarded as the product of a theory of morality.

*   *   *

(2) *The practical viability of individual rights.* It is one thing to argue for a theory of rights; it is something else altogether to bring this theory to practical fruition. Politics, as it is conducted in the real world by actual politicians, is not primarily governed on the basis of moral, political, or philosophical principles. Those who make the important decisions in politics could care less about some purely abstract theory of rights. What most men in politics are concerned about is maintaining their position within the ruling elite. If this desideratum can only be accomplished by violating somebody's rights, then somebody is going to have his rights violated, and that's all there is to it. Anyone who thinks that such a violation can be prevented by philosophical argumentation is living in a fool's paradise.

Pareto's truculent realism provides a refreshing contrast to the usual political twaddle presented by soft-headed idealists like Rand and her followers. "So as between the various social classes no principle of 'right' can be found to regulate the division of social advantage," Pareto shrewdly explains. "The classes that have the greater strength, intelligence, shrewdness, take the lion's share. It is not clear how any other principles of division could be logically established and even less clear how once they were established logically they could be enforced or applied in the concrete. Every individual certainly has his own principle of division that would seem ideal to him. But such a principle is nothing more than an expression of his individual sentiments and interests which he comes to conceive as 'right.'" (1916, §1509)

Pareto here hits the nail so firmly on the head that it would be difficult to improve upon his analysis. Let us merely amplify some of the points he makes, supplementing our discussion here and there with corroborative evidence.

Pareto begins by assuming that the problem of rights involves the issue of dividing social advantage between the classes. Objectivists would reject this approach from the outset. In their view, rights are purely moral concepts: they deal, not with the regulation of social advantage, but with the moral requirements of man's life. According to Objectivism, only a collectivist social order which fails to observe individual rights needs to worry about the regulation of social advantage. That issue never arises in a free society, because in a free society there are no social classes benefiting from special advantages which require regulation.

This view of the matter, however, does not accord with the facts. All societies, whether "free" or not, have social classes, some of which gain more from the prevailing social order than others. In a free society, those who are adept at using their wits tend to gain more from freedom than those whose talents lie elsewhere. In other words, the social advantage of freedom is greater for people who are intelligent than for people who are not intelligent. Now while it may be true, as Rand would argue, that the unintelligent still end up gaining more from living in a free society than they would from living in a state of despotism, this hardly matters. As long as the benefit of living in a free society is greater for the intelligent than it is for the less intelligent, there will exist resentment and conflict between the two groups. This is a fact that must be recognized by anybody who wants to understand the nature of human society.

Following his remark about the futility of discovering a principle of right to regulate the social advantage, Pareto notes how the classes with "the greater strength, intelligence, ability, shrewdness" end up taking the lion's share, regardless of considerations of principle. This may strike some as a rather cynical way of looking at the matter. However, I must point out that what is at issue is not whether Pareto's position is cynical, but whether it is true. A view may be as cynical as you please, but if it accords with reality it has to be accepted. It is my contention that Pareto's view accords with the facts of reality, as I will seek to prove over the course of this chapter.

Pareto's next statement is even more revealing. "It is not clear how any other principles of division could be logically established," he argues, "and even less clear how once they were established logically they could be enforced and applied in the concrete." This, in a nutshell, constitutes my entire argument against Rand's theory of rights. I seriously doubt whether her theory of rights can be established logically; yet even if this were possible, it would still leave open the question of how the theory could ever be implemented in practice. Rand concerned herself almost exclusively with the logical problem of rights, for the most part ignoring the practical problem or merely touching upon it with a casual remark here or there. She apparently assumed that if she could just provide a logical solution to the problem of rights, the practical implementation would follow as a matter of course. This assumption, which Rand rationalized in her theory of history, is extremely dubious. It amounts to believing that social conditions can be changed through philosophical argumentation.

If only it were that simple! If only our social problems could be solved merely by proving the validity of the "right" philosophical ideas, just think how easy it would be to save the world! "To save the world is the simplest thing in the world," we find Leonard Peikoff declaring at the end of his treatise on Objectivism. "All one has to do is think." (1991, 460) But if the solution to the problem of saving the world is so simple, why hadn't anyone thought of it before?

It should be obvious that Rand and her followers have little, if any, notion of how many real-life obstacles stand in the way of the implementation of their theory. In the first place, it is entirely gratuitous to assume that you can persuade more than a handful of people to accept a theory on logical grounds alone. Human beings are motivated, not by logic, but by desire and sentiment. If a given theory of rights conflicts with an individual's desires and sentiments, no amount of logical argumentation will ever persuade him to accept the theory in question.

History consists of one long and uninterrupted testimony to this fact. Everywhere in history we find individuals governed either by sentiments (e.g. sentiments of religion, nationalism, humanitarianism, etc.) or by desires (e.g., economic interests, political ambition, vanity, sex drives, etc.). Whenever there exists a conflict between an individual's abstract convictions and his sentiments and desires, it is always the sentiments and desires that win out. This is plainly seen in the effect that Christianity had on the feudal barons of the Middle Ages. Nearly everybody in that era, including the feudal barons, believed speculatively in the doctrines of Christianity, including the doctrines of chastity and non-resistance. If the feudal barons had been at all concerned with logic, they would have given up their violent mode of life and become pacifist monks living in the manner of the lilies of the field. This, of course, is not the path they took. Instead, they simply ignored the contradiction and went about their business believing one way and acting another. In the twelfth century, the uncouth feudal barons of Northern France were encouraged by the Pope to invade the rich and blossoming lands of Southern France in order to stamp out the Albigensian heresy. What started out as a religious crusade soon became an exercise in rape, conquest, cruelty and plunder. Examples of this sort of behavior are quite common among partisans of many other religions and ideologies besides Christianity. It is especially common among individuals in the ruling class. Nor should it be surprising that this is so. After all, few people become part of the ruling class by strictly adhering to religious or ideological principles. Power and morality do not mix well. Those who wish to dominate their fellow human beings cannot afford to have too many moral scruples, because if they do, they will simply find themselves under the thumb of someone less scrupulous than themselves.

This has been proven again and again throughout human history. Only under very exceptional circumstances do the "best," morally speaking, make it to the top. Most political leaders throughout human history have either been corrupt and dishonest or bloody and cruel. In order to succeed in politics, you have to be at least one or the other. A politician who is neither corrupt and dishonest nor bloody and cruel would be at a severe disadvantage against any rival who excelled in these vices. A politician, if he is to survive in the competition for political power, must be willing to avail himself of all the means necessary to maintain power, including those that are commonly regarded as immoral; because if he is not willing to avail himself of these immoral means, he will be at a disadvantage against those who are willing. A moral conscience is a luxury that few political leaders can afford.

Now just because morality has little to do with politics doesn't mean that all political leaders are unadulterated criminals who are incapable of decency. There are many politicians who sincerely try to do as much good as they can and who, in private life, are very upstanding citizens. However, when they are put in the position where they *have* to do something underhanded merely to maintain their status within the ruling elite, politicians rarely allow moral scruples to get in their way. There is something else to keep in mind here as well. There exists no such thing as a disinterested politician. Politicians, like everybody else, have economic and political interests that they are eager to cultivate. Since their position within the ruling elite makes it much easier for them to look after their interests than it would be if they were part of the subject class, there may exist quite a few politicians who entered politics for purely "selfish" reasons. But even those politicians who have entered politics for purely idealistic reasons will generally, over time, be corrupted by the economic advantages which their position in the ruling elite brings them. As they and their families become accustomed to living well they soon find themselves loath to give up these advantages, and this puts them at the mercy of anyone who can take away their privileges, whether by fair means or foul.

The bearing of all this on the problem of rights should be fairly obvious. Rights cannot be implemented simply by persuasion alone. Even Rand acknowledged the need of an institution capable of implementing and enforcing rights. Rights can only be implemented by providing protection against force. "If a society provided no organized protection against force," wrote Rand, "it would compel every citizen to go about armed, to turn his home into a fortress, to shoot any stranger approaching his door—or to join a protective gang of citizens who would fight other gangs, formed for the same purpose, and thus bring about the degeneration of that society into the chaos of gang rule, i.e., rule by brute force, into the perpetual tribal warfare of prehistorical savages." (1964b, 108)

In order for society to provide the organized protection necessary to protect individual rights, it must set up a government expressly designed for this purpose. It is to government, then, that Rand looks for the solution to the problem of rights.

But what makes Rand think that such a government is even possible? Here again we find Rand guilty of ignoring the concrete realities of the situation. Governments are run, not by philosophical principles or moral laws, but by men motivated by sentiment and desire. In order to have a government that devotes itself exclusively to barring force from human relationships, you must have political leaders exclusively devoted to this end. Now given what we know about the nature of political power and its influence on those who pursue it, what reason do we have to believe that there will ever exist a group of political leaders exclusively concerned with using their political power for upholding individual rights? What could such individuals possibly gain from being part of a government of this description?

Rand spent ever so much rhetoric defending the egoistic motivations of businessmen. But what about the egoistic motivations of government officials? Rand never seems to have given much thought about what egoism means in the context of government. Her theory of government, if examined closely, provides very little opportunity for government officials to exercise their moral obligation to be selfish. Rand even went so far as to argue that a "proper" government would not even be allowed to collect involuntary taxes. It would have to depend on charity, lotteries, and *voluntary* user fees for the enforcement of contracts. (1967b, ch. 15) But if this is so, government officials would likely find themselves in a very precarious position. Underpaid, insecure, despised, they would be held in contempt by everyone in the community. Why would any egoist want to be a part of such a government?

If a government of this description were in fact possible, it is likely that its existence would prove extremely precarious. Most intelligent and capable individuals prefer to enter the most remunerative fields of endeavor which society has to offer. In an Objectivist society, this would mean big business. Government would be left to the incompetent and the mediocre. The results of such a situation are easy to predict: either an internal revolution led by men who abhor any theory of politics which weakens the government to the point of emasculation—or a foreign invasion by nations eager to plunder the immense wealth produced by Rand's capitalist economy.

Another serious threat to a government operated by Objectivist principles would be corruption by big business. Many corporations in an unregulated Objectivist economy would have an enormous amount of money at their disposal to use to bribe impecunious government officials into giving them special treatment. Sooner or later, some business interest or another would offer a bribe and somebody in government would accept it. Once, however, one business interest had gained through bribery, other interests would be forced to engage in bribery simply to keep up with the competition. Once this whole process is set in motion, it would not take long for the government to become completely corrupted by big business interests eager to take advantage of government favors. Government on the basis of Objectivist principles would soon give way to government on the basis of plutocratic principles.

Rand attempts to meet this threat to her system of government by insisting on the importance of constitutional checks and balances and on objectively valid legal principles prescribing what is permitted to governmental officials. "This is the means of subordinating 'might' to 'right,'" she tells us. "This is the American concept of 'a government of laws and not of men.'" (1964b, 110) Whether it is an American concept or not, the phrase *a government of laws and not of men* is hardly an American reality. It is hardly a reality anywhere in the world. (Pareto, 1916, §466) All governments are and must be of men. All attempts to prevent government misconduct through constitutional prohibitions will always be doomed to eventual failure. Sooner or later, government officials will find a way of circumventing constitutional law. There is no constitutional government on record where this has not happened. Constitutions, like treaties between foreign governments, are mere pieces of paper. They have no binding force of their own. They depend for the viability on those men whose responsibility is to observe and uphold them. As soon as it ceases to be in their political interest to observe the legal prohibitions of the constitution, governing elites cease to observe them. Constitutional checks and balances may prevent these elites from immediately undermining the constitution, but it will not stop them forever. American constitutional history demonstrates this in spades.

Defenders of constitutional government always blame the degeneracy of constitutional law on legal flaws in the constitution itself. Rand, for example, speaks of "certain contradictions in the Constitution [which left] a loophole for the growth of statism." (1964b, 114) But to believe that constitutional law in America was undermined through loopholes is to demonstrate an astonishing ignorance of American history. The American Constitution was not undermined because of loopholes. It was undermined because America's plutocratic ruling elite found it less and less convenient to observe its strictures as time went on. Had there been no loopholes the result would have been the same. Loopholes are not required to circumvent constitutional law. Adept jurists can always think up rationalizations for evading this or that constitutional precept. Since the precepts themselves are none too exact, they can easily be interpreted to mean whatever those in power wish them to mean. And this is precisely what has happened in American constitutional history. (Nock, 1935, 95) Supreme Court justices have never been at a loss to justify their particular interpretations of constitutional law.

Rand's failure to understand why her theory of rights is not realistic stems from her moralistic approach to politics. She was so wrapped up in proving what *ought* to be that she wound up blinding herself to what *is*. This led her to adopt premises that have little, if any, relation to reality. One such premise is her conviction that "there are no conflicts of interest among rational men" in a free society. (1964b, 50, 56) Rand adopted this premise in order to assure everyone that her morality of rational selfishness could never be a threat to anyone's rational interests. As long as we all agree to be rational, every last man of us can be selfish without anyone getting hurt. In making this assumption, I fear Rand bit off more than she could chew. To begin with, there is the problem of defining precisely what constitutes a "rational" man. How is a rational man supposed to be distinguished from an irrational man? Rand provides what is, at best, only an abstract—and, therefore, intolerably vague—solution to the problem. It turns out, on closer inspection, that the term *rational man* is any man whose interests Rand approved of, while a non-rational or irrational man is any man whose interests Rand did not approve of.

This purely subjective solution to the problem of defining a rational man is not the only thing wrong with Rand's premise that there exist no conflicts among rational men. There is another problem that Rand, in her eagerness to rationalize her subjective preferences, did not even notice. This problem could be described as *the heterogeneity of human nature.* No two human beings are exactly alike in character and disposition. Some are different in many important respects. This being the case, it appears very likely that the interests of men, whether "rational" or not, will, at some point in time, conflict. If Peter's nature (or character, if you prefer) fails to coincide in all respects with Paul's, there will always be a chance that at some point in time their interests will conflict. To claim that no conflict will arise as long as both Peter and Paul remain "rational" is entirely gratuitous, because such a claim assumes that it is not rational for Peter and Paul to have different natures. Yet this is absurd. How can they help but have the nature they are born with? An individual has no choice but to be what he is. Certainly, you cannot expect him to be *other* than he is.

This point can best be illustrated by a concrete example. There have existed throughout human history certain individuals who have thrived on using force to satisfy their needs. This was true of the individuals who made up the ruling elites of Sparta, Macedonia, the early and middle periods of the Roman Republic and the feudal barons of the Middle Ages. It is also true of the professional mercenaries—the so-called *condottieri*—of Renaissance Italy. One of the characteristics very common among individuals skilled at using force is that they are rarely skilled at using their wits. As long as the battle is one of strength and force, such individuals have a very good chance of prevailing. But if it is a battle of wits and cunning, such individuals will usually find themselves at a disadvantage. Historically, nations governed by ruling classes dominated by individuals adept at using force tend to be culturally and economically backward. The classic example of this is Sparta, which was legendary for its courage and perseverance in battle but despised for its lack of culture.

The precise opposite is true of those individuals in history who have thrived on intelligence and cunning. Such individuals are usually not as skilled in the use of force as they are in the use of their wits. The most prominent historical illustration of this is Periclean and post-Periclean Athens. This famous city-state had a very high concentration among its citizenry of individuals adept at using their wits but not very adept at using force. As a result of this state of affairs, Athens, even while developing one of the richest literary and intellectual cultures on record, could not defend itself from its foreign enemies, succumbing in turn to Sparta, Macedonia, and Rome. Individuals who thrive on using intelligence and cunning to satisfy their interests are perfectly fine as long as they are left free to exercise their intelligence; but as soon as they are called upon to defend themselves with force, they find themselves at a disadvantage. This was true not only of Athens, but also of Carthage, twelfth century Provence, Renaissance Italy, and France of the Second Empire, all of whom were conquered by nations governed by ruling elites well stocked with individuals adept at using force.

Now let us suppose that Peter is adept at using force but not so adept at using his wits, while Paul is adept at using his wits but not so adept at using force. Given these parameters, it is impossible that the interests of these individuals should not in some respects conflict. It is in Peter's interest to live in a society that rewards individuals adept at using force, while it is in Paul's interest to live in a society that rewards individuals adept at using their wits. Peter would be better off living under a military oligarchy eager to make use of his talents, while Paul would be better off living under a system of democratic capitalism where he would be free to prosper by the use of his wits.

Rand's conviction that there are no conflicts of interest among rational men enables her to dismiss Peter's interest in living under a military oligarchy as "irrational." But in doing so she merely expresses her own personal preference for the kind of society most in harmony with the interests of Paul. It still remains unclear why Peter's preference for living in a society which rewards those who are adept at the use of force should be considered irrational. No doubt Rand would have argued that it is irrational to want to thrive on the basis of one's talent for using force, because force is antithetical to human survival. (1967, 17) However, there is some question whether this is really true. Obviously, not everyone could live on the basis of force, but that is not what the advocates of force desire. They prefer that the use of force be restricted to a small ruling elite which would govern over a large class of people living on the sweat of their brow. To assume, as Rand does, that such a social arrangement could not possibly work because "force is the antonym and negation of thought" is to assume what is palpably not true. The Spartan oligarchy used force to maintain its dominance over the subject class for over five centuries. (Pareto, 1916, §2490) Rome likewise flourished on the basis of force for many centuries, and only collapsed when it stopped being good at using force and could no longer defend itself. The fact of the matter is, force is not anywhere as irrational or impracticable as Rand supposes. It has been an effective instrument of domination and plunder throughout all of human history. Only an individual whose understanding had been debauched by wishful thinking could believe otherwise.

These remarks should not be construed as a moral defense of the use of force, but merely as a description of the way things actually are. As I have already indicated, I am perfectly willing to concede that force *ought* to be barred from human relationships. The question remains, however, whether force can in fact be barred from human relationships. And to that question only a negative answer seems warranted.

           *   *   *

(2) *Class-circulation.* In analyzing the practicability of any political ideal, it is important to examine how the implementation of that ideal will effect class-circulation. Every society tends to reward certain types of individuals at the expense of others. A militaristic society, for example, tends to reward men of strength, discipline, and courage at the expense of intelligent men who are deficient in these

qualities. The process by which certain types of men rise to the top of a society while others sink towards the bottom is called *the circulation of elites*, or *class-circulation*. It is a greatly under-appreciated factor in the evolution of societies. The character of a society's ruling elite is determined by class-circulation—that is, by the type of individuals which various social mechanisms promote into the ruling elite. When these social mechanisms fail to promote individuals endowed with the qualities necessary to defend the social order from its enemies, foreign or domestic, the social order is put into grave danger. Any system of society, therefore, which, through the process of class-circulation, allows its ruling elite to be taken over by individuals incapable of defending the social order will find itself in imminent peril of dissolution.

Let us suppose it were possible to construct a social order in which Rand's ideal of barring physical force from human relationships holds sway. What effect would barring physical force from social relations have on class-circulation?

The most obvious effect would be on those individuals adept at the use of force but not so adept at using their wits. Such individuals would not likely achieve as much social status in a society governed by Rand's political ideals as they would in a militaristic or feudal society which would allow them to profit by their skill at physical coercion. In fact, they would probably find themselves occupying a relatively low position on the societal totem poll. Meanwhile, individuals adept at using their wits in speculation or in entrepreneurship would be making piles of money and enjoying preeminent positions within the social elite. It does not take a great deal of insight into the nature of human psychology to realize that this would create a highly unstable and potentially catastrophic situation. On the one hand, you would have an enormously wealthy social elite dominated by individuals adept at using their wits but not very adept at using force. On the other hand, you would have a veritable underclass made up of those individuals who are extremely adept at using force but not so adept at using their wits. How do you suppose these individuals adept at using force will view their predicament? Obviously, they will be resentful about it. At least some of them will regard their comparatively lower position in society as unjust. Why should all the status and honor of society go to men who are adept at using their wits—men who, in other words, are (from the viewpoint of the man of force) mere clever swindlers, lacking all the manly virtues of courage, strength, and fortitude? It is only a matter of time before the men of force will get fed up with always having to settle for an inferior position in the pecking order and will start flexing their muscles. Inevitably, a conflict will arise in society between those individuals who are adept at using their wits and those individuals adept at using force.

No one has analyzed this conflict between intelligence and force better than Pareto: "Suppose a certain country has a governing class, *A*, that assimilates the best elements, as regards intelligence, of the whole population. In that case the subject class, *B*, is largely stripped of such elements and can have little or no hope of ever overcoming the class *A* as long as it is a battle of wits. If intelligence were to be combined with force, the dominion of the *A*'s would be perpetual....But such a happy combination occurs only for a few individuals. In the majority of cases

people who rely on their wits become less fitted to use violence, and *vice versa*. So concentration in the class *A* of the
individuals most adept at chicanery leads to concentration
in the class *B* of the individuals most adept at violence;
and if that process is long continued, the [social order]
tends to become unstable, because the *A*'s are long in cunning but short in the courage to use force and in the force
itself; whereas the *B*'s have the force and the courage to use
it, but are short in the skill required for exploiting these
advantages. But if they chance to find leaders who have
the skill—and history shows that such leadership is usually
supplied by dissatisfied *A*'s—they will have all they need
for driving the *A*'s out of power. Of just that development
history affords countless examples from remotest times all
the way down to the present." (1916, §2190)

The type of social order advocated by Rand would be
extremely vulnerable to the process described above. But
as a result of Rand's ignorance and naiveté about the
nature of man and society, she was not even aware of this
threat to her political ideals. She assumed that in a free,
non-coercive society, everyone would be so much better
off, economically, that you would not have to worry about
anyone trying to destroy the existing social arrangement.
The trouble is, even if everyone were better off economically, there would still exist individuals dissatisfied for
other reasons. After all, it is not as if human beings are
concerned solely with their economic well-being. Some
are also preoccupied with social status. And since no society can promise everyone a place in the social elite, there
will always exist a number of individuals who will believe,
rightly or wrongly, that they haven't been given their just
due. In the type of society Rand advocates, the people

most likely to be shut out of the elite are precisely those who are most adept at using force. Had these men of force lived in a militarist society, they would have enjoyed a much higher social status than they would under Rand's system of laissez-faire. True, they might have been poorer under a militaristic regime, and maybe they would not have lived as long, but men adept at using force do not normally give such considerations much weight. In their minds, only weaklings and cowards care about wealth and personal longevity. To the man of force, a "glorious" death on a battlefield is much more preferable to a humiliating death in old age.

Rand's inability to understand the violent man's point of view renders her oblivious to the threat he poses to her political ideals. She would like to conjure him away by accusing him of irrationality. But the man of force cannot be disposed of so easily. Rand's political theory of rights is impracticable in large part because it fails to explain how a social order dominated by men adept at using their wits but short in the courage to defend their wealth and power is expected to keep in check those elements in society which, although not terribly skilled in the arts of cunning, are ready and eager to use force.

*   *   *

(3) *Capitalism.* The greatest obstacle confronting the critic of Rand's economic views is the complete lack of empirical evidence from which to draw conclusions one way or the other. As Rand herself has admitted, the brand of capitalism she advocates—so-called "laissez-faire" capitalism—has never existed. (1967, 48) One of the advan-

tages of advocating an economic system that has never existed is that you can make nearly any claim you please about it without ever running the risk of being refuted on empirical grounds. This advantage comes, however, with the corresponding defect of not being able to corroborate any of your claims with factual evidence. The best you can do in regards to a system that has never existed is to isolate certain factors of the system in question and examine how these would interact with each other under simplified circumstances approximating real conditions. This is what theoretical economics attempts to do—with moderate though not complete success. I have also availed myself of this method on several occasions throughout this book— most recently, in my discussion of the effects of Rand's principle of individual rights on class-circulation. In this section, I will have no choice but to make use of it once again.

Central to Rand's defense of laissez-faire capitalism is her insistence that capitalism is the only "moral" system. Since I have already made clear that I will concede to Rand all her moral claims, I will not question Rand's ethical defense of laissez-faire. Nor will I question the purely economic claims made on behalf of this system. I am perfectly willing to concede that laissez-faire capitalism is the most efficient of all economic systems, despite the complete lack of empirical corroboration for this view and the existence of plausible arguments showing that, at least under special circumstances, a moderate amount of government intervention may actually increase economic production. (Pareto, 1916, §2208-2218, 2316) My argument, instead, will focus on the question of the practical viability of laissez-faire capitalism judged from a *political*, rather than from a moral or economic point of view. Objectivists assume that all you have to do in order to demonstrate the practical viability of laissez-faire is to prove that capitalism is morally and economically superior to all other systems of political economy. But they have completely forgotten the problem of capitalism's *political viability*. Given the nature of political reality as it is revealed to us by history, is there even the remotest chance that any government will *ever* allow a system of complete and unadulterated laissez-faire capitalism to prevail? I don't believe there is. Laissez-faire capitalism may be the most moral and most efficient economic system ever; but this does not mean those in power will consider the implementation of such a system to be in their interest. If history can be our guide in such matters, the ruling elite will always tend to favor having at least some degree of state interventionism in the economy. The very fact that laissez-faire capitalism has never existed tends to corroborate this view of the matter. If it has never existed in the past, what are the chances that it will ever exist in the future?

If we go a little further into the question and ask ourselves *why* laissez-faire capitalism has never existed, we can get a much better grasp of the immense political and social obstacles standing in the way of the implementation of such a system. I have stated that some degree of government interventionism will *always* be in the interest of the ruling elite. Why is this so? If laissez-faire is really the most efficient economic system, wouldn't it be in the interest of the ruling elite to prefer such a system?

In order to answer this question, we have to examine a little more closely the nature of ruling elites. Nearly all ruling elites enjoy various economic advantages due to their superior status in society. Whether they are aristocratic warriors, theocratic priests, princes of commerce, cunning plutocrats or demagogic politicians, they have always used their power as members of the ruling elite to feather their own nests. This is true even under conditions of widespread economic freedom. Wherever men are left free to pursue their economic interests, wealth tends to concentrate into the hands of a select few, who can then proceed to use this wealth to corrupt government officials and turn the state into their own private plaything. This sort of thing is so common in history that there is hardly any need to emphasize it. Even Shakespeare complains of it in some memorable lines from *Hamlet*:

> In the corrupted currents of this world,
> Offence's gilded hand may shove by justice;
> And oft 'tis seen the wicked prize itself
> Buys out the law.

That is precisely what takes place: the law is literally bought out, as if it were a commodity on the open market. Hence arises the phenomenon of plutocracy.

Economic freedom almost inevitably leads to rule by plutocracy. The most unscrupulous, cunning, and brilliantly manipulative entrepreneurs and speculators will always take the lion's share of the profits, some of which they will use to corrupt judges, legislators, and other government officials. This is what occurred in America during the Nineteenth Century. At the beginning of the century, American businessmen enjoyed a high degree of economic freedom. From the start, the most successful of them nearly always turned to government in the hope of thereby securing themselves some kind of advantage over their competitors. Cornelius Vanderbilt, for example, during his days as a steamboat magnate, used to bribe New York Common Council officials into denying dock privileges to his competitors. (Myers, 1909, 279) Later, he blackmailed his competitors into paying him as much $480,000 a year for agreeing not to compete with him in certain geographical areas. (Myers, 1909, 287) During the Civil War, Vanderbilt charted or sold to the government ships for troop transport that were in appalling condition. "Despite his knowing that only vessels adapted for ocean service were needed, Vanderbilt chartered craft that had hitherto been almost entirely used in navigating inland waters," we are told. "Not a single precaution was taken by him or his associates to safeguard the lives of the soldiers." (Myers, 1909, 296)

I have chosen Vanderbilt as an example because he is one of the nineteenth century plutocrats defended by Rand in her essay "Notes on the History of American Free Enterprise." (1967) Rand confines her discussion to Vanderbilt's struggle with the New York City Council and the New York State Legislature, claiming that Vanderbilt had to bribe members of these two political bodies in order "to buy the removal of some artificial restriction." While this may be true in regards to that issue, it does not appear to be true in regards to all of Vanderbilt's dealings with the government. On other occasions, Vanderbilt did not scruple to use the government to gain an unfair advantage over his competitors; nor did he scruple to defraud the government during wartime.

One of Rand's most tenaciously held assumptions is her belief that most businessmen just want to be left free to compete on the open market. In her view, it is not the titans of industry, but government, spurned on by power-hungry intellectuals, that has done the most to sabotage capitalism. Businessmen, she would have us believe, are not the perpetrators of government intervention, but its victim. Using railroad builders as an example, Rand claims that "those who started out with private funds...did not bribe legislators to throttle competitors nor to obtain any kind of special legal advantage or privilege. They made their fortunes by their own personal ability—and if they resorted to bribery at all...it was only to buy the removal of some artificial restriction....They did not pay to *get* something from the legislature, but only to get the legislature out of their way. But the builders who started out with government help...were the ones who used the government for special advantages and owed their fortunes to legislation more than to personal ability. This is the inevitable result of any kind or degree of mixed economy [i.e. government interventionism]. It is only with the help of government regulations that a man of lesser ability can destroy his better competitors—*and he is the only type of man who runs to the government for economic help.*" (1967, 108, emphasis added)

There is no evidence to suggest that only men of lesser ability run to the government for help. Historically, almost all the major industrialists and businessmen, regardless of their entrepreneurial expertise, tried to get the government to help them in some way or another. It is simply good business to do so. The astute businessman uses every means possible to make an extra buck. He will try to profit both from his entrepreneurial genius and from his skill at manipulating government officials.

There is some question whether American industrial development would have been quite as rapid if it had not been for the fact that its industrialists used political means to raise capital. The subsidies, the land grants, the credit manipulations, the unpunished fraud, and the onerous tariffs from which the industrialists of nineteenth century America profited enabled them to raise the capital necessary to fund their economic endeavors. In the absence of this capital, industrial development in the United States would have been stymied, and the American people would have been deprived of most of the comforts and even necessities of modern life.

Rand believed it would be possible to prevent businessmen from using the government to gain an advantage in the market by merely forbidding the state from having any involvement in the economy whatsoever: "It is not a matter of accidental personalities, of 'dishonest businessmen' or 'dishonest legislators' [which has caused the abuses of government intervention on behalf of business]. The dishonesty is inherent in and created by the system [of government intervention]. So long as a government holds the power of economic control, it will necessarily create a special 'elite,' an 'aristocracy of pull,' it will attract the corrupt type of politician into the legislature, it will work to the advantage of the dishonest businessman, and will penalize, and, eventually, destroy the honest and the able." (1967, 108)

In other words, it is the government's capacity to intervene in the economy that leads to all the abuses associated with plutocratic capitalism. If you could forbid the government from interfering in the economy, then all the corruption would stop. However, this view of the matter misses the main point. I am perfectly willing to concede to Rand that it is only government intervention that makes economic corruption possible. Where I differ from her is in regards to whether it is possible to do away with government intervention. I do not think it is possible. I believe that wealthy businessmen will always seek to use government to gain an advantage over their competitors, and that no constitutional or legal restrictions prohibiting government involvement into the economy can possibly prevent this from happening. Rand would have us believe that only incompetent businessmen would ever seek government assistance. But history shows that most businessmen, regardless of their skill in economic production, are eager to take advantage of political power in order to get an extra edge over their competitors.

Rand's conviction that only businessmen of lesser ability will ever turn to the government for help stems from her rather romantic view of entrepreneurial integrity. In her novel *Atlas Shrugged*, she portrays all productive businessmen as men of ruthless integrity who, although eager to drive their competitors out of business, want to play fair and give everybody a sporting chance. Dagny Taggert, the heroine of the book, is devastated when she learns that one of her competitors was ruined by the political pull of her brother. In a mournful conversation with the ruined man, she confesses that "I would have fought you, if I could make a better [rail]road than yours, and not given a damn about what happened to you. But this…Oh God,…I don't want to be a looter!" (1957, 80) This is hardly the attitude which the Vanderbilts, Carnegies, Morgans, and Rockerfellers had towards *their* competitors. They had no scruples as to the methods they used in order to maintain their preeminent position in the market. Fair means or foul—it was all the same to them. As long as they came out top-dog—*that* is all they really cared about.

To believe that entrepreneurial genius and moral integrity go hand in hand and that only an entrepreneur of lesser ability would ever stoop to seeking government help is to evince a naiveté about human nature so staggering that it can only be accounted for on the basis of wishful thinking. Men of entrepreneurial genius desperately require capital in order to take full advantage of their business acumen. An entrepreneurial genius without capital is like a great painter without paint, brushes, and canvas. It is only by having access to capital that the entrepreneur can develop and use his innate talents. But unless the entrepreneur inherits a fortune, where is he supposed to find the capital necessary to make full use of his genius? No investor will give money to some fledgling entrepreneur just starting out. How, then, is the fledgling entrepreneur ever going to get the chance to develop and use his talent if he cannot persuade anyone to give him the capital necessary to get started? One enormously effective method used by many of the great industrials of the nineteenth century is by resorting to some kind of immensely clever scheme of fraudulent manipulation.

Typical in this respect is James Jerome Hill, a self-made industrial magnate who built the Great Northern Railroad and was instrumental in developing the American Northwest. There can be little doubt that Hill was an entrepreneurial genius of the highest order. His greatest achievement was the construction of a railroad connecting Minnesota with Puget Sound, the only transcontinental railroad built without the aid of a special land grant or government subsidy.

It may be wondered how Hill ever managed to raise the capital necessary to build what would become the Great Northern Railroad. At the beginning of his career, he was virtually penniless. Within the space of a couple years, however, he managed to gain control of a railroad and 2,586,606 acres of land that a circuit court judge estimated to be worth $20,000,000 or more. (Myers, 1909, 675) How did a man who could not have been worth more than a few thousand dollars gain control of a $20,000,000 property in just a couple of years?

The evidence would suggest that Hill acquired the railroad in question through conspiracy and deceit. The railroad had gone bankrupt through gross mismanagement and malfeasance. Like so many railroads of that period, it had been chartered largely as an instrument of plunder. Its directors had been too incompetent, however, to make use of the plunder. The railroad and its lucrative land grants had been mortgaged to a syndicate of Dutch Capitalists for $13,380,000, but even this money had been diverted for fraudulent transactions, causing the line to go into bankruptcy once again. It is at this juncture that Hill made his move to get control of the property. The only problem was that he had no money and was therefore forced to rely solely on his wits to bag the plunder. His scheme was brilliant in all respects. He began by persuading the court appointed general manager of the railroad to sabotage the line in order to bring the price down. He then bought out the bondholders of the company at an absurdly low price, paying as low as three per cent of the bonds value, without however making any immediate cash payments. This was all part of a deal that had been made to pay the bondholders only after the railroad had been reorganized under Hill's control.

Once he had secured control of the railroad, Hill next turned his attention to securing the railroad's land grants from the threat of forfeiture. The Minnesota Legislature had passed an act declaring that unless a specified number of miles of track were laid by a certain date, the railroad and all its land grants and other special privileges would be immediately forfeited to the State of Minnesota. In order to save his investment, Hill went to enormous lengths to begin laying track. No one knows for certain where he got the $1,016,300 necessary to finance the 125 miles of rail that completed the line and connected St. Paul to the Canadian railway system, but some of it might have been raised illegally through the bank of Canada. (Myers, 1909, 672-675) Hill personally supervised construction of the line, driving his workers very hard but gaining their respect by calling them by their first names and also by grabbing a shovel and working with them for hours at a time.

With the completion of the railroad, Hill found himself a wealthy man: for not only did he own a railroad connecting important lines in Canada to the United States, but he also owned thousands of acres of land as a result of the government land grants secured by the extension of the line to Manitoba. In 1891, the Supreme Court declared that this land grant extended to some of the most fertile areas in the Dakotas—areas, moreover, which had long been settled by farmers. Once Hill had secured, through government favoritism, (Myers, 1909, 679-680) the rights to this land, Hill issued an order compelling anyone already settled on the land to leave within a few weeks: "The settlers appealed to Congress," wrote the socialist historian Gustavus Myers. "That body passed an act to allow the railroad company to select an equal area of lands in lieu of those settled upon. This act, although apparently passed for the benefit of the settlers, was precisely what the Great Northern Railroad Company was waiting for. The lands relinquished by the company were non-mineral; the act of Congress therefore, provided that the lands [taken] in exchange...should be non-mineral. But when the exchange was made it was discovered that the company had selected the most valuable timber lands in Idaho, Montana and Washington—lands worth far more than the Dakota lands—and that on some of these lands rich mineral deposits underlay the timber." (1909, 680-681)

Hill completed his Great Northern Railroad two years later, in 1893. To what degree his acquisition of valuable timber lands rich in minerals in Idaho, Montana, and Washington facilitated the construction of his great railroad will probably never be ascertained, but it is no stretch to suggest that the acquisition of these properties, made possible only through the bribery of government officials, might have assisted Hill to at least some degree. And while it is true that Hill received no land grants in association with his line from Minnesota to the Puget Sound, he did, as we have seen, receive grants for the line he completed from St. Paul to Winnipeg. For this reason, it is somewhat misleading to present Hill as someone who earned his fortune *entirely* without government assistance. Like most of the other titans of American industry, Hill profited from government corruption and venality. Had Congress been

willing to authorize land grants for his Great Northern
Railroad, he would have taken them, just as he took the
lands grants for his railroad to Winnipeg. Nor is this necessarily a bad thing. Hill was a man of extraordinary productive genius. Those economic resources that he attained
by fraud and government favoritism were immeasurably
enhanced by his control of them. Had they remained in
the hands of government bureaucrats or incompetent
businessmen, they would have remained totally useless.

I say this neither in defense of Hill nor in denigration
of him. I am merely trying to portray him and those of his
class as they really were and are. The trouble with thinkers
like Rand is that they are too wrapped up in promoting a
specific political or economic agenda to give a damn about
whether their views correspond with the facts. They can
see only the good in men of Hill's stamp. The darker side
of such men they either refuse to accept or find some
means of explaining away. Rand explained away the dark
side of American capitalism by insisting that it was all the
government's fault. "The evil's popularly ascribed to big
industrialists were not the results of an unregulated industry, but of the government power over industry," she
maintained. "The villain in the picture was not the businessman, but the legislator, not free enterprise, but government controls." (1967, 102) What Rand here fails to
acknowledge is the fact that it was big business that
encouraged legislators to interfere with free enterprise in
the first place. It is big business that has enjoyed the lion's
share of the power and influence in this country since its
inception, and it is businessmen who have done the most
to undermine the free market. As Edwin Sutherland noted
in his classic study of corporate and business crime, *White*

Collar Crime: "The primary loyalty of businessmen has been to profits, and they have sacrificed the principles of free competition and free enterprise in circumstances where they believed they could secure a pecuniary advantage by doing so. Moreover, they have been in a position of power and have been able to secure these advantages. Although businessmen had no intention to change the economic and political systems, their behavior has produced this result." (1949, 91)

Whether this is good or bad from the viewpoint of economic efficiency can only be determined on the basis of who ends up controlling most of the economic resources. To the extent that government interventionism allows men like James J. Hill to get their hands on a good chunk of the nation's capital, to that extent is it economically beneficial. To the extent that government interventionism distributes capital into the hands of incompetent businessmen and bureaucratic dolts, to that extent is it harmful. Whether interventionism is "moral" or "right" or "just" has no bearing on the matter whatsoever. The Objectivist view that only the moral is practical is only valid if you define morality as whatever succeeds. The industrialists who directed the economic development of the United States were hardly paragons of virtue in the Objectivist sense of the word. Many of them were involved in all sorts of "shady" transactions. Yet without these "immoral" industrialists America would still be a backward, largely agricultural community incapable of supporting more than 80 or 90 million people. Transportation would be perilous and difficult, farming risky and onerous, and survival hard and precarious. America's leading industrialists might not have maintained, in their business affairs, the most immaculate degree of honesty; they might have engaged in all sorts of crimes, including bribery of government officials, commercial blackmail, fraudulent stock manipulation, tax evasion, suppression of strikes and labor unions, misrepresentation in advertising, patent infringement and manipulation, coercive discriminatory pricing, violations of special war regulations, and conspiracies of trade, but they were also the primary architects of the American Industrial Revolution. It is not entirely clear that they would have been as successful in building the country if they had kept at all times to the straight and narrow. While certainly not all of their crimes benefited economic production, some of them probably did. It may be a melancholy fact of life, yet it is true nonetheless that honesty is not always the best policy, as has been well demonstrated by those handful of thinkers (e.g., Machiavelli, Mandeville, Nietzsche, Pareto) who have been courageous enough to face up to the truth and accept it like real men.

*   *   *

(4) *Freedom*. Rand's entire political philosophy is centered around her passionate espousal of freedom. In her ideal society, all men would be free to do whatever they pleased, provided they did not initiate physical coercion against anyone else. Rand acknowledges no exceptions to this ideal of freedom. "There can be no compromise between freedom and government controls," she maintained; "to accept 'just a few controls' is to surrender the principle of inalienable individual rights and to substitute

for it the principle of the government's unlimited, arbitrary power, thus delivering oneself into gradual enslavement." (1964b, 68)

Whether Rand's view on this matter accords with the facts hardly matters, since, as I have explained throughout this chapter, the ideal of absolute freedom espoused by Rand is impractical and unfeasible in the extreme form in which she defended it. No ruling elite would ever countenance such a state of affairs for very long. The most that partisans of freedom can ever hope for is a social order that comes close to Rand's ideal of perfect laissez-faire without, however, precisely matching it.

Even then, there are all sorts of obstacles that could end up preventing the realization of such a society. No one single person can determine the type of social order that prevails in a given society. Such things are determined by a complex web of interdependent factors involving the interplay of the sentiments and interests of various factions within the social order. By himself, the lone individual has virtually no effect on the determination of a society's political and economic institutions. He is merely one man acting among millions.

Although the isolated individual may be powerless to change society all by himself, he may be able to exercise a very real influence as part of a group of other like-minded individuals. It all depends on whether external conditions are propitious to the ideals he espouses and the degree to which the group he belongs to takes account of all the relevant facts in its attempts to influence the determination of the social order. Ideological movements usually fail either because they did not have a chance to begin with or because of poor leadership. The history of the Marxian ideological movement illustrates this quite well. The movement failed in Western Europe and the United States because conditions were not propitious. It failed in Central Europe (e.g., Hungary under Lenin's disciple Béla Kun) because of a combination of unfavorable circumstances and poor leadership. In Russia, however, it succeeded only where it was well-commandeered—i.e., within the Bolshevik segment of the Marxist movement. All other Marxist-inspired socialist movements failed miserably, its partisans being among the first victims of the new Bolshevik state.

If the Objectivist movement is going to exercise more than a merely marginal influence on society, two things are requisite: (1) Conditions must be propitious—or at least not too unpropitious; and (2) the leaders of the Objectivist movement must formulate strategies which take account of all the relevant realities. Let us examine the extent to which the Objectivist movement meets these two requisites.

(1) *Social conditions.* Edmund Burke frequently noted the importance of framing laws "to suit the people and the circumstances of the country, and not...to force the nature, the temper, and the inveterate habits of a nation to a conformity to speculative systems concerning any kind of laws." There are certain conditions under which even an approximation to Objectivist ideals may prove utterly impossible. For example, a nation cannot be free if it is always in imminent danger of foreign invasion or if a large portion of its citizenry is cowardly and weak. Nor can a nation be free for very long if there does not exist in the hearts of its citizenry an ingrained passion for freedom.

Where this passion fails, no ideology of freedom can have any appreciable influence.

Unfortunately, there exists no way of instilling men with the courage, strength, and passion necessary for the success of social, political, and economic freedom. Either an individual has all these elements, or he doesn't. If he doesn't have them, all the preaching in the world won't make up for their lack. Words alone cannot transform a weakling and coward into a man of courage and strength. Nor can you inflame an incurably phlegmatic man with a passion for freedom with mere patter. Freedom thrives best when harsh circumstances have toughened men and taught them to depend largely on themselves and to regard their own possessions as something inviolable. The American tradition of liberty has its roots in the ornery, defiant character of the medieval Saxon yeomanry of England. The French historian Hypolite Taine well-described these medieval Saxons when he wrote of them: "If they have acquired liberties, it is because they have conquered them; circumstances have assisted, but character has done more. The protection of the great barons and the alliance of the plain knights have strengthened them; but it was by their native roughness and energy that they maintained their independence....Observe, moreover, that these people, in each parish, practiced the bow every Sunday, and were the best archers in the world—that from the close of the fourteenth century the general emancipation of the villeins multiplied their number enormously, and you may understand how, amid all the operations and changes of the great central powers, the liberty of the subject endured. After all, the only permanent and unalterable guarantee in every country and under every

constitution is this unspoken declaration in the heart of
the mass of the people, which is well understood on all
sides: 'If any one touches my property, enters my house,
obstructs or molests me, let him beware. I have patience,
but I have also strong arms, good comrades, a good blade,
and, on occasion, a firm resolve, happen what may, to
plunge my blade up to its hilt in his throat.'" (1896,
I:109-113)

It is precisely this "firm resolve" to defend one's property with physical force, "happen what may," that serves as
the foundation of freedom. Once this resolve weakens,
freedom may continue to exist on the strength of custom
and habit, but eventually it will degenerate into a system
characterized by the toleration of all kinds of government-
sponsored abuses. Preaching may delay this process, but it
cannot prevent it altogether. When people no longer have
the courage and the passion to defend freedom with their
lives, liberty cannot long exist. And history demonstrates
again and again that this courage and passion tend to
diminish by virtue of the very freedom that it creates.
Freedom brings about greater economic productivity, but
this greater productivity begets wealth, luxury, and ease,
all of which undermine the courage and strength necessary
to maintain freedom. Thus does the very success of freedom tend to undermine liberty and bring about its degeneration and ruin. This is what happened to freedom in the
ancient world, and this is what is happening to it in the
modern world as well.

(2) Supposing, however, that current social conditions
are not so unfavorable as to render freedom utterly unfeasible, even in the more viable, mitigated form of its realiza-

tion, what kind of strategies might prove effective in reducing restrictions on the freedom of the individual?

As I explained in chapter 2, Rand believed she could change social conditions by refuting the theories which, she claimed, had brought those conditions about. From this conviction, Objectivists have deduced a strategy for bringing about the political and social changes they crave. They believe that if they can just "spread" the ideas of Objectivism around the culture, their political ideals will follow as a matter of course. "[I]f we spread the right ideas now, we each will have a share in bringing about the shining future," Leonard Peikoff once assured an audience of hopeful Objectivists. (1995, 14)

In concrete terms, "spreading" ideas means: discovering ways of exposing individuals to the ideas of Objectivism. Rand encouraged her followers to "Speak on any scale open to you, large or small—to your friends, your associates, your professional organizations, or any legitimate public forum." "Do no pass up a chance to express your views on important issues," Rand insisted. "Write letters to the editors of newspapers and magazines, to T.V. and radio commentators and, above all, to your Congressman (who depend on their constituents). If your letters are brief and rational (rather than incoherently emotional), they will have more influence than you think." (1982, 202)

Since Rand's death, the Objectivist movement has fallen into the hands of former or current college professors who have emphasized the importance of getting Objectivism taught at American universities and colleges. I have already explained why I do not believe such a strategy would work (see chapter 2, sec. I). Rand and her followers are mistaken in their belief that men are primarily motivated by speculative philosophy. Men are primarily motivated by their sentiments, their interests, and their desires. Speculative ideas are simply not as real to them as hunger, social status, sex and money. To think otherwise is to be completely out of touch with reality.

The ineptitude of the Objectivist strategy for reducing restrictions on freedom is best illustrated by comparing it to another strategy more suited to the relevant facts of the matter. In order to have any chance of bringing about greater freedom in society at large, you must begin by taking account of the actual conditions at hand. You will not get anywhere if you pretend these conditions are other than they really are. Even if they turn out to be extremely unpropitious to your heart's most treasured ideal, you nevertheless have to face up to their reality. They will not go away merely because you do not like them.

Societies are made up of individuals, groups, and institutions manifesting varying sentiments, interests, and desires. Those who are eager to change the course of society must discover ingenious ways of manipulating those individuals, groups, and institutions so that at least an approximation of the desired end can be reached. By *manipulation*, I mean: appealing to the sentiments, interests, and desires actually existing in society itself in such a way as to encourage behavior conducive to the end in view. If greater freedom is your goal, you should seek to trick members of the ruling elite (as well as important groups in the non-ruling mass) into supporting and enacting measures which, directly or indirectly, might help lessen restrictions on the individual. I will not deny that such manipulation—such "trickery," if you will—requires an immense amount of skill and intuitive insight into the precise nature of human beings and the workings of political institutions.

This intuitive insight, I need hardly add, can only be attained by "hands-on" experience. This would seem to rule out, from the very start, the intellectual whose experience is confined to rationalizing his sentiments and desires. Those whose experience is confined to mere ideas have no business taking part in the practical affairs of the world. Their attempts to meddle with social affairs will likely prove either inefficacious or, if they are allowed access to power, disastrous.

It is the practical inexperience of intellectuals like Rand and her followers which, when combined with their intransigent *hubris*, encourages them to believe that their abstruse chatter can exercise a tangible effect on the course of history. A man of experience would never accept such nonsense. He knows from many years of observation that you cannot alter an individual's basic sentiments, interests, and desires merely by preaching. An individual's basic psychological motivations must be accepted as an unalterable fact. You will never change it by trying to reason with it. Instead, you must try to channel its motives into less destructive pursuits.

Let me give a concrete example in order to more precisely illustrate what I mean. Suppose an astute political leader is eager to bring about more freedom in contemporary America. What is one way he might succeed in realizing this end?

The greatest obstacle to freedom in America stems from the fact that most of the individuals in the ruling elite benefit from restrictions on freedom. It is therefore in their interest either to maintain the status quo or, if they are inclined to make changes, to support increased restrictions on the individual. Moreover, as members of the ruling class, they will *ipso facto* have a greater say in such matters than will members of the subject class.

What, then, is the partisan of freedom to do? Everywhere he turns, he is opposed by a ruling elite which benefits from restrictions on the freedom of the individual and which will fight tooth and nail in order to maintain these restrictions. His only alternative is to accept the ruling elite as it really is and try to strategize accordingly. If ruling elites oppose freedom because they believe their interests would be jeopardized by it, the only way to get around this obstacle is by trying to use these very interests as the means of fomenting division within the ruling elite itself. It would be a mistake to assume that ruling elites are homogeneous bodies characterized by perfect cooperation. Within every ruling elite there is a hierarchy made up of individuals competing for positions of leadership and supremacy within the elite. By skillfully taking advantage of these competing interests, it is sometimes possible to bring about greater freedom in the subject class.

In the United States, the competition between rival interests within the ruling elite is in some respects instituted into the very system of government. These instituted rivalries are more commonly known under the concept of *checks and balances*. The most effective of these checks and balances in relation to the problem of freedom is the division between the states and the federal government. If the partisans of freedom could somehow manage to decentralize federal power to the individual states, this might prove an enormous boon to the cause of freedom, even if in some states restrictions on the freedom of the individual actually increased. This might strike some as paradoxical, so let me explain why decentralization could very well prove beneficial to freedom.

If each state had the right to decide for itself how much government intervention and tax-funded entitlement programs it wanted, this would create institutional incentives encouraging politicians and government officials to make political decisions beneficial to freedom. Those states which embark on a policy of intense government intervention coupled with generous entitlement programs would end up attracting to their state large numbers of the most lazy and shiftless individuals in the country, while at the same time driving from their state the bulk of their most hardworking, productive citizens, many of whom would choose to move to states with less government interference and a lower tax burden. But any state that attracted the lazy, the indigent, and the parasitical while at the same driving away the hardworking, the wealthy, and the economically sufficient would soon face ruin and bankruptcy. Somebody has to pay for all those welfare checks; but if all the state's most productive citizens have been driven out because of high taxes and intense business regulation, the tax base will disappear and state revenues will plummet. A state put in such a position would have no choice but to quickly adopt the precise opposite policy of cutting back entitlement programs and making conditions in the state propitious to business. The only alternative would be complete destitution. Government officials, merely to save their own salaries (if for no other reason) would be forced to adopt measures propitious to business and the freedom of the individual. Creating a sufficient tax base for their political schemes would demand such measures.

Meanwhile, those states that refrained from harmful business regulation and did away with entitlement programs altogether would attract a large contingent of the most productive and hardy citizens of the nation, while at the same time driving out all those shiftless, lazy, or incompetent individuals eager to live at the expense of others. Such states would flourish economically, thereby providing a further incentive for more freedom and less taxes among those states that had followed the opposite policy.

The problem with allowing the federal government to decide how much welfare and taxes and government regulation the entire country must endure is that, short of emigration from the country, there exists no way for the individual to escape the burden of so much government interference in his private life. At least with the state's rights approach, individuals can choose what sort of government they want to live under. If they want to live under a government that has a lot of compassion for the poor, they can move to state which has a legislature and bureaucracy sympathetic to such aims. If, however, they prefer to live under a state which allows a great deal of freedom to their citizens, they can move to a state where there are few regulations and fewer entitlements. The federal government, meanwhile, would content itself with defending the country as a whole, leaving the lion's share of domestic policy to the discretion of the states.

The only difficulty with such a scheme would be getting it implemented. Obviously, it would be useless to get it implemented on the basis of persuasion alone. A more subtle method would be required, one which works by cunning and deceit. Instead of trying to talk the ruling elite into decentralizing government power to the states, one would have to manipulate them into doing it. Admittedly, this would be very difficult (if not impossible) to do; but if somehow the partisans of freedom could create divisions between those elites who might benefit from greater state power and those who currently benefit from greater federal power, perhaps they might attain some level of success. Those who want greater freedom for the individual in this country should do everything in their power to foment divisions between state governments and the federal government. This means supporting any measure that might lead to a serious conflict between the states and the federal government, even if that measure is itself contrary to freedom. One issue which may prove an extremely fertile source of conflict between the states and the federal government involves the controversy over national immigration policy. The four states along the border of Mexico are suffering from what many believe is a veritable invasion of America. If the partisans of freedom had any strategic sense at all, they would do everything in their power to incite the political leaders of those states into usurping the federal government's role in policing immigration. This could lead to a major conflict between the states and the federal government—a conflict moreover which might, if circumstances are favorable, force the federal government into making concessions to the states, thereby leading to greater power for the states and, *ipso facto*, greater leverage in demanding further concessions.

It should not come as a surprise to anyone who understands how thoroughly Rand's view of man is contaminated by utopian currents that her political philosophy would oppose using the strategy outlined above. Never mind whether the strategy might work, the very fact that it involves the advocacy of state's rights makes it unacceptable to Objectivism. "The Jeffersonian theory that states must be sovereign regarding local matters cannot be sustained philosophically," argues Objectivist spokesman Harry Binswanger. "What *moral* justification could there be for requiring the federal government to look the other way while a state tramples on the rights of American citizens? The federal government, having the power to stop local rights-violations, stands charged morally with the responsibility to do so upon the citizen's appeal, whether the rights-violator is a state, a foreign nation, or a plain criminal. A federal government that allows states to violate rights—rights by its own standards—undercuts its moral legitimacy and moves in the direction of anarchy." (1987, 13)

Mr. Binswanger wonders what *moral* justification there could possibly be for allowing the states to trample on the rights of American citizens. But it is not really a question of morality. Mr. Binswanger's penchant for viewing every-thing in moral rather than factual terms renders him inca-pable of understanding this. Because the federal government *ought* to protect the rights of individuals, he naively concludes that the federal government *will* protect the rights of individuals. But how can he be sure that this is so? What if the federal government chooses not to pro-tect the rights of its citizens? Where are individuals going to turn for protection if that happens? At least under decentralization of federal power, there will be fifty states to choose from, some of which will probably refrain from serious violations of an individual's freedom. And so if the citizen is oppressed by one state, he can choose to move to a state where he will escape such oppression.

Mr. Binswanger, by his opposition to the doctrine of states rights, has, in effect, adopted the strategy of putting all his eggs in one basket. He is gambling that the federal government will seek to observe the rights of all Americans. Unfortunately, there is no reason to believe that the federal government will ever do such a thing. Institutional forces within the federal government itself encourage policies inimical to freedom. Politicians, in order to get elected, must pander not merely to their constituents, but to wealthy economic interests. This puts the federal government at the mercy of those individuals eager to profit from special government privileges. Under such circumstances, what are the chances that the rights of the individual will continue to be respected?

While it is true that these dangers to freedom exist in regards to state governments as well, at least under federal decentralization there would exist institutional counterforces that might help mitigate the effect of the social forces leading to corruption and abuses of power. Since all fifty states, in order to create a sufficient tax base, would have to create a hospitable environment for productive individuals, it would be in the interest of state politicians to advocate legislation that promotes freedom. These incentives would not exist if power were concentrated on the federal level, because there would be no place within the country at large where the productive citizens could escape for shelter from oppression. As I noted earlier, emigration would be their only alternative, and the federal government could easily take away that option from them if it so desired.

In the final analysis, we must regard Objectivism's opposition to states' rights as evidence of a serious lack of strategic sense among the Randian fold. This lack of strategic sense undoubtedly stems from Rand's utopian theory of human nature and her verbalistic mode of thinking. By regarding human beings as better than they really are and by assuming that man's problems can be solved by the verbalistic manipulation of epistemological and moral conceptions, Rand and her followers have rendered themselves utterly useless to the cause of freedom.

CHAPTER 7:

▼

THEORY OF AESTHETICS

"The realm of culture is the realm of meanings, the effort in some imaginative form to make sense of the world through the expressiveness of art and ritual, particularly those 'incomprehensions' such as tragedy and death that arise out of the existential predicaments which every self-conscious being must confront at some point in his life."

—Daniel Bell

Rand's theory of aesthetics, like nearly all her philosophical theories, was primarily devised to justify her own personal prejudices—in this case, her personal prejudices about art, music, and literature. Rand believed that only *her* aesthetic tastes were "rational." Anyone with different aesthetic tastes she regarded as "irrational." How she reached this conclusion and what is wrong with it will be the primary focus of this chapter.

*   *   *

(1) *Sense of life.* Rand believed that every individual has what she called a "sense of life," which she described as "an emotional, subconsciously integrated appraisal of man and existence." (1975, 25) Rand held that it is a man's sense of life that provides the basis of his emotional appraisal of a given work of art: "It is the artist's sense of life that controls and integrates his work, directing the innumerable choices he has to make, from the choice of subject to the subtlest details of style. It is the viewer's or reader's sense of life that responds to a work of art by a complex, yet automatic reaction of acceptance and approval, or rejection and condemnation." (1975, 35)

Rand held that it was possible to distinguish a "valid" sense of life from an "invalid" one. A "valid" sense of life would be one that coincided with an individual's rationally formulated convictions about life and man. An invalid sense of life would be one that did not coincide with a "rational" view of man and existence. (1975, 29-31)

According to Rand, a rationally formulated view of man and existence must involve what she called the "benevolent universe premise." Basically, what this premise entails is the view that the achievement of man's values is the norm of human life and that pain, suffering, failure, disaster, and tragedy are "unnatural" and without "metaphysical" significance. As Leonard Peikoff explains: "The 'benevolent universe' [premise] does not mean that the universe feels kindly to man or that it is out to help him achieve his goals. No, the universe is neutral; it simply is; it is indifferent to you. You must care about and adapt to it, not the other way around. But reality is 'benevolent' in the sense that if you *do* adapt to it—i.e., if you do think, value, and act rationally, then you can (and barring any accidents will) achieve your values. You will, because those values are based on reality." (Binswanger, 1986, 51)

Contrasted to the "benevolent universe premise" is what Rand chose to call the "malevolent universe premise," which Rand defined as the view "that man, by his very nature, is helpless and doomed—that success, happiness, achievement are impossible to him—that emergencies, disasters, catastrophes are the norm of his life and that his primary goal is to combat them." (1964b, 48) Rand regarded the malevolent universe premise as irrational and debilitating. Those who suffered from a "malevolent" sense of life required, in her opinion, psychological counseling.

A rational individual, Rand contended, will espouse the benevolent universe premise, and this will be reflected in his sense of life and in the kind of art that he admires. The rational man will seek art that gives him "the pleasure of contemplating the objectified reality of one's own sense of life [and] feeling what it would be like to live in one's ideal world." (1975, 38) In other words, the rational man will seek art that portrays the world not as it *is* but as it *ought* to be.

An irrational individual, on the other hand, will espouse the malevolent universe principle, which will lead him to admire art which projects a malevolent sense of life. "For an irrational man, the concretized projection of the malevolent sense of life serves, not as...inspiration to move forward, but as permission to stand still," noted Rand; "it declares that values are unattainable, that the struggle is futile, that fear, guilt, pain and failure are mankind's predestined end—and that *he* couldn't help it." (1975, 39)

From these principles Rand forged a theory of aesthetic response that enabled her to use *ad hominem* tactics against anyone whose aesthetic tastes differed from her own. Her own aesthetic tastes she regarded as good and rational; everyone else's tastes, to the extent that they differed from her own, were denigrated as bad and irrational. Works of art she disliked were, for the most part, dismissed as "malevolent"—i.e., as the kind of art that only an irrational person would like. This included most of what passes for the great artistic masterpieces of Western Civilization. Rand considered anyone who admired Rembrandt or Van Gogh, Beethoven or Wagner, Shakespeare or Mark Twain as suspect. I have alluded to this trait of Rand's before when I discussed her mania for conformity (see chapter 3, sec. iv). She simply could not abide having any of her friends admire art she didn't like.

Rand believed that an individual's artistic tastes revealed their innermost souls. If this is true, what does Rand's artistic tastes reveal about *her* soul? What are we supposed to think of an individual who regards most serious art as "malevolent" or worse? And what are we to make of her belief that "rational" art should give one the pleasure of living in one's ideal world? In the next section, we will seek answers to these questions.

*   *   *

(2) *Rand the philistine.* If we define philistinism as the incapacity or unwillingness to appreciate and admire great art, then there can be little doubt that Ayn Rand was a philistine. Although she pretended to be a champion of art, even going as far as to describe art as a "profound need" of man's life, (1975, 45) it should be clear from what we know about her artistic tastes that Rand did not really like great art—that, a few exceptions notwithstanding, she despised most of the great artists, composers, and writers of Western Civilization and had no use for their artistic creations. What other conclusion can we come to concerning someone who regarded Van Gogh as too undisciplined, chaotic, and wild to qualify as a great artist; who dismissed Rembrandt's art as "grim, unfocused malevolence"; who excoriated Shakespeare for his "abysmal failure" to portray men as *she* wished them to be, rather than as they actually are; and who chastised Beethoven for his "tragic sense of doom"? (Branden, B., 1986, 269) Rand only cared for art in the abstract sense. Concrete instances of art she usually disliked. In this sense, she was like those humanitarians who love mankind in the abstract yet never fail to mistreat and oppress actual individuals. As long as art was a mere concept, Rand could regard it as a good thing; but as soon as it became manifested in a particular painting, book, or musical score, she could only abhor it. Exceptions to this were few and far between. Among serious novelists, she responded enthusiastically only to Victor Hugo. She disliked the novels of nearly all the great realists of the past two centuries (e.g., Tolstoy, Balzac, Drieser, Flaubert, Zola, Hemmingway, Thomas Mann). Although she was willing to admit that some of them were "writers of genuine literary talent,"

(1975, 119) she regarded their unwillingness to write the kind of fiction she approved of as evidence of "determinism," which she considered a bad thing. (1975, 99-102)

There would be nothing objectionable about Rand's hatred of great art if she had been content to keep it to herself. But she was not so content. She had to justify her intransigent philistinism on "rational" grounds. This is where all her arguments linking "rationality" with "benevolence" come in. These terms are simply masks designed to conceal the prejudicial nature of Rand's appalling aesthetic tastes. When Rand describes a work of art as "benevolent," she is merely saying, in a roundabout way, that she likes and approves of it; while, on the other hand, whenever she castigates a work for being "malevolent," she is merely expressing her disapproval of it. These terms have no other significance than as expressions of Rand's aesthetic tastes.

That this is so should be clear from Rand's own notion of what constitutes "benevolence." Rand once described her benevolent universe premise in the following terms: "There is a fundamental conviction which some people never acquire, some hold only in their youth, and a few hold to the end of their days—the conviction that *ideas* matter....That ideas matter means that knowledge matters, that truth matters, that one's mind matters....[The consequence of this fundamental conviction] is the inability to believe in the power or triumph of evil. No matter what corruption one observes in one's immediate background, one is unable to accept it as normal, permanent or *metaphysically* right." (1971b, 118)

Let us examine a little more closely what Rand is saying in this passage. The "fundamental conviction" she writes about is, of course, the very "benevolent universe" premise which, she here claims, is tantamount to the belief that ideas, knowledge, and truth all matter. Now what could she possibly mean by saying that ideas, knowledge, and truth *matter*? Basically, what she is trying to convey is her conviction that the right ideas will win out in the end and evil will be vanquished. In other words, she is merely asserting her own doctrine of history, which posits her belief that Objectivism will ultimately triumph over all its ideological enemies. It is the acceptance of this theory of history, along with all its sundry implications, which constitutes, for Rand, the benevolent universe premise. The universe is benevolent because Objectivism will ultimately triumph.

At the base of Rand's doctrine of history is her theory of man. Because man is fundamentally a "rational" being, he will ultimately accept Objectivism as his philosophy of life. The benevolent universe premise therefore entails the acceptance of Rand's theory of human nature.

What if the individual neither accepts Rand's doctrine of history nor her theory of human nature? Does this mean that he must have a *malevolent* sense of life? Apparently so. Consider the implications of such a view. As I explained in the first two chapters of this book, neither Rand's doctrine of history nor her theory of man accord with reality. Men are not, nor could they ever be, as Rand wished them to be; nor is history determined by speculative philosophy. Yet Rand claims that anyone who does not believe in these doctrines is guilty of accepting the malevolent universe premise. This is tantamount to saying that realism, by its very nature, is malevolent and that true benevolence can only be reached through wishful thinking.

Although elsewhere in her philosophy Rand defended realism, in her aesthetics she tended to regard it with suspicion and hostility. Literary realists she accused of denying man's volition and depriving the novelist of the freedom to choose the subject of his work. (1975, 165) This latter charge contains a grain of truth: literary realism does in fact limit the novelist's choice in subject matter: it restricts it to the known, the factual, and the real. This was a restriction Rand could not abide. She believed art should only portray that which is worth contemplating in life. "That which is not worth contemplating in life, is not worth re-creating in art," she insisted. "Misery, disease, disaster, evil, all the negatives of human existence, are proper subjects of *study* in life, for the purpose of understanding and correcting them—but are not proper subjects of *contemplation* for contemplation's sake. In art, and in literature, these negatives are worth re-creating only in relation to some positive—but *not* as an end in themselves." (1975, 166-167)

If this contemplation theory of aesthetic appreciation were to become widely accepted and practiced, the results would be a tremendous depreciation of the cultural heritage of Western Civilization. If art were simply contemplation for contemplation's sake, there would be no reason for anyone to appreciate the tragedies of Aeschylus, Sophocles, or Shakespeare; the poetry of Homer, Dante, and Milton; the novels of Balzac, Dostoevsky, and Kafka; the music of Berlioz, Bartok, and Shostokovich; or the films of Welles, Tarkovsky, and Bergman. All these artists produced works of art in which very disturbing things take place, from patricide and child molestation to the torments of the damned and the persecution of innocence. If art were simply a matter of contemplation, only a sadist would care to contemplate the horrors portrayed in such works as the *Orestia* trilogy of Aeschylus, Shakespeare's *King Lear*, the *Inferno* of Dante, the *Symphonie Fantastique* of Berlioz, the *Miraculous Mandarin* of Bartok, or Bergman's *Cries and Whispers*. But art is about much more than mere contemplation. Art confronts, challenges, and disturbs: it does so, not in order to project a "malevolent" view of life, but to help the individual learn how to deal with some of the less pleasant aspects of existence. One does not have to regard man and existence in a malevolent light to realize that life is not all cakes and ale. Even individuals with an uncompromisingly benevolent sense of life will experience, at some point in their life, personal tragedy. The certain fate of all, benevolent or malevolent alike, is death. But even worse than personal death is the death of loved ones. Most individuals who do not die young will experience, at some time in their life, the death of someone they love. They are also likely to suffer from various personal crises, from broken relationships to financial hardship and poverty. The universe may not be malevolent, but bad things do occur in it nonetheless, and human beings require solace in the face of tragic adversity. This is precisely the role that so-called "tragic" art fulfills in human life. The individual does not merely contemplate tragic art: he experiences it vicariously. He feels the despair, the heartache, the sorrow of the characters portrayed by the artist. When he leaves the theater after watching a tragedy or the cinema after seeing a heart-wrenching film, he may feel emotionally and spiritually drained, but he will also feel uplifted and purged. The experience, in the main, will generally be regarded in a positive light. Indeed, if he has felt especially moved by the performance, he may regard it as one of the highlights of his aesthetic life. Although this might seem, to a superficial observer, rather paradoxical, yet it is confirmed many times over by experience. Many human beings regard the vicarious experience of tragedy through art to be somehow uplifting and spiritually therapeutic and profound. For some people, no higher aesthetic compliment can be made to an artist than to say that they are moved by his work.

Ayn Rand would like to dismiss such aesthetic experiences by setting them all down as products of an "irrational," "malevolent" sense of life. But what grounds are there for believing that an individual who is moved by the tragic strains of Shostokovich or by the unhappy plight of Shakespeare's Hamlet is motivated by a malevolent sense of life? Why is someone who feels moved by tragic art necessarily malevolent? If anything, the capacity to be moved by tragic art demonstrates a higher level of emotional maturity than is displayed by those superficial smatterers who cannot tolerate the representation of tragedy in art because they have never learned to confront and deal with the tragic side of existence. The eagerness with which Rand accuses those who appreciate tragic art with being "malevolent" suggests to me that Rand had trouble dealing with the tragic side of existence. Although she admitted the existence of pain, suffering, and failure, she could never bring herself to consider them as important: such phenomena, she insisted, were without "metaphysical significance": they do not, according to her protégé Leonard Peikoff, "reveal the nature of reality." But if pain, suffering, and failure exist in reality, how can they not reveal at least a *part* of reality? And what on earth can Rand possibly mean by denying the "metaphysical significance" of the tragic side of existence? Rand here seems to be trying to have it both ways, accepting the existence of tragedy in one breath and then denying its significance in the next. But if pain, suffering, failure and tragedy exist, then of course they must have significance. To think otherwise is to embrace a philosophy of evasion and emotional repression.

Throughout this book I have emphasized the important role which Rand's idolatry of her "ideal man" played in the formation of her philosophy. Not surprisingly, we find evidence of this in her esthetic theory as well. A great deal of her animus toward realistic and tragic art is merely an expression of her disgust with any kind of art that projects a view of man that is not as exalted (and as meretricious) as her own. This is clearly demonstrated in her intense dislike of the works of Shakespeare. As she admitted to Barbara Branden in a taped interview, what she despised most about Shakespeare was not the "tragedy and malevolence," but "that he is a detached Olympian who takes no sides. When we were taught in classes [at the University of Petrograd] that Shakespeare holds up a mirror to human nature, *that set me even more against him....I had no admiration for any of his characters.* Caesar and Mark Antony are stock, cardboard characters, they are official bromides, they are what you are historically suppose to admire, but they are not alive; there is nothing individual about them. *I refused to believe that Lear and*

MacBeth represent what man really is." (1986, 45; emphasis added)

It is clear from this confession that Rand's dislike of Shakespeare was largely motivated by the fact that his view of man differed from her own. Especially revealing in this sense is her statement about not admiring any of Shakespeare's characters. She refused to believe that Lear and MacBeth represent "what man really is" because Lear and MacBeth fail to accord with her view of the ideal man. She despised Shakespeare because Shakespeare had the gall to portray men realistically, as they really are in the empirical world of fact, and not how Rand wished them to be.

Rand's hostility towards any realistic portrayal of human nature in art is further illustrated by her admiration of what she chose to call "romanticism," which she defined as "a category of art based on the recognition of the principle that man possesses the faculty of volition." (1975, 99) Rand's romanticism has little, if anything, to do with the romantic cultural movement that swept through Europe during the first three or four decades of the nineteenth century. Although Rand attempted to connect her concept of romanticism with the nineteenth century cultural movement, there exists no scholarly justification for such a linkage. Rand's romanticism is one thing, the historical romanticism of the nineteenth century something else altogether. (Babbitt, 1919; Barzun, 1961)

What did Rand mean be describing romanticism as the "category of art based on the recognition that man possesses the faculty of volition"? Volition, for Rand, is merely a synonym for "free will," which is itself merely a synonym for Rand's belief in the primacy of the intellect, the cardinal doctrine of her theory of human nature. Romanticism, then, as far as Rand is concerned, is that category of art which projects, in some form or manner, Rand's view of man.

Opposed to romanticism is what Rand chose to call "naturalism," which she defined as the category of art which denies man's volition. Again, we must beware of trying to connect the literary movement of naturalism led by such writers as Taine, Zola, and Drieser with Rand's own version of naturalism. Rand's version is merely a straw man she constructed to attack writers she didn't like. In her hands, naturalism emerges as a thoroughly distorted caricature of literary realism. The naturalists, she claimed, were progressively more and more "journalistic" and "statistical" in their subject matter, eventually replacing characterization with the "indiscriminate recording" of trivia. (1975, 117) Even more objectionable to Rand was the refusal of naturalists to write novels with exciting plots. According to Rand, the plotlessness of naturalism stems from its belief that man's choices are the product of forces beyond his control. (1975, 100-101) Only literature based on the premise that man's choices are determined by himself can have a plot, Rand maintained.

If by naturalism we mean literary realism, there is little if any truth in Rand's strictures. None of the major literary realists of the last two centuries tried to replace characterization with the indiscriminate recording of trivia. Nor does her remarks about the plotlessness of naturalism and its alleged relation to the question of choice have much ground to stand on. In the first place, it is simply not true that the literary realists based their work on the premise that man's choices are determined by forces beyond his control. All they did is merely attempt to portray men as they actually are. And since men in fact make their own choices in real life, literary realists have always strived to portray them doing just that. Where Rand picked up the idea that literary realists, or "naturalists" as she calls them, believe that men are mere puppets whose choices are determined by forces beyond their control is anyone's guess. While it is true that a handful of literary realists might have entertained such a doctrine on a purely speculative level, hardly any of them ever applied such speculative beliefs to their actual literary work. Even a diehard mechanist like Drieser didn't portray human beings as mere choiceless automatons. (Vivas, 1955)

It remains only to consider Rand's contention that naturalist fiction (i.e., *realist* fiction) must always be plotless. That this is untrue can easily be demonstrated. There are many plays and novels which, though Rand would probably have considered them "naturalistic," nevertheless have plots. Not all literary realists rejected plot. Most of the English and American realists strove to write novels with plots, and some of them were pretty good at it. Prominent examples include Henry Fielding's *Tom Jones*, George Eliot's *Silas Marner*, George Meredith's *The Egoist*, Henry James' *The Bostonians*, Frank Norris' *McTeague*, and Joseph Conrad's *Nostromo*. I suspect that Rand's primary objection to such writers would not be for the alleged plotlessness of their novels, but that they had the nerve to portray men as they really are rather than as Rand wished them to be.

     *   *   *

(3) *Conclusion.* That Rand's aesthetics is merely a rationalization of her own idiosyncratic tastes should be obvious. For the most part, Rand only cared for the kind of art that portrayed men as she wished them to be and which avoided emphasizing the tragic side of existence. Since very little art comes all that close to meeting Rand's narrow tastes, she wound up either indifferent or hostile to most of the great artistic masterpieces of Western Civilization.

Although I have little if any respect for Rand's aesthetic tastes, I would not have objected to them or accused Rand of philistinism if she had not presented herself as a champion of art. It is, I must insist, absurd to regard her as such. I must also insist very emphatically that anyone who regards Rand as a champion of art has absolutely no notion of what art is and is every bit as much a philistine as Rand was herself. In order to be a champion of art, you must like art and encourage others to like it as well. Rand, to the extent that she was able to wield a palpable influence, did everything she could to discourage the love of art. "I would see her convince so many [individuals] of the invalidity of their artistic tastes," reports Rand's biographer and former confidant, Barbara Branden. (1986, 243) Is this behavior consistent with the love of art?

The consequence of Rand's refusal to tolerate different aesthetic tastes within her inner circle only served to intensify the aesthetic sterility of the Objectivist movement. This is somewhat ironic, given Rand's opinion of herself as a "bridge" to the next aesthetic renaissance. (1975, v-viii) But as long as Rand continued to harass and persecute all those within her inner circle whose aesthetic tastes were not as narrow and immature as her own, there would never be a viable aesthetic movement connected with her name. Any aesthetic movement that begins by rejecting most of the art of the past will be doomed from the start to complete insignificance. The attempt to restrict aesthetic creation to the narrow parameters set down by an extremely prejudiced aesthetic despot can only lead to the subversion of creative development. This is well testified, not only by the utter failure of the Objectivist movement to produce any kind of significant art, but also by individuals within the movement itself who experienced first-hand the effects of Rand's philistinism on the development of talented young artists: "I could see that Ayn's artistic tastes, and the impressive logic with which she backed them, were impeding the development of my students," testified one such individual. "It disturbed me very much to see young artists, some of whom were very talented, struggling to do 'benevolent' pictures in the style of Dali, not daring to develop their own way of expressing themselves for fear of being judged irrational." (Branden, B., 1986, 387)

Now that Rand has passed from the scene, it will be interesting to observe whether any artists of genuine distinction ever emerge from the Objectivist movement. To the extent that Rand's influence still persists, I would regard the prospects for Objectivist-inspired art as extremely slim. For it was not merely Rand's aesthetic prejudices which subverted any effort on the part of her followers to develop a viable artistic movement; the principles she devised to justify her prejudices also played a part in this subversion. An Objectivist artistic movement, to the extent that it actually tries to follow Objectivist aesthetic principles, would be a veritable contradiction in terms.

CHAPTER 8:

▼

FINAL THOUGHTS

"[T]hose who frame political or religious or aesthetic systems ought not to expect that they should be long carried out or widely accepted in the spirit in which their authors conceived them. They must reckon with their host, with the unaccountable, ever young, irrepressible individual."

—George Santayana

Ayn Rand sincerely believed that she had developed a rational, empirically-based philosophy that could withstand any effort to refute it. In this belief Rand was mistaken. Her philosophy, far from being rationally and empirically sound, is laced with contradictions, misinterpretations of fact, and verbal sophistries; many of Rand's doctrines, including her theory of human nature, are presented without the benefit of a single scrap of relevant empirical evidence. Her theory of history is based on assumptions that no individual with extensive experience of men could possibly take seriously. Her theory of human knowledge often reads like an inept rationalization of a largely verbalistic mode of cognition, with vague generalizations being elevated above precise observation and the accumulation of scientifically validated facts. Rand tended to believe that questions of fact could be determined by the manipulation of vague terms. This tendency is most clearly illustrated in her so-called "metaphysical" theory of reality, in which she tries to demonstrate the objectivity of reality and validate causality on the basis of cognitively empty tautologies such as "existence exists" and "A is A." Rand also makes good use of her verbalistic method of reasoning in her ethics, where she introduces three distinct ultimate values, none of which are logically compatible. First she tells us that survival is the ultimate value; then she qualifies this by claiming that only a "rational" survival is proper to human beings; after which she concludes by insisting that happiness is man's "highest moral purpose." The confusions of her ethical theories are reproduced in her political ideology. Having convinced herself that she had solved the moral problems of politics in her ethics, she assumed that the solution of all political problems would follow as a matter of course. Politics, she declared, consisted of nothing more than the application of morality to questions of social relations. If you can prove that a certain political ideal *ought* to prevail, then it eventually *will* prevail.

Despite all the many errors, obfuscations, sophisms, contradictions, and violations of fact with which Rand's Objectivist system abounds, it would be a mistake to consider everything Rand said to be untrue or her philosophy as entirely worthless. As I noted in the introduction, many of Rand's convictions contain an *element* of truth. She was not wrong about everything. And even if she had been, this would not necessarily make her philosophy worthless. A philosophy cannot be solely judged on the basis of its accordance with reality. Philosophies serve other purposes besides the illumination of mundane truth. The utility of a philosophy may depend on its ability to console or inspire, or on its intrinsic beauty or poetical significance. Plato's philosophy contains many elements that diverge quite sharply from reality, but this does not mean that his philosophy is entirely worthless.

In the first section of this chapter, I will examine the question of Objectivism's utility. Can belief in Objectivism actually improve an individual's life? And if so, in what way? And what about the errors of Objectivism? Isn't it harmful to believe in errors? And if believing in errors is harmful, wouldn't belief in Rand's errors be harmful?

In the second section I will turn to the question of the future prospects of the Objectivist movement. Does Objectivism have a future? And if so, what kind of future is it likely to enjoy? As usual, my answers to these questions will derive from the naturalistic assumptions held throughout this book. My focus will consist entirely on determining what *is most likely* to occur, not on what *ought* to occur. Some of Rand's detractors no doubt believe that Objectivism *ought* to be completely forgotten by future generations. Although these detractors may be right, I find that I have little interest in what Objectivism's future prospects *ought* to be. I am far more interested in what these future prospects actually will be.

*   *   *

(1) *Utility of Objectivism.* Throughout this book I have concentrated primarily on the question whether the main doctrines of Objectivism correspond with empirical reality. In this section, I will focus on an entirely different issue—namely, the issue of whether Objectivism benefits or harms those who believe in it.

It is often assumed that if a doctrine is false, then no benefit can be gained from believing it. Indeed, it is widely thought that belief in false doctrines is dangerous. This, however, is not always the case. It all depends on what sort of belief we are talking about. False beliefs about lethal substances, such as poisons or explosives, can be very dangerous. But false beliefs about purely philosophical issues are rarely dangerous and in some instances might even prove beneficial.

While this might strike some as paradoxical, it is nonetheless true. An individual may believe in some of the most palpably absurd philosophical doctrines imaginable and yet achieve a high degree of success in his practical endeavors. The reason for this has to do with the fact that philosophical beliefs rarely play a very large role in determining the practical behavior of the individual. Knowledge concerning how to achieve practical ends comes, not from abstruse philosophical principles, but from day-to-day experience. Hardly anyone ever learns how to earn a living or take care of a household or raise a family from reading Plato or Kant. They learn how to do such things through imitation and practice.

Does this mean that philosophy has no effect on practical conduct? No, not quite. Under certain conditions, philosophy may exercise a very real effect on conduct. It usually does so, however, not by influencing the means by which a given end is pursued, but by increasing the individual's morale, that is, his spiritual inspiration. By instilling within the individual faith in his ultimate success, a philosophy can provide him with that extra bit of courage necessary to prevent him from giving up. This is well documented in the case of serious illnesses. Individuals who have no faith in their prospects for recovery run a greater risk of dying than do those individuals who continue to believe, even in the face of overwhelming evidence to the contrary, that they will somehow recover. This is true even when, from a purely objective point of view, there is no reason to believe that a recovery is possible. While most individuals in such circumstances do in fact die, the few exceptions who miraculously beat the odds and end up surviving generally come from that group which continued to have faith.

What is true in regards to terminal illnesses is no less true in many circumstances in life. Faith does not assure success; but to the extent that faith inspires individuals with the conviction that they will succeed in the end and that any reverses they experience will be only temporary, to that extent does faith increase the chances that the individual will achieve greater utility for himself. Now although a philosophy cannot, all by itself, give people faith, it can intensify whatever faith they already have; and it is in this way that a philosophy which does not accord with the facts may exercise a beneficial influence.

This does not mean that the effect of an inspirational, though untrue, philosophy will *always* be beneficial. It all depends on the circumstances. If a philosophy helps instill enough faith and hope in order for the individual to enter medical school and train to become a doctor, then it will have exercised a beneficial effect. If, on the other hand, a philosophy merely provides the inspiration to go out and tilt at windmills or beat one's head against walls, then it will have exercised a deleterious effect. In order to be beneficial, a philosophy must inspire conduct that actually benefits the individual.

A false philosophy can also be harmful to the extent that it affects the individual's practical judgment concerning everyday matters. It is rare for philosophy to exercise an influence in this area of life, but it occasionally happens. Once in a while, some idealist will try to apply this or that utterly impracticable philosophical principle to everyday life and will end up causing all kinds of trouble for himself and others. The attempts by the Bolsheviks to impose communism on Russia represent a *partial* example of this. Much more common is the attempt to apply impractical *religious* or *supernatural* principles to everyday life.

The harmful effects of erroneous philosophical principles might be called *the dark side of faith*. Although faith has many beneficial effects, it can occasionally cause individuals to ignore important realities. This is precisely what you have to worry about in regards to any philosophy that, like Objectivism, preaches false principles. As long as these false principles serve no other purpose than to instill hope and courage, then their effect may prove beneficial. But if an attempt is made to use these principles as a guide to practical conduct, then they will tend to be harmful.

Let us now turn to the question of whether Objectivist principles are harmful or beneficial to those who accept them. Judged merely as inspiration, I believe Objectivism has been, in many cases, beneficial. It's emphasis on self-initiative and self-responsibility; its uncompromising defense of achievement and personal happiness; its passionate opposition to conformity, stale tradition, and mysticism; and its implacable faith in the "benevolent universe" premise: all such convictions, as long as they are not interpreted too dogmatically, can help the individual succeed in life by giving him enough courage to resist harmful pressures to conform. Any society, even one as tolerant and geared to self-gratification as contemporary American society, will usually place a high premium on conformity to certain social norms. An individual's family, friends, peers, etc. will all expect conformity to *their* idea of what constitutes a "normal" person. Failure to conform can result in harassment, persecution, and ostracism.

Although it is fashionable to deride these social pressures to conform, it would be a mistake to conclude that all of them are bad. To a certain extent, at least some amount of conformism is absolutely necessary for the maintenance of the social order: for if there were no standards of conformity at all and each person in society could go his or her own separate way, society would fall apart. At the same time, if you had total conformity, there would be no room for progress. Under such conditions, society would be incapable of adapting to new circumstances. The rigidity of its conventions would inevitably destroy it.

A certain amount of individualism is therefore necessary, not merely for the individual's happiness, but for the survival of society. Social pressures to conform exercise a harmful effect by discouraging useful innovations or by forcing individuals to pretend to be what they most emphatically are not. To the extent that Objectivism instills within its partisans the courage to resist harmful pressures to conform, to that extent is it beneficial.

If I am not mistaken, this is precisely the effect produced by Objectivism on many occasions. The stories one occasionally hears about individuals whose lives have been dramatically changed for the better by exposure to the ideas of Ayn Rand are explicable on these grounds alone.

Many followers of Rand erroneously believe that they have benefited from Objectivism because it gives them a greater insight into reality. I do not believe this is the case at all. On the contrary, a much better case could be made for the precise opposite conclusion. Rand's philosophy, far from increasing one's insight into reality, tends instead to narrow one's vision and encourages a more naive outlook on life. This naiveté may have beneficial effects in regards to giving Objectivists the courage to face the challenges of life, but it does not give them insight into *how* to meet these challenges. The knowledge of how to meet these challenges must come from practical experience. It cannot come from Objectivism. Those people who get the most benefit from Objectivism are those who draw from Rand's philosophy the inspiration to move forward and, by resisting harmful pressures to conform, go on to realize their unique potential while at the same time deriving all their knowledge of *how* to attain their values from practical experience. Individuals who, on the other hand, attempt to apply specific doctrines of Objectivism to everyday life are likely to run into difficulties at some point. An individual, for example, who attempts to apply Rand's verbalistic method of reasoning to the problems of running a complicated business or to the analysis of a troubled girlfriend will probably get himself into a whole heap of trouble before long. The same is true of those individuals who attempt any sort of strict adherence to the principles of Objectivist morality. No man who is not a pathological fanatic can possibly expect to succeed in life if he becomes as obsessed with personal integrity as Objectivism counsels him to be. Howard Roark's integrity, though inspirational, is beyond what most people can hope to achieve. And anyone who, in a fit of misguided idealism, tries to live up to the moral standards of the heroes of Rand's novels will likely have a very hard time of it in a world that constantly demands compromise and flexibility. The principles of Objectivism can only be "followed" in everyday life if they are interpreted very loosely and in conformity with the individual's practical sense of what is needed in the situation confronting him at a particular moment in time.

Whatever problems Rand's followers have experienced in their efforts to be good Objectivists are largely the consequence of trying to adhere to some kind of "strict" interpretation of Rand's creed. Since the tenets of Objectivism do not accord all that closely with experiential reality, any attempt to follow them literally may result in serious problems.

One of the most harmful of Rand's principles in this respect is her theory of human emotion. From this theory a number of Objectivists have concluded that their emotions ought to harmonize with their thinking, and when this doesn't happen they become depressed and demoralized. "Over the years," noted psychologist Nathaniel Branden, Rand's closest associate for nearly two decades, "I encountered many men and women who, in the name of idealism (Objectivist or otherwise), crucified their emotional life to conform to their professed values. Inevitably, this entailed massive self-repudiation, which students of Objectivism are appallingly expert at, notwithstanding their talk of 'selfishness.'" (1989, 413) Further corroboration of this view is provided by another of Rand's former associates, the psychologist Alan Blumenthal. "For many years, I had been aware of negative effects of [Rand's] philosophy on my Objectivist patients," Mr. Blumenthal informs us. "At first, I attributed them to individual misinterpretations. But then I began to see that the problem was too widespread. Objectivism's insistent moralism had made many patients afraid to face their own conflicts and that was counterproductive in psychotherapy....They experienced, to an unwarranted degree, feelings of inadequacy and guilt and, consequently, they repressed massively. This led to a tragic loss of personal values. Instead of living for their own happiness—one of the ideas that attracted them to Objectivism in the first place—they sought safety by living to be 'moral,' to be what they were supposed to be and, worse, to feel 'appropriate' emotions. Because they had learned the philosophy predominantly from fiction, the students of Objectivism thought they had to be like Ayn Rand heroes: they were not to be confused, not to be unhappy, and not to lack confidence. And because they could not meet these self-expectations, they bore the added burden of moral failure." (B. Branden, 1986, 387-388)

According to my theory of human nature, the individual's conduct proceeds, not from some abstract principle that has been imposed, arbitrarily, on his psyche, but from his inner character. This is precisely where Rand's wrong-headed theory of human nature gets some of her more scrupulously literal followers into trouble. Rand's conviction that man creates his character from the basic premises of his mind encourages her followers to believe that what is important is not who they are but what they can become. However, any attempt to assume a type of character that is not in accordance with the individual's real, *congenital* character can only lead to emotional repression, neurosis, and misery. If the individual wants to achieve his highest potential, he must, as Nietzsche once put it, *become what he is*. But in order to do this, he must first determine the true character of his inner nature and then discover the best way of realizing this true character in a world that demands compromise at every turn.

By denying the existence of this fixed, rooted, congenital inner nature, Objectivism discourages individuals from coming to any kind of understanding of their fundamental character. It is in this sense that Objectivism winds up opposing, unwittingly perhaps, the Socratic dictum, *nosce te ipsum*, know thyself, which forms the very kernel of philosophical wisdom.

To sum up. The utility of Objectivism depends on how the individual uses Rand's ideas. If he uses Rand's principles merely as a kind of vague form of inspiration, then he may profit from them. If, on the other hand, he tries to apply Rand's principles in a narrow, excessively literal sense to specific problems of everyday life, he is likely to get himself into trouble. This is particularly true regarding

Rand's principles of human nature and human emotion. Such principles, if taken too literally, can encourage individuals to adopt unrealistic expectations about themselves and others, leading to dysfunctional behavior and emotional repression.

*   *   *

(2) *Prospects for Objectivism.* Among her followers, Rand is regarded as a world-historical figure whose ideas will ultimately change the course of history. (Peikoff, 1995, 14) Among her detractors, Rand is seen as a mere cult figure who will be remembered—if she is remembered at all—as the author of a handful of excessively romanticized novels projecting a pretentiously adolescent sensibility towards the great questions of life. While no one can say for certain how Rand will be viewed by future generations, my guess is that the verdict of history will lie somewhere between these two extremes. On the one hand, I do not believe there is any chance of Rand becoming a major influence on the course of history: her philosophy simply does not have a wide enough appeal to attain such influence. On the other hand, I cannot imagine future generations ignoring Rand completely or setting her down as a mere contriver of ideological potboilers. As long as Western Civilization rests on a techno-industrial economic base, there will always exist a steadfast minority who will attempt to keep Rand's name alive to posterity.

In order to understand why Objectivism will never attain more than a modest following, it is necessary to grasp why it is that certain people become admirers and followers of Rand's philosophy in the first place. Contrary to what Objectivists might tell you, the majority of Rand's followers do not become partisans of her philosophy because of its truth and logic. They may sincerely believe this to be the case, but their sincerity does not make them right. People become Objectivists for purely emotional and sentimental reasons, that is to say, because the ideals of Objectivism conform to their personal sentiments and interests. Had these sentiments and interests been different, they would never have become Objectivists.

What sort of sentiments and interests does Objectivism cater to? Let us begin with the sentiments. Objectivism appeals to a variety of sentiments prominent in certain strains of human nature. First of all, it appeals to utopian sentiments regarding the future and to moralistic sentiments regarding the efficacy of virtue and the impotence of vice. It appeals to the need for eternal verities and absolute standards of right and wrong. It appeals very strongly to sentiments of freedom, individualism, and self-responsibility. And lastly, it appeals to various sentiments associated with the romantic idolatry of heroic individuals. The interests Objectivism appeals to are largely economic in nature. Objectivism appeals most strongly to the economic interests of individuals of the professional classes: e.g., writers, artists, computer programmers, and doctors. It has little or no appeal for blue collar workers, bureaucrats, people on welfare, or politicians. Objectivism is an ideology for young aspiring professionals and entrepreneurs who are too secular and worldly in their outlook to find solace in religious doctrine and too individualistic and egocentric to buy into humanitarian ideologies like liberalism and socialism.

Even more important is the type of people who would likely be turned off by Rand's philosophy. Objectivism has little if anything to offer to people who are religious or socialistic in their thinking. It has even less to offer to those who have endured great suffering or to those who have learned, from hard-earned experience, the true nature of man and his social and political institutions. It is also useless to those who know how to think critically or are familiar with the facts of history and the social sciences.

By the time you sift through all the different types of people who would likely be turned off by Rand's ideas, you don't have many people left. During her lifetime, Rand aroused an immense amount of hostility to her ideas. This, in and of itself, is conclusive proof of Objectivism's failure to appeal to most people.

Rand and her followers tend to blame the hostility aroused by her philosophy on the "corruption" of the times. Contemporary intellectuals, we are told, are so corrupt that they feel obliged to oppose anyone who, like Rand, stands for "reason." But in the future things will be different: "reason" will win out and Objectivism will become the dominant ideology of the age.

In chapter 2, I refuted the theory Rand devised to support this conclusion. Further evidence against it can be provided by noting the dominance of religion and faith over the minds of most individuals throughout human history. Virtually every society known to man from the most primitive to the most advanced has been infused with religious or mystical ideals and beliefs. Even today, when religion is supposed to be on the wane and secular values predominate, religious belief remains widespread. In Europe and North America, where secularism and religious skepticism are supposedly the fashion, religious belief still dominates among the masses of people. In North America, over ninety percent of the population regards itself as religious. Christian belief remains high in both Europe and North America, where more than four out of every five persons continue to regard themselves as followers of the gospel. Even more interesting is the tiny minority who regard themselves as atheists—less than half a percent in North America! Most nonbelievers are agnostics who profess complete indifference to the issue of religion one way or the other.

Let us stop and reflect on this for a moment. Throughout human history, the overwhelming majority of human beings have accepted some kind of mystical or religious belief system. Even today, in one of the most secular periods in human history, nearly eighty percent of the world's population professes some kind of religious belief. (World Almanac, 1999) Such evidence suggests that there is something rooted in the very nature of most human beings that predisposes them towards religious belief. Further confirmation of this view is provided by the fact that, where religious belief wanes, belief in secular equivalents of religion (e.g., Marxism, nationalism, liberalism, Darwinism, Objectivism, etc.) rises. Very rare is the individual who believes only in what can be established by empirical observation and the logico-experimental method. Nearly all human beings are characterized by a profound need to overstep "empirical" realities in some manner or form.

Rand and her followers are no exception to this. Despite all their denials to the contrary, Objectivism has its articles of faith just as any religion does. The problem is, these articles of faith are not designed to appeal to the majority of human beings. What most people want is a faith that assures them that there is an afterlife and a God who will look after them. What Objectivism gives them, instead, is the promise of a utopian future that would heavily favor entrepreneurs, professionals, and property owners. For most people, this is not enough. A faith should provide solace for human suffering and mortality. Only a religious faith like Christianity can offer solace of this kind. Secular faiths like Objectivism, which deny both God and an afterlife, are quite useless in this regard.

If history is to be our guide in such matters—and what other guide can there possibly be?—then we have no choice but to conclude that the future prospects of Objectivism are not terribly good. Throughout history, nearly all men have believed in some kind of religious or mystical faith. This would suggest that religious belief is necessary to most men and any attempt to replace it with "reason" or some other kind of secular faith will most likely result in failure. It will be on the rock of religion that Rand's hopes for an Objectivist future will ultimately founder.

Founder though it may, it will not disappear entirely from the sight of man. Objectivism may not have what it takes to appeal to the masses at large, but it should for many centuries continue to appeal to a select minority whose sentiments and interests accord with Objectivist ideals. Human nature, though largely fixed and unalterable, is not homogeneous: many different types make up its totality, and among those types are certain individuals who are more or less congenitally predisposed to Objectivist doctrine. They are those romantic, egocentric, utopian individualists in search of eternal, absolute values I referred to earlier. They flourish in techno-industrial societies, but only in small numbers. If they should ever flourish in large numbers, they will probably cause a great deal of harm, because few if any of them would want to do any of the dirty work of society. You will never find many Objectivists among garbage collectors, charwoman, and janitors, because such vocations do not square well with the sentiments which find expression in Objectivist ideals. Objectivism places a high premium on human creativity. But what about all those jobs which require little, if any, creativity? Who's going to fill such jobs in an Objectivist society? Fortunately, most human beings are not constituted so as to be predisposed towards Objectivist ideals. Consequently, they have little trouble accepting employment that is boring, unglamorous, and uncreative.

Although it is unlikely that Objectivism will disappear altogether in the course of future centuries, it would be naive to expect it to remain what it is presently. During her lifetime, Rand desperately sought to preserve the integrity of Objectivism from those eager to develop its implications. The heir to her estate, Leonard Peikoff, has continued this policy of discouraging growth and elaboration within the Objectivist movement. How long such a policy will remain feasible is an open question. In less than 35 years, Rand's works will enter the public domain and Rand's estate will no longer enjoy the sole monopoly of the royalties from her books. Under such conditions, it will be very difficult for Peikoff's successors to maintain their status as the only official spokespersons for Rand's ideas. Other nominally "objectivist" groups will spring up declaring themselves as Rand's "true" spokespersons.

There will be endless squabbling between the various Objectivist factions, as each accuses the other of "tampering" with Rand's ideas and trying to cash in on Rand's reputation. There may even come a time when the most serious threat to Objectivism will come from Objectivism itself. Such are the fruits of preaching that man can be certain: such talk only encourages individuals to regard anyone who diverges ever so slightly from the prevailing orthodoxy as a scoundrel. Since human beings can rarely come to any kind of precise agreement, it is best to show some tolerance for divergences of opinion. Intolerance only divides potential allies and wastes valuable energy in futile disputes between individuals who believe virtually the same thing anyway and who are only arguing because neither is willing to admit the possibility of error.

*   *   *

(3) *Concluding assessment.* Just before the publication of her novel *Atlas Shrugged*, Rand told Nathaniel Branden: "If I don't break through this time—if the book doesn't get the understanding it deserves *from someone*—I mean, from some serious minds, not just 'fans'—then I'm finished; finished with this society and this century." (1989, 228) Following the publication of *Atlas*, Rand became increasingly depressed. "In many of our discussions, from the summer of 1958 and into the next two years, [Rand] would begin to cry while describing her perception of the world and her place in it," Branden would later recall; "and she confided that she cried almost every day." (1989, 238) "The problem is that not one first-class brain has

stood up for me in public to defend me," Rand would complain. (1989, 241)

At first glance, Rand's depression would seem entirely anomalous. According to the standards of her own philosophy, there was no reason for her to be depressed. She had just finished the major work of her life, *Atlas Shrugged*. The book was doing extremely well—in fact, it had been on the best seller list for months. Enthusiastic fan mail poured in from all parts of the country. Thousands expressed interest in learning more about her philosophy. And yet, her despair was so great, that she admitted to weeping every day! What is this all about? Why would Rand become so depressed at the very moment of her greatest triumph?

The reason is quite simple: she was depressed because no eminent person, no "first-class brain," as she put it, had come forth to validate the greatness of her achievement. For Rand had convinced herself that *Atlas* was a great work that would someday leave its mark on the course of human history. But if this were the case, why hadn't any of Rand's distinguished contemporaries noticed the fact and announced it to the world?

It seems plain to me that the reason no great mind, no man of eminent reputation and stature came forth to herald Rand's novel as a great and important masterpiece is because the novel is, in fact, neither great nor important. It is, to be entirely frank, a rather ridiculous and overblown philosophical fantasy populated by stock figures whose resemblance to anything human is merely coincidental. The book, for all its ingenuity of plot, cleverness of integration, and brilliance of style, remains, at its core, essentially juvenile—an exercise in unintelligent, excessively romanticized hero-worship. Such, in any case, would likely be the estimate of any great mind.

I suspect that somewhere deep within her, Rand knew this to be the case. She was not a stupid woman. She could not have been completely ignorant of the baselessness of her view of human nature. But she had invested so much in her conception of the heroic, "ideal" man that she could not face the bitter truth of his unreality. She had hoped that the publication of *Atlas* would help prove that her ideal man did in fact exist. *He* would read the novel and seek Rand out. Together, they would strive to bring about a world governed by reason and rational self-interest—or rather, *he* would lead the fight and she would be his indispensable side-kick. "I never wanted to be a general, let alone a commander in chief," Rand once remarked. "My dream has always been to be the ideal lieutenant—to my kind of man." (N. Branden, 1989, 215)

Unfortunately for Rand, since her ideal man did not exist, her dream of being his lieutenant could never be realized. Following the publication of *Atlas Shrugged*, this became much clearer to Rand. Hence the two-year long depression when she cried every day. "Do you know what it's like to have no one to look up to—always to look down?" she was heard complaining in the final years of her life. "Can you understand what it means still to hope, always to hope, and never to find it?" (B. Branden, 1986, 386) There is something immensely tragic in all this. Rand devoted her entire life to the pursuit of a figment. No wonder she was depressed!

It would have been best for Rand if she had simply owned up to the fact that her ideal man was a mere phantom of her overly romantic sensibility and to seek to base her philosophy on something for less impalpable. But she was too proud, too self-willed, too implacable to do any such thing. She stuck to her guns to the bitter end, insisting with increasing vehemence that only she was right and that all the great geniuses of intellectual history who had arrived at very different conclusions regarding the nature of man were either complete ignoramuses or vicious, evil man-haters. Rand's idolatry of her "ideal" man set her against nearly every important thinker and scholar, past and present, of Western Civilization. If you go through the entire Objectivist literature, you will find one denunciation after another of the best minds which our civilization has produced: Hume, Kant, Burke, Schopenhauer, Kirkegaard, Tolstoy, Tocqueville, J. S. Mill, Nietzsche, Weber, Michels, and Hayek are just some of the eminent figures whom Rand and her followers have seen fit to deride or denounce. Only Aristotle, Aquinas, Locke, the Founding Fathers, and a handful of pro-capitalist economists were regarded by Rand as worth studying. All the other classics of Western thought could have been left to rot in some library, as far as she was concerned. She had no use for them, and what she had no use for she regarded as beyond the pale.

In coming to a critical assessment of Rand's philosophy of Objectivism, I cannot ignore her contempt of most of the great thinkers who preceded her. It demonstrates, to a very considerable degree, her fundamental lack of culture. It was not merely the "malevolent" art of Western Civilization that she disapproved of; she detested most of what passes for humane knowledge as well. She opposed it not simply out of boorishness or intellectual laziness: she opposed it as a matter of principle—because it projected a view of human nature that she could not abide. Why could she not abide it? *Because it was and is true.* Human beings are not, nor can they ever be, as Rand wished them to be. Rand's inability to accept this fact is what drove her to oppose the naturalistic conception of human nature; and from opposing this concept there was only a short step to opposing what it represented in reality. Rand's worship of the "ideal" man drove her eventually to despise or denounce most *real* men. This is seen clearly in her contemptuous reference to what she called "the folks next door" and to her inability to sustain relationships with her closest friends and associates.

It was this hostility of Rand's toward the phenomenon of human nature that inspired me to entitle this work *Ayn Rand Contra Human Nature.* For that seems to me what her philosophy—and her life in general—amounted to in the end: one long and futile struggle against the old Adam in every one of us. This hostility towards human nature affects nearly every aspect of Rand's philosophy: it affects her theory of history, her ethics, her politics, and her aesthetics, all of which are based on the premise that man is a rational being whose emotions are the product of his thinking. More importantly, it affected the way she thought and argued. Since she could not establish the reality of her ideal man scientifically, she had no choice but to resort to sophistry. In this way, her entire philosophy became infected by her verbalistic mode of argumentation. And so even those parts of her philosophy which are largely true, such as her metaphysics, were defended by a false and pernicious method of validation.

What, then, is my final critical assessment of Rand's philosophy of Objectivism? I fear it must not be a very good one. If judged solely on the basis of how much insight it gives us into the nature of man and the universe, I would give Objectivism very low marks. Her admirers will not be pleased with this, but I regard it as a just estimate nonetheless. In any case, it is based on years of hard work and study. Those who believe I am being unfair to Rand can go out and do the hard work for themselves. Let them read the philosophers Rand so cavalierly denounces; let them study the history she claims is determined by ideas; let them familiarize themselves with the best that has been said and thought in the disciplines of political science, sociology, and psychology. If they are intelligent enough to profit from their labors, they will see that, whatever errors I might have committed in regards to this detail or that, in the main, I am justified in my low assessment of Rand's philosophical achievement. No one who is well educated in these matters and is endowed with the ability to think critically can ever regard Objectivism as anything other than a mistake.

FINIS

BIBLIOGRAPHY

———————▼———————

Babbitt, I. (1919) *Rousseau and Romanticism*. New York: Meridian Books, 1955.

Barzun, J. (1961) *Classic, Romantic, Modern*. Chicago: University of Chicago Press.

Binswanger, H. (1986) *The Ayn Rand Lexicon: Objectivism From A to Z*. Edited by Harry Binswanger. New York: Meridan.

Binswanger, H. (1987) *Objectivist Forum*. December, 1987.

Branden, B. (1986) *The Passion of Ayn Rand*. Garden City, N.Y.: Doubleday.

Branden, N. (1989) *Judgment Day: My Years with Ayn Rand*. Boston: Houghton-Mifflin, 1989.

Buchanan, J. & Tullock, G. (1960) *Calculus of Consent: Logical Foundations of Constitutional Democracy*. Ann Arbor, MI: University of Michigan Press.

Ellis, A. (1968) *Is Objectivism a Religion?* New York: Lyle Stuart, Inc.

Ferguson, A. (1767) *An Essay on the History of Civil Society*. London.

Hayek, F. (1967) *Studies in Philosophy, Politics, and Economics*. New York: Simon & Schuster.

Hume, D. (1739-40) *A Treatise of Human Nature*. London: Penguin Books, 1969.

Hume, D. (1751) *An Enquiry Concerning the Principles of Morals*. Indianapolis, IN: Hacket Publishing Company, 1983.

King, C. (1984) *The Philosophic Thought of Ayn Rand*. Edited by D. Uyl & D. Rasmussen. Chicago: University of Illinois Press.

Konner, M. (1982) *The Tangled Wing: Biological Constraints of the Human Spirit*. New York: Henry Holt.

Lakoff, G. & Johnson, M. (1999) *Philosophy in the Flesh: The Disembodied Mind and its Challenge to Western Thought*. New York: Basic Books.

Levy-Bruhl, L. (1931) *The Making of Man*. Edited by V. F. Calverton. New York: Random House.

Michels, R. (1915) *Political Parties: A Sociological Study of the Oligarchical Tendencies of Modern Democracy*. Translated by Eden and Cedar Paul. Gloucester, Mass: Peter Smith, 1978.

Mitcham, S. (1996) *Why Hitler?* Westport, CN: Praeger Publishers.

Myers, G. (1909) *The History of the Great American Fortunes*. New York: Random House, 1936.

Nietzsche, F. (1885) *Beyond Good and Evil*. Translated by Walter Kaufmann. New York: Modern Library, 1968.

Nock, A. (1935) *Our Enemy the State.* Tampa, FL: Halberg Publishing Corporation, 1983.

Oakeshott, M. (1962) *Rationalism in Politics and Other Essays.* Indianapolis, IN: Liberty Fund, 1991.

Pareto, V. (1916) *The Mind and Society.* Translated by Arthur Livingston and Andrew Bongiorno. New York: Harcourt, Brace and Company, 1935.

Peikoff, L. (1985) Philosophy and Psychology in History. *Objectivist Forum.* October 1985.

Peikoff, L. (1991) *Objectivism: The Philosophy of Ayn Rand.* New York: Dutton.

Peikoff, L. (1995) *Objectivist Forum.* October, 1995.

Pinker, S. (1997) *How the Mind Works.* New York: W.W. Norton & Company.

Pirenne, H. (1925) *Medieval Cities: Their Origins and the Revival of Trade.* Translated by Frank D. Halsey. Princeton, NJ: Princeton University Press.

Polanyi, M. (1958) *Personal Knowledge: Towards a Post-Critical Philosophy.* Chicago: University of Chicago Press, 1974.

Popper, K. (1934) *The Logic of Scientific Discovery.* New York: Routledge, 1992.

Popper, K. (1945) *The Open Society and its Enemies.* Princeton, NJ: Princeton University Press, 1966.

Popper, K. (1963) *Conjectures and Refutations: The Growth of Scientific Knowledge.* New York: Routledge, 1991.

Popper, K. (1979) *Objective Knowledge: An Evolutionary Approach.* Revised Edition. Oxford: Clarendon Press.

Popper, K. (1983) *Realism and the Aim of Science.* New York: Routledge, 1992.

Rand, A. (1957) *Atlas Shrugged.* New York: Random House.

Rand, A. (1961) *For the New Intellectual: The Philosophy of Ayn Rand.* New York: Random House.

Rand, A. (1964a) Alvin Toffler's Playboy interview with Ayn Rand: A candid conversation with the Fountainhead of "Objectivism." *Objectivist,* March 1964.

Rand, A. (1964b) *The Virtue of Selfishness: A New Concept of Egoism.* New York: New American Library.

Rand, A. (1967) *Capitalism: The Unknown Ideal.* New York: New American Library, 1967.

Rand, A. (1971a) *The Objectivist.* September 1971.

Rand, A (1971b) *The New Left: The Anti-Industrial Revolution.* Revised Edition. New York: New American Library.

Rand, A. (1975) *The Romantic Manifesto.* Revised Edition. New York: New American Library.

Rand, A. (1982) *Philosophy: Who Needs It.* New York: New American Library.

Rand, A. (1990a) *The Voice of Reason: Essays in Objectivist Thought.* New York: Meridian.

Rand, A. (1990b) *Introduction to Objectivist Epistemology.* 2nd ed., expanded. Edited by Harry Binswanger and Leonard Peikoff. New York: New American Library.

Rand, A. (1995) *Letters of Ayn Rand.* New York: Dutton, 1995.

Rand, A. (1997) *Journals of Ayn Rand.* Edited by David Harriman. New York: EP Dutton.

Santayana, G. (1923) *Scepticism and Animal Faith.* New York: Dover Publications, 1955.

Santayana, G. (1926) *Dialogues in Limbo.* Ann Arbor, MI: University of Michigan Press, 1957.

Santayana, G. (1942) *Realms of Being.* New York: Cooper Square Publishers, 1972.

Santayana, G. (1940) *Egotism and German Philosophy.* New York: Charles Scribner's Sons.

Santayana, G. (1946) *The Idea of Christ in the Gospels.* New York: Charles Scribner's Sons.

Santayana, G. (1969) *Physical Order and Moral Liberty.* Edited by John and Shirley Lachs. Vanderbilt University Press.

Schopenhauer, A. (1847) *On the Fourfold Root of the Principle of Sufficient Reason.* Translated by E. Payne. LaSalle, Il: Open Court, 1974.

Sciabarra, C. (1995) *Ayn Rand: The Russian Radical.* University Park, PN: Pennsylvania State University Press.

Sumner, W. (1906) *Folkways: A Study of the Sociological Importance of Usages, Manners, Customs, Mores and Morals.* New York: New American Library, 1940.

Sutherland, E. (1949) *White Collar Crime.* Yale University Press, 1983.

Taine, H. (1896) *History of English Literature.* Translated by Henri Van Laun. New York: A. L. Burt Co.

Turner, H. (1996) *Hitler's Thirty Days to Power: January 1933.* New York: Addison-Wesley Publishing Co.

Vidal, G. (1961) Comment. *Esquire,* July 1961.

Vivas, E. (1955) *Creation and Discovery*. Chicago: Henry Regnery Co.

Weber, M. (1904-5) *The Protestant Ethic and the Spirit of Capitalism*. Translated by Talcott Parsons. New York: Charles Scribner's Sons, 1958.

Wilson, E. (1978) *On Human Nature*. Cambridge, MA: Harvard University Press.

Made in the USA
Lexington, KY
14 August 2012